Stones Alive!

A Reference Guide To Stones
for the New Millennium

———————

From Their Hearts to Our Hands
New Uses and Applications

with

Twintreess

Presented by

AhhhMuse/Twintreess
2340 US Hwy 180 E. #171
Silver City, NM 88061 USA

We give thanks to the spirits of the stones who asked for this book to be written and allowed us to participate in that co-creation. Our lives are incredibly enriched and we share that with all the readers, in appreciation.

First Edition.
Printed in the United States of America.

ISBN# 1-890808-09-1

Cover photo: Susan L. Newman
Contributing artwork: Crystal Karl (*pp. 30, 44, 11, 120, 146, 193*);
Joyce Morningstar (*pp. 39, 74, 123*); Daniel Krasofski (*pg. 133*)

Very special thanks to Don Karl, for writing the Physical Descriptions of almost all of the stones and most importantly, for his constant joy!

Graphic Design: Charlotte Krebs/Salmagundi Design

We offer the information included in this book, based on intuition and personal experience. We do not intend for you to use it to replace your own judgment or your doctor's prescriptions or advice. Honor this book and yourself by utilizing it to explore more deeply your own life and your connection to the earth.

A Journey of Thanks

We offer this magical story to those that we and "Stones Alive!" wish to thank. If you recognize yourself, smile and share that warmth with someone else. If you don't recognize yourself here, then just put yourself in any place along the way, for surely you have your own mystical piece in this journey....

I lay down next to the fire. It warmed my bones and promised a story...

I blinked at the rough night and the soft flaming colors. There was something there; I could almost see it.

"Want some soup?" she smiled.

"Yes, please," I replied. "What's your name?"

"Anna."

The soup warmed me more than the fire. It filled me with so much love I could taste it. Anna's eyes surveyed me brightly, "What are you doing so far away from home?"

"Writing a book," it sounded weird even to me and I had heard it already.

Anna just nodded kindly, "Yes, I can see it. A magnificent book. A book made in the dreamtime. Can I read it sometime?"

"Of course, I think that it's a book for everybody," I smiled back.

"Okay, then, I'll stay here by the fire and I'll make this camp your home. Whenever you need something to feed you, I'll be here."

Before I could wonder at her soft generosity, she was gone to gather more wood. I sighed and walked away from the fire to be closer to the stars. Two men stood before me gazing at the heavenly lights.

"It's about time you got here," Brad exclaimed, "Mercury's going direct soon and I want to help you organize all your pages then."

Don shook my hand, "I'm not an expert in astrology, but I do love the stars. On behalf of their beauty, I dedicate all my love of writing to your endeavor."

"Perfect. You can tell stories of what makes up the stones and where they came from. Every good story has to have its roots in the earth. You'll be the roots AND the stars, and I will be grateful."

When I went back to the fire, two beautiful women, Joyce and Crystal, sat there drawing the stones next to the flames. Rather than distract their art, I slipped back into woods, bumping into a tree sprite.

"Watch where you're going!" she shouted. "You could hurt someone."

"Sorry. I'll be more careful," I jumped back very quickly.

"No need for that," Ursela twinkled. "I said that I would watch where you're going and let you know when you're on the right path." Before I could say thanks, she was gone. I wandered deeper in the woods, looking for the next chapter. After a few more turns, the fire was gone. I couldn't hear anybody else's voices and I felt lost.

"This is a fine story," the gypsy laughed, "Lots of people will enjoy it."

I had no idea how she had gotten a hold of my book.

Now she was giggling, "Of course I'm the one to find your book. I'm the one who finds the magic in between the pages and puts it all together so that it is a story that people will love for a very long time. I'm Charlotte, the overseer. When you run out of magic, come to me and I'll always give you mine." With that, she was gone.

With that, I was gone out of the woods. Once again I was lying before the fire. Charlotte was already there, surrounded by a crowd of happy, eager people, "Let me introduce you to the helpers who will bring the extra magic and stories." She pointed gracefully, " This is: Lee, Fran, Jennifer, Jeanice, Colleen, Peter (he's brought you some flowers), Ron, Karen, Robert, Lisa, Colene, Jim, Kate, Linda (she's got a whole company with her), Ellen, Crazy Colleen, Sage, MaryAnn, Gary, Daniel, Geoff, Keran, all the readers and finally, the Linda who brought the dragon. And you know, once the dragon is here, the fire will never die."

With that, I awoke to find that the dream had not left. It had just begun.

Table of Contents

Welcome

Like all fine books this one has its own spirit and its own heart. When you open its pages, you enter its home and word by word you uncover its special, unique wisdom. After you leave, you know more about the world and about your own growing heart.

That's how it is with stones, for us.

They come to us in soft and loud colors, in smooth and jagged shapes, in pebbles and boulders, and each one reads like a very fine book. Stones are the libraries of the earth. They hold the wisdom of all her seasons, storms and growth. You just need to listen, in stillness, to their language- a patient recording that has accumulated over thousands of years- one word at a time.

So that's our (Twintreess) piece in this book. We listen to the earth's record-keepers and translate them into human words. Why?.... because the stones wanted to give their wisdom to people who couldn't hear them yet.... because our world, right now, is changing more rapidly than we can record, or imagine, or accept. We need to understand the language of the seasons, in order to flow with the earth changes. Maybe as a species, we have struggled against the earth and its beings for far too long.

When we peacefully listen to the stones, we join with them; we walk into their life stories. Then we know the seasons of this earth and it is, finally, our home.

We breathe fully again.

We join with all life and change, which is the pulse of life, itself.

We invite you to enter this book and our heart. May you find your own peace. A connection to life awaits you, here. Listen.

Enter the Adventure

Thank you for entering this book and its life story. We want you to know that it comes to you as a gift from the stones, themselves. All things have consciousness and each one expresses itself in its own unique way, weaving itself perfectly into the overall pattern of life. The stones asked us to share their essences through this book, so that we, as humans, could feel the incredible interconnectedness of everything on this planet.

Every word in this book is a co-creation between the stones' spirits and our own. Listen to that. Take that with you. Try it on. Adjust it for your own life and see what you learn. Certainly don't accept our experience as the only possibility. "Stones Alive!" has arrived in your hands to invite you to listen to another consciousness that is so different from yours (and yet so alike, too) that you not only change, you transform. You embrace change so delightedly, that you don't change your thoughts, you transform the way you *think*.

That means that as we enter the new millennium, we may enter it with the wisdom of the earth. We can walk through this new season, like all the others, knowing that we are conscious, co-creating adventurers.

Adventurers

Hello fellow adventurers~

Something miraculous happened on the way to writing a reference guide; it turned into magic. We don't think it swooped down in a poof. It just slipped in a day at a time, word by perfect word...

We agreed to this adventure, out loud and full of trust. When the stones told us that they wanted to give us their stories, we said, "Yes." When they said, "It will be a co-creation of our words in your language and your definitions," we said, "Yes." Then they smiled and told us that all of that together would be a reference guide. Yes, yes.

So, we just lived with the stones, day by day, storing their wisdom in ways that we didn't know how to measure (nor needed to, actually). They whispered that the book was one way to offer their services to humans at a time when they could use help. No matter what words the humans read, the underlying invitation would ring in their hearts: Join with us. With our true unlimited natures revealed, we can co-create a magnificent, peaceful earth now.

Then the stones announced that all was ready and that "Stones Alive!" wanted to be launched immediately. Suddenly we had a few weeks to make it so; we said, "Yes." When we laid out the schedule of events, it didn't seem possible (notice, we didn't say "impossible") to create it all in that short a time. So we gave up expectations, found some more trust and just began.

We wrote this blindly - no time to edit or to compare notes in the usual way. We let the words make their own way in the world, a sentence at a time. Did they make sense? Were they connected? We gave that job to the stone spirits...

That's when the miracle unfolded. It was there all the time, but it was easier for us to see when the book was all in one piece/peace. ***This reference guide reads like an adventure!*** All of the quotes from the stones form a glorious poem. All the physical and emotional integrations weave a story of reality and magic united on the earth (where we insist on tangible evidence of both). Science and mystery embrace each other and find that they never were strangers, after all. All the Stone Stories speak of the consciousness deep inside the earth, where life is based, where we all sustain ourselves, even when we think otherwise.

It is the strong, clear voice of the earth's beings greeting a new millennium. When we read "Stones Alive!" from start to finish (like a novel, instead of like a reference book where you just pull out an occasional, disjointed piece to answer a single question) we realized that all the beings on the earth know that we all stand on the precipice of an evolution never before seen. This is the moment when we meet our destiny, if we choose it...if we choose to co-create it together.

The stones feel the change coming and they greet it like every season- with all their heart. That's why it's an adventure.

They put in their full essence here. Drink in all of it and you will be on adventure, too. If you put your fullness boldly and lovingly into this, then your story will change because of it. You may find that your way to the next millennium is through risks and challenges and laughter. The stones gave us a doorway to all of it, right there, in the first quote, the first sentence. Your doorway is, and always has been, in your gorgeous, open heart. Go ahead. Go on in. Give it all a chance. Find yourself a page at a time. Say yes.

The Mystery

The Stone Totem Stories ~ Okay, we're all adventurers in this book; we have established that already. Now here comes the part where everything gets interesting. This is where mystery enters, and no matter how many words we add here, we can't really explain it.

The stones have taken care of that, for all of us. Welcome to the Tibetan Tektites (for an introduction to them, see page 192), who have offered, graciously, to serve as the totems of this book. They are our special allies in this adventure. In our personal lives, we have divine guardians who always watch over us, even when we can't see them, hear them, or even appreciate them. They're just there for us.

It's the same thing with the Tibetan Tektites...almost. They have presented themselves as our totems/guardians, which means that they will help us to feel safe while we risk learning new things (Don't underestimate the potential fear here. New ideas might be the only real fears we find in life.). What's different about this guardian arrangement is that it is conscious. We know about it before we even begin the adventure; we know we have help along the way. What that means is that we must be ready for something really big, something wondrous. Going even further, that means that we may have evolved enough to receive guardianship that can lead us to glorious transformations that, by ourselves, we could not imagine.

So be it. Periodically throughout "Stones Alive!", the Tibetan Tektites will share their guidance in The Stone Totem Stories. They offer it in whatever form we most need at the moment (like the Stone Story category). It will come in a conversation, a question, or even an elegant allegory. It seems mystical, because they use our human language (infused with respect) to paint the broadest, brightest picture possible, to honor our hearts and our spirits, not just our minds. They guide us with messages that will grow with our growing wisdom.

One day, long after reading this book, we may find utterly new meanings in their words that will bring us to the next adventure and the next. The Tibetan Tektites' answers lead us to greater mysteries, which brings us to the core of life itself.

Once there, we can do anything.

We can enjoy all of it, even when we don't understand it.

Welcome to the mystery, which is the spirit in everything and that's what makes an adventure, an adventure.

After all, if we knew everything about the journey in advance, why would we even go on it?

The Treasure of the Adventure

When you have finished exploring all the single stones, A-Z, the adventure doesn't end. Like all truly magnificent quests of the heart, when you come to the end of it, you discover that it begins again on a new path, that is bigger, brighter and even better. Whenever you follow your heart (as you are in this book), all the wisdom you have gained allows you to find other adventures, ones that expand on your past knowing, exponentially. All that you have learned with the single stones leads you to how they join with each other to co-create even more possibilities. This is where you find the buried treasure at the end of the first adventure that makes the next adventure possible...and the next...and the next...

The Stone Combination Section— is one of the exponentially expanding adventures (you are another) of "Stones Alive!" Whenever any life forms on this planet combine with each other to celebrate the glory of life, miracles happen. They drop right out of the sky and land on the earth and grow new flowers or crystals or whatever is needed to give us a sudden smile on a down day. If you're looking for them (the miracles), they will land right next to you; or if you're really trusting, they'll land right in your hand, and you can put them to good use right off. If you aren't looking for them they might bop you in the head. One way or the other miracles arrive plentifully and they will get your attention sooner or later.

The Stone Combination Section is dedicated to the stones, who when joined, asked to have their services recorded like this:

Uriel's Wisdom (the title they conferred upon their union in this example)

"Let us walk together, hand in hand,

upon the earth and see all there is—

love creating perfection."
(their joint message offered as a gift to anyone who would like to be officially introduced
to them.)

Moss Agate is the sweetness of the earth inside of us.

Rutilated Quartz is the communication of our guides in everyday events.

Moldavite is seeing with the eyes of our heart.

Angelite is the peace of knowingness.

(the list of their services, not the ones that they perform individually, but the ones they offer to the whole {Uriel's Wisdom} when combined this way.).

There, that's some of what their miracle looks like approximately (for the rest of the information, go straight to the *Stone Combination Section* and enjoy.).

Each of the combinations offered in this book has come to us as a specific gift to help humans with their most pressing needs of the moment. It's like part of the philosophy of macrobiotics: Eat according to the seasons around you, because your body is already a part of those seasons. The stone combinations present themselves now, as we all are living in a dramatic initiation (the 2000's). They're feeling the evolution that is being demanded of them, of us, and of all beings on the planet. So, they're evolving by providing and altering their services to meet the greatest, current needs.

If you're really paying attention to miracles, this may be obvious. You're already down the road, adventuring with the stone beings. Enjoy.

If you're not quite seeing the miracles before they hit, let's talk about this some more. When the stones consciously combine their essences, they increase their abilities to support all life on this planet. As they do that, so can you...

If you open up your heart and join with the stones, you can co-create a new, ever expanding peace that will affect all the cycles of life and the earth. Whenever any of us gathers together for respect and love, it makes more respect and love available to the consciousness, and, therefore, it's available to every single, being, too...whether they realize it, or not.

Just like the hundredth monkey results, when we fill the world with enough bliss, something deep inside of all of us delights, unconsciously, or consciously. It's the same part of us that innately responds to the earth's seasons and allows us all to share some of the same experiences. And yet, because we also differ in some ways, those differences will complement other beings. That's how we co-create the essential harmony of being on this planet. As humans, we can choose to participate in that actively, intentionally, or not. However, when we jump full-hearted into that harmony, that's when the adventure exponentially expands and expands.

So, if we (Twintreess) could share our essences with you (and we are), we would invite you to realize that this book is a true adventure. That adventure is a new and incredible chance to embrace the gifts of the stone people,— not just for the sake of the stones — but to connect deeply to all life at a time when we and the earth are evolving beyond all possibilities. We need the support and maybe, they need or want ours, too, because we already are connected.

Take the wisdom you acquire here and stretch it. If something doesn't fit for you, throw it away. Go find what your truth really is. When you look at the combinations, pay attention. Seek out the ones that will work directly with you. Listen, we have a very good friend, Robert, who is an excellent cook. He generously shares all his recipes and says that his favorite part of that is when people come back to him and say, "I loved that recipe! I loved it so much, that I changed it around. I took out the tomatoes, threw in some more garlic and seeds..." Pretty soon, they have created a labor of love that's nothing like the original one. Yes! Robert totally, delightedly celebrates that.

That's exactly how we feel about you and the *Stone Combinations* and any of the adventures of "Stones Alive!" Take them and make them your own and that exponentially enriches all of us. Yes. Thanks Robert, thanks to the stones and thanks to all of us. He has written a marvelous cookbook called, "Flavors of the Southwest Vegetarian Style," by Robert Oser.

Well, now, we want to present you with a general guide (sort of a road map) for this book- something that will help you to learn about the stones and maybe to enjoy them even more:

1. *Every stone is different.* Of course every fluorite shares common traits with every other Fluorite; however remember that the naming of the types of stones just sorts our knowledge (For instance, we know that a Diamond is a Diamond partly because it formed under great pressure.). Once we understand certain classifications then we can take that basic data and stretch it into a wisdom that covers all the earth and its cycles.

    Getting back to the differences, every stone is unique (like every human is unique). So listen to each of their stories with respect, but know that the information presented speaks to the general qualities of the listed stone. In reality, when you handle a specific Fluorite, it still will tell its own specific story. One way to let this all unfold easily is to allow the information here to open your heart so you can explore the uniqueness of all beings in the world.

2. *This is one of many references available to you.* This book/adventure has been co-created to expand your possibilities, including new connections with nature and life. As with anything new, test it out responsibly. Honor yourself. Let the Physical and Emotional Integrations simply guide you. Do not take them as medical advice. Consult a doctor for that, if you choose. Respect all parts of your being with careful thought and action.

3. ***Develop your own senses.*** We all are interwoven with all life (including rocks) and all we have to do to connect deeply with everything is to just choose that connection. Right now, right here, decide that you want to understand the changes happening on the earth this moment. Once you choose that, your senses will hear your declaration and they will re-energize. You will alert yourself to things you never even noticed before; suddenly everything in the world stands before you as a very exciting, synchronous exploration.

4. ***What to do if you don't know what to make of this information.*** Read on, of course. Remember that every new belief started as a puzzle that you may have rejected completely at first. Then the next time you saw the puzzle it wasn't quite so alien. After repeated exposure to it, you eventually figured that it did apply to your life. Sometimes the difference between an accepted idea and an abandoned one is having just a little extra time to get used to the idea.

    Remember, you may have defenses whose job is to disregard unusual notions. That's fine but if you always reject different things, how are you ever going to see any miracles?

5. ***Read all the stories, start to finish.*** Of course, we can't make you do that, but as hosts of this adventure, we would be remiss if we didn't suggest this, strongly, to you.

    Something amazing happened while this book wrote itself. As the stones unfolded their glorious life stories, they gave us something beyond a reference guide—they gifted us their essences and their life services. When you realize that, then you can absorb their fullness (instead of just referring to only parts of their stories), and that can change your life. You can receive their wisdom and actually use that to transform yourself.

    That's where you meet the true adventure of "Stones Alive!" If you simply cite some of the stones' words in your life, then "Stones Alive!" is a book for you (and if that's enough for you, perfect.). However, if you joyfully join with the earth record-keeping and the unique wisdom of the stones, then you are *adventuring* with another wondrous life form that has chosen to offer its support to you and to the earth, consciously.

That, my friends, is what "Stones Alive!" is all about. That's why we're doing this. That's why the stones are here. And maybe that's why you're here, too. Of course, just like our suggestion, "Read all our stories start to finish," it's up to you. It's all up to you and like all of your free choices, it reminds you that you are unlimited and you have all the help and resources you could ever need to express that.

In short, that means if you don't duck, miracles will land on you. Congratulations to all!

Stones A-Z

Tools for the Adventure

As a reference guide for the new millennium, "Stones Alive!" is not just a book, it gives life stories. As you embrace it, it is your adventure. It is your life, and your life is leaping into an incredible unknown...

Congratulations on your choice to follow your own heart!

Along the way, you will find some tools that will help you to feel supported and ever more capable of exploring. We offer them, freely, from our own experience, and in the incredible journey that is called "Stones Alive!" they are named: Physical Description; Physical Integration; Emotional Integration; Millennial Uses; Affirmation of Support; Personal Story; Stone Story, and Summary. Each category/tool presents itself to you like a magic key. When you speak these words, they open up vast worlds that you didn't know even existed a second before. Each of these intentionally chosen tools bridges the space where you are at (along with the way that you currently understand the world) to the unknown...to a boundless mystery-sparked-into-life that directly offers you the eternal wisdom of the stone beings. In their world, we discover that they are and have been the base of life and of matter on this planet. Through the magic of these tools, we will (together) explore exactly what the experiences of the stones have to offer us now:

The Quote: "the Doorway"~ Each stone entry begins with a quote from the stone itself, like the one from Carnelian, *"Together we are passions and instincts living in focus."* This is the doorway to the heart of Carnelian; it shouts to us of its service in the world and of what our potential could be when we join as human and stone in this earth adventure.

Just as every human is utterly unique, so, too, is every stone. Therefore the Quote (the doorway) for each is unique. Some whisper the way to enter. Some shout it. Others welcome us so immediately that the door already lies wide open and they begin by speaking of what will happen after we enter. They tell us what it will be like when they unite their story and their consciousness with us. They show us their picture of what it could be like when we choose to co-create our parts of the world, together, joyfully.

However they speak, note that the Quote begins the adventure. It readies you for the unknown by talking to you in the universal language of the heart. If you're only in your head, it might not make sense. If you're just reading it "physically", you might race right on by it, never imagining that this is a signpost. Still, if you listen to the Quote with your heart, you never will fail to find its exact meaning for you and just for you. There may be no exact, scientific, mass media explanation for that; it just jumps into your feeling and absorbs itself so thoroughly into your life, that you just practice it and love how it expands you.

So, one of the best ways to enter these stories, is to stop.
Stop.
Blink.

Drop your worries (if you truly like them with you that much, you can check them at the door and pick them up later when you really might use them).
Breathe.
Breathe again.

Breathe like you mean it. Breathing not only enables us to survive (a short time without air shows us quickly how fragile we really are...), but when we give all our loving attention to it, it *enlivens* us. It grants our existence the richness that makes our souls want to stay with our bodies. It bestows us with new awareness and that awareness can lead us into expanded brain wave states that open us to the unimaginable.

So, the first tool to use with the Quote, is breath. Breathe fully. Allow the doorway to present itself to you, automatically. Enter.

Physical Description: *"The Form"*~ This tells you how to identify each stone through its: color, hardness, geographical location, shape, composition, etc. It's where you meet each other as fellow beings on the earth. Let the information just flow through you so freely that, later, you might find that the stone's color and form may be more than just identifying marks. After all, rocks that possess certain hardness have certain uses; rocks that possess certain shapes also have corresponding properties. The key, here, is that the uses and the properties will begin with physical traits and then will evolve beyond that into more. That's the reward of a fine adventure.

Physical Integration: *"The Synchronicity"* ~ With the Physical Description, you and the designated stone meet each other. Now that you're familiar with each other, the next categories/tools for exploration focus on, "How do we come together? What happens when we combine our possibilities?"

The Physical Integration shows you the services that this stone can offer your body and how you might blend that potential into your life to transform your day-to-day reality. In order for this adventure to mean something, it needs to produce practical results in the world. That's what you'll find in the Physical Integration.

One of the best ways to work with the Physical Integration is through the simplicity of synchronicity. Carry the key phrases with you everywhere and release any expectations about them. Then when they suddenly **fit** into your day you'll know it, and you will remember it. The Physical Integrations will light up new meanings and possibilities for you and your life. This is the pathway of the adventure.

Emotional Integration: *"The Heart"* ~ This category/tool tells us how the qualities of each stone serves us emotionally. It tells us how these stones will *feel* to us. Once we enter their hearts, we won't just learn about the properties of stones, we truly will explore ourselves, as well, and in that newfound ease, we will connect, joyfully, with the earth, with all beings, and with peace.

So, the key to absorbing the fullness of the Emotional Integrations is to read them with the eyes and the ears of your heart. Let the innate wisdom underlying each phrase fill you. Let the deep knowingness that goes beyond written or spoken language guide you to your own, completely individual meanings. When you dig even deeper, do what we (Twintreess) do: read the spaces between words. The unlimited energy there speaks directly to the heart. Within an adventure, this is the moment when you fully know it's right, beyond all reason, to be journeying down this path.

Millennial Uses: *"The Evolution"*~ Every stone, every human, every being in life has a service to provide. Some of us are great builders, others are great nurturers. Regardless of what our unique gifts are, they serve the whole of life, perfectly; it is, in fact, what makes up life and fulfillment on this planet.

The nature of life is to evolve according to the seasons on the earth. Through evolution, our tendencies are honed to support the needs and desires of all, flawlessly, and at precisely the ideal time. Millennial Uses lists the gifts of the stones and, specifically, how they continually evolve in order to assist all of us in this exciting, challenging time. By witnessing how they stones grow and change with the seasons, we, too, can learn how to transform ourselves in a way that will ready us for the future, right now.

So, the key to working with this category/tool is to evolve. Acknowledge that you and the earth are changing ever more rapidly and even when it doesn't feel like that, it is a natural season of great change and birthing. In a really fine adventure, this is the place where you see the bigger picture of your involvement.

The Electrical Body Alignment: *"Oneness"* ~ When you are connected with something, body, mind and heart, you open yourself to full intimacy. Then you align with your electrical bodies.

The electrical body is the unlimited essence of you that is superimposed over your form and goes beyond it; it unites all that you are to your spirit, the source of your life force and of your vast, free self. The energy of your electrical body appears to be invisible and yet is immensely powerful. To acknowledge it means that you are practicing complete unity with self; therefore you can allow all the wonder of life to be activated within and around you.

So, one of the best ways to work with the Electrical Body Alignment, is to trust that you are infinite (as is all consciousness) and exquisitely interwoven with all beings, like the stones. Their presence, here, provides you with the opportunity to acknowledge, freely and happily, your oneness with all life, through all your actions. This is the sacred space in the adventure when you realize all that you're doing *is* the adventure.

The Affirmation of Support: *"Co-creation"* ~ In this book/adventure, you will read about the services of the stones and you will feel their purpose in life. That inspiration can lead you to why are you here and how you can turn that into the most thrilling, fulfilling adventure you can imagine.

Listen to the Affirmations of Support. They are created specifically for you. In integrating all these new, unusual realities/qualities, you may feel alone at times. When you need support, use these affirmations. Let the words show you how to co-create your life in a way that nurtures you thoroughly just as you are and as the you that you are becoming in the future. Feel free to change these words to suit you perfectly as you and your needs evolve. This is the point in the adventure when you find the magic words that endow you with all the riches and friends that you require to carry on.

The Stone Story: *"Wisdom"* ~ This tool/category comes directly from the hearts of the stones. We can't explain this, entirely. The stones offer their words so freely that they transcend storytelling; they *are* their stories, and all of their natural, glorious wisdom is bestowed upon us. It's up to us to choose how to use it to expand our own awareness.

Sometimes the Stone Story presents itself as a poem. Sometimes it directly spurs us on and/or questions us. It is unpredictable because it is not just a collection of sentences, it's their experience. Stone Story is the stones welcoming you into their: doorways, forms, synchronicities, hearts, evolution, oneness, co-creation, along with the wisdom to use all of their gifts exceedingly well. Perhaps their gifts will lift us to the next millennium with such inspiration and love that we will find ourselves at the end of the adventure- with a real future that once was unimaginable.

Thanks to all~

Totem Stories from the Tibetan Tektites

Greetings friends and adventurers~

In every adventure (and everything on the earth is an adventure) we join you.

We join you because we descended upon this planet to know more love and passion.

Like you, we want to be here.

We feel so honored to be here.

Now we choose to extend to you an invitation~

we invite you to come closer to us.

Feel our hearts reaching for you.

We request your presence-

such casual words-

however our meaning rings loudly.

We request your PRESENCE.

Have you even asked this of yourself?

Adventurers, walk on the earth path with us.

Regardless of what happens,

we ask you to be here,

to be fully here,

to be fully here with us

to be fully here with yourself.

And that is the most we can ask of you.

Adamite

"I catch the sparkles of a hundred different glories.
Everything upon the earth shines before me like an infinite miracle."

I am a basic arsenate of Zinc, often accompanied by Copper. I am usually found with Limonite and Calcite, and my colors are light, honey, and brownish-yellow, pale green, yellowish-green and, on rare occasions, colorless. Notable for wedge-shaped drusy crystals and brilliant yellow-green fluorescence, my structure is thorhombic, usually prismatic or horizontally elongated. My hardness is 3.5 and my cleavage is good in one direction, while poor in the second. I am named after the 18th century French mineralogist Gilbert-Joseph Adam, and my most superb crystals have been found near Hyeres, France, as well as in Mexico, Utah, and California.

Physical Integration: Increases receptivity to various energies and stimuli. Connects the body to the earth. Clears the skin.

Emotional Integration: Unites the inspiration of dreams with the abilities to manifest them. Combines inner child joy with adult responsibilities. Constantly refreshes perspective.

Millennial Uses: Adamite combines strength and vulnerability, childlikeness and wisdom and unimaginable dreams in day to day reality. It comes to us now as a bridge between what we have known, into the unknown. As we co-create a new world (out of the chaos of the old), this stone reminds us that we are surrounded by miracles and that we can continue to create more in any circumstance, no matter how challenging it appears.

Electrical Body Alignment: Connects our passions and instincts to our unknown inspirations.

Affirmation of Support: *"I am a miracle on the earth and I am creating more miracles every moment."*

Stone Story:

As you read this, a million different voices whisper behind mine. They tell you to read left to right, to expect periods at the ends of the sentences. They let you know that most things in the world are black or white or some other very well practiced polarity. In the white spaces between these words, I am listening. I hear your expectations even though you don't. I have been listening to them for a long, long time. I have placed them in my heart and warmed them up and now I give them back to you. I tell you that this is the time of timelessness. Now we can bridge the black and the white, the body and the spirit, the earth and the sky. Listen to me and we will be the bridge together.

Summary: Adamite unites body and spirit.

Ajoite

"I am the heart of the earth."

I am a gorgeous stone known for my lovely blue phantoms of many different mineral inclusions such as: Limonite, Yellow Clay, Hematite and Copper. Though I am found in the Messina mine in South Africa, supposedly I am named for some micro-copper quartz crystals located in Ajo, AZ. The story goes, that when I was discovered I reminded them of the colors of the copper crystals from Ajo.

Physical Integration: Opens the sinus passages. Removes blocks, obstructions, congestions. Increases appetite for all things.

Emotional Integration: Pulls hidden feelings to the surface for safe expression. Gives the courage to be your honest self. Sharpens dreams and the memories of their learnings.

Millennial Uses: In some societies, the peoples of the earth have pulled away from knowing the inner-connectedness of all life. Ajoite insists, lovingly and fully, that we embrace the earth. It instills in us the knowledge that all of the elements that make up the earth, make up our bodies. In these times, Ajoite symbolizes the heart of the earth. Therefore, it imparts compassionate generosity.

Electrical Body Alignment: Connects our intuition with the cycles of the earth.

Affirmation of Support: *"I feel my feelings align with the seasons of the earth."*

Stone Story:
Come to me and appreciate the wonders I see. Fly with an eagle. Blaze with the sunrise. Weep with the rains. I treasure all these things and so they breathe and beat in my heart every moment. I give that to you. I shed that essence in this song. As I praise all things, I also praise you. We are the wonders of earth.

Summary: Ajoite stands for the heart of Mother Earth.

Amazonite

*"No matter what the reality, I look for more....
I aim higher, then I am that reality."*

We are the finest crystals of Microcline—Potassium Aluminum Silicate, one of the four potash Feldspars. Light bluish-green in color, we are also called Amazon Stone. We are an important rock-forming mineral in plutonic, volcanic, and metamorphic rocks. Commonly incurring in granite pegmatites and carbonatites throughout North America, we usually form intergrowths with quartz and albite. Our finest examples occur in Russia; in North America they exist in the pegmatites of Pikes Peak, Colorado; Amelia, Virginia; and in Pennsylvania.

Our system is triclinic with twined crystals forming perfect cleavage in two directions; our specific gravity is2.5 to 2.6, our luster is vitreous, and our hardness is 6 to6.5.

Physical Integration: Being able to listen to the body and its needs. Overall toning of the metabolism. Supports the thyroid and the parathyroid.

Emotional Integration: Celebrates every physical and emotional experience. Engenders quiet compassion. Releases harsh self judgment.

Millennial Uses: During the last part of the 20th century, many people have turned to anything outside of themselves for entertainment, validation and fulfillment. Amazonite empowers us freely and invites us to see ourselves as the source of our own contentment. It reminds us that, with our attitude, we can change any situation. Therein lies the potential for true freedom.

Electrical Body Alignment: Connect us to our own power, joyfully.

Affirmation of Support: *"I love myself to allow myself a respectful, happy life."*

Stone Story:
I accept you.
I love you and I celebrate you.
I admire you enough to ask you to admire yourself.
You are a timeless human,
an adventurer of the soul,
a heart full of passion,
and an ever learning child.
See yourself.
Tell yourself the wonder of you.
Then, no matter what happens,
you are free.
You are free to be your magnificence
despite the fears
or pain of anyone,
even yourself.

Love.

Summary: Amazonite symbolizes our true selves—free and happy.

Amber

*"I remind you that you are not so different from the stonepeople.
You are also ancient, wise ones."*

I begin as an organic, gummy resin, generally from conifers, secreted when my tree is injured; I seal the wound against insects, disease and desiccation, and under certain conditions I will harden into a honey-colored globule of amber. I am transparent to translucent with a greasy luster; typically I am yellow or brown in color, yet I may also have had a red or white tinge. I am usually cloudy in appearance due to air spaces. When rubbed I will produce a detectable negative electric charge.

People have prized amber back to Paleolithic times on Earth, drawn to both the color and the story of my creation. With a hardness of only 2.5 I carve easily; this and the fact that I polish beautifully make me a desired choice for jewelry. To the world of human science, I am valued for the unrivaled view I provide of prehistoric insects: trapped within my essence, they are perfectly preserved and display an astonishing detail, as well as a rare and vivid glimpse into other lives long since passed.

I am mined extensively along the Samland Coast near Kaliningrad, Russia, and I am found along shorelines worldwide, after rising from the seabed and floating along innumerable ocean currents.

Physical Integration: Increases left/right brain integration with joy and ease. Supports all brain functions. Expands cellular connections to other parallel realities/dimensions.

Emotional Integration: Helps to connect us with the sources of our joy. Increases spontaneous laughter. Opens up to new wisdom.

Millennial Uses: Stones serve as the earth's record-keepers. They observe everything and open themselves up to wisdom. Amber is an ancient ally to wisdom. It can help us to *really* witness what is happening around us. If we choose to empty ourselves of expectations, we can learn anything (including how to live in the 2000's) from whatever is around us.

Electrical Body Alignment: Links us to our ancestors and to eternal wisdom.

Affirmation of Support: *"Every moment, I grow wiser and happier."*

Stone Story:
There is no time;
there is only life measured by each experience.
You can measure that in time.....
If you value life then it comes to you in awareness.
It expands you beyond measurement.
You remember to participate in it,
to live it so utterly
that descriptions give way
to sheer pleasure.

Summary: Amber represents timeless wisdom.

Amethyst

"When you touch me,
you find joyous upliftment and the awakening of all possibilities."

I am Quartz—Silicon Dioxide, and in the silica group which includes Opal and Chalcedony. Silicates are the largest and most widely distributed class of minerals, comprising 25% of all known mineral species, and 95% by volume of all minerals in the Earth's crust. I am violet to red-purple in color, and my family includes Rock Crystal (colorless), Rose Quartz (pink to rose red), Citrine (clear yellow), Smoky Quartz (pale brown to black), and Milky Quartz (white), as well as Aventurine (glistening with mica or hematite), Cat's Eye (opalescent from asbestos), and Tigereye (with lustrous yellow to brown parallel fibers).

My hardness is 7, and I have little or no cleavage. My crystal system is trigonal, my specific gravity is 2.65, and my luster is vitreous. As with all quartz, I am piezoelectric; under pressure I will develop an electric charge. Another characteristic of quartz is enantiomorphism—left or right-handedness, which is detectable by the position of small faces. A pervasive rock-forming mineral, I develop in a wide variety of environments. I am a common constituent of both granite and sandstone, and I am found in abundance in Brazil and Uruguay, as well as in the Ural Mountains of Russia, Namibia, Western Australia, Sri Lanka, Zambia and Germany.

Personal Story

For me, Amethyst is a stone of openness and attraction. Its purple color always attracts me and makes me feel happy and gives me a rich warmth inside. When I wear it I feel open to whatever may come along and alert to other possibilities. Amethyst always seems to attract attention, wherever it is.

~from Mary Rydman

Physical Integration: Releases old habits and old patterns. Frees us from headaches and addictive desires.

Emotional Integration: Uplifts perspective beyond expectations. Encourages integration with our spirit. Promotes a love of service. Decreases delusions.

Millennial Uses: Amethyst is more than a stone for easing addictions and painful illusions. Like all lifeforms on this planet, it is evolving. Its service now includes exploring how and why we separate ourselves (hence creating addictions of all types) from life. Amethyst leads us into our innate power (beyond domination and victimhood) by reminding us that we are spirit in a form. That's where we find phenomenal new worlds to explore in any millennium.

Electrical Body Alignment: Puts us in touch with our true inspiration.

Affirmation of Support: *"I live with spirit!"*

Stone Story:
Everything forms on this earth perfectly.
I amplify every swirling vibration of me to a single tip.

All of my existing meets at one point-
spirit.
I am alive
because I am a face
a thought
a smile of spirit.

Visit me whenever you like.
Ask me whatever you wish.
We will remember your glorious lifetimes, past and future.
All that we do will meet with spirit,
the source of life.

Summary: Amethyst puts us in touch with our spirit.

(See *Stone Combination Section* for Amethyst in "Connecting to Your Guides," and "World Peace").

Ametrine

*"Come run across the bridge from unknown to known
and play in the indescribable reality."*

I am a variety of Quartz that contains both Amethyst and Citrine sectors in the same crystal. Only known since the 1980s, when I was first found in Bolivia , I am colored by minute amounts of Iron (about 40 parts per million). I develop color when Quartz containing Iron is exposed to ionizing radiation which arises from the gsmma rays produced by the decay of Potassium. An inventive lapidary can cut me in such a way as to create unusual and very striking color effects, and it is even possible to produce a bicolored gem, with one part distinctly yellow-orange, and the other Amethyst.

I form in veins of dolomitic limestone, and to date the only known significant source of natural Ametrine is the Anahi mine in eastern Bolivia. I am also produced synthetically in limited quantities in Russia.

Physical Integration: Helps to release allergies and sensitivities. Supports the adrenals. Strengthens the diaphragm.

Emotional Integration: Expands on the use of breath for meditative states. Lets go of the emotional attachment to unhelpful cravings.

Millennial Uses: Perhaps the greatest thing we could leave behind in the 20th century would be fear as a way of life. Ametrine relaxes the body and the mind enough so that we may approach the future with joy. This joy encourages us to go through our fear of change, consciously, freeing us up to hear our truth— no matter the distractions. It focuses us on our most inspired dreams and inspirations and leads us to the practical ways to manifest them.

Electrical Body Alignment: Combines intuition and spirit with everyday life.

Affirmation of Support: *"I allow my spirit to lead me in life."*

Stone Story:
*Every crystal is programmed with
the breath of spirit.*

Welcome to my world~
Here I see how the broken paths of separation
in your bodies
and your minds
are still whole.

You learned to play with limits,
yet you remain unlimited.
Hear me,
I am the echo of your truth,
that you pleaded to know again.
I echo that echo
that knows you, too.
Take all that you know,
grasp the unknown with it
and make the practices that will inspire your perfection.

Summary: Ametrine connects our knowledge with wisdom and with our personal guides.

Apophyllite

"When I come out from the earth, rings of fairies join me."

I am Hydrous Calcium Potassium Flurosilicate, and I often contain small amounts of iron and nickel. My name is from the Greek words for "off," and "leaf," alluding to the fact that I flake apart when heated. My colors range from reddish, yellowish and greenish, to gray, white and colorless. My luster is vitreous. I have an average hardness of 4.5 to 5 and my crystals are tetragonal. I have perfect cleavage in one direction, where cubelike crystals exhibit a pearly luster.

I form at low temperatures and am commonly found in basalt cavities of volcanic rock, commonly associated with prehnite and zeolites. My best known crystals originate in the igneous rocks of Bombay, India, and I am also found widely in Mexico and the United States.

Physical Integration: Nourishes the scalp and hair. Promotes lightness of movement.

Emotional Integration: Increases openness to intuition. Fosters the remembering of important dreams. Trusts in unseen realities.

Millennial Uses: In traditions throughout time, throughout the world, people have shared stories of other-worldly beings, (fairies, gnomes, sprites) who live upon the earth. Recently, the workers at Findhorn Garden in Scotland told of how devas (the spirits of the plants) helped their crops grow abundantly in a less than ideal climate and soil.

Apophyllite connects us to the spirits of the land and reminds us how to speak to them. In speaking to them, we can work together to create harmony for all beings of the earth.

Electrical Body Alignment: Links us to the spirits of the earth.

Affirmation of Support: *"I allow magic to touch me every day."*

Stone Story:
Whatever you believe in, I believe in you.
I come before you to announce my love.
My spirit speaks to you now.
Do you know that I speak to you whenever you most need it?
My voice lands upon your heart,
any way that you allow.

Come to me freely.
Find me in soft dreams.
However you discover me,
the richness of our meeting
will enchant your days and nights forever.

Summary: Apophyllite represents the invisible magic of other dimensions of life

(See *Stone Combination Section* for Apophyllite in "Celebration of Fairies," "Judgement," and "Open Heart").

Aquamarine

*"I touch the earth. I dance the skies.
I pull their union into me and create magnificence."*

I am Beryllium Aluminum Silicate. I am a pale blue to greenish blue gem, due to iron impurities, and in the mineral world I am known as Beryl, (from the Greek word for green gemstones), along with Emerald (green), Golden Beryl (golden yellow), Heliodor (yellow to brown), Morganite (pink to light purplish-red), and Goshenite (colorless). I am a hard gem at 7.5 to 8 on the Mohs Scale and I possess a vitreous to resinous luster, with a weak, basal cleavage. My system is hexagonal, and my generally six-sided prism crystals are striated lengthwise and are often large and flawless.

I develop primarily in pegmatites and metamorphic rocks and usually with quartz. My best gem-quality examples emerge from Minas Gerais, Brazil, found as alluvial deposits, and in the Minsk Urals. Other common locales for my discovery are Argentina, Burma, Northern Ireland, China, Namibia, India, Madagascar, Norway, Pakistan, Tanzania, Zimbabwe and the United States.

Physical Integration: Evens out the rhythms of breath. Calmly integrates vision and hearing with action. Aligns muscles and vertebrae in the neck.

Emotional Integration: Releases biases. Promotes free, harmonious feelings. Continually connects the emotions to peaceful detachment. Inspires & uplifts.

Millennial Uses: According to some traditions we now are entering a time of brotherhood among all peoples of the earth. Aquamarine lives and breathes peaceful equality for all. It continually refreshes our spirit, allowing us the freedom to choose harmony always. Aquamarine gently but insistently lifts our perspective until we embrace peace as the one way for all of us to survive (past our domination urges) into the future.

Electrical Body Alignment: Integrates our past with the future, compassionately.

Affirmation of Support: *"I always choose inner and outer peace, from this moment on."*

Stone Story:
Be who you are.
Be that so fully
that all that is left to think about is breathing.
Breathe consciously
so that you inhale peace
so that you exhale calm...........
Now you live your destiny.
While all your experiences are wisdom's tools,
you never needed to live in fear.
You never were designed to die frightened and alone.

You beacon love across your countenance
and across the waves of the universe.
Yes.
This is your freedom just to be:
You are created in and from complete love,
from thought to flesh to spirit- whole, perfect.
Take up the life of love. Choose it every moment.
You are choosing yourself, from the mirror of eternity.

Summary: Aquamarine stands for continual inner and outer peace in the world

(See *Stone Combination Section* for Aquamarine in "Listening").

Aragonite

"Welcome to the science of timelessness, dreams and magic."

Named after the Aragon province of Spain where first found, I am a low-temperature orthorhombic form of Calcium Carbonate. My colors are white, gray, colorless, yellow, pale green, violet and brown; my luster is vitreous and resinous. My hardness is 3.5 to 4, my specific gravity is 2.9 to 3, and my cleavage is good in one direction and poor in two others.

I am dimorphous with calcite, but less common, and created in

(con't from previous page)

stop sign. It just purred all the way home. Since he hadn't done anything differently, he figured that the aquamarine must be a totem for his car. So he took a nice one and wire wrapped it inside his car's engine. Not only did his vehicle run smoothly, it used less oil and needed fewer repairs from that moment on.

~from Marilyn

far fewer environments. I am found near the surface, formed from hot springs and geysers, in gypsum beds and iron ore deposits, in veins in serpentine, in basalts, as stalactites, and in sulfur deposits as celestine. I occur in evaporite deposits of chemical sedimentary rocks with gypsum and calcite, in blue schists of regional metamorphic rocks with Albite, Lawsonite and Glaucophane, and with Cuprite, Azurite and Chalcopyrite in massive hydrothermal replacement deposits.

I appear worldwide, with fine crystals found in Alston Moor, Cleator Moor and Frizington, in Cumbria, England. Other fine deposits are to

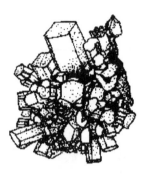

be found the Magdalena district in Socorro County, New Mexico.

Physical Integration: Clears the thinking processes. Assists those with dyslexic patterns and supports brain functions.

Emotional Integration: Maintains the confidence to pursue every experience to its logical and unimaginable end. Enlivens curiosity. Allows for healthy detachment.

Millennial Uses: Aragonite encourages us to explore life through all means. It pushes us on to find the limits and then pass through them. It tells us that we have all the tools necessary to study anything if we choose to do so.

Electrical Body Alignment: Connects our mind and our brain to all knowingness.

Affirmation of Support: *"I combine my reason and my intuition to explore new joys."*

Stone Story:
You understand certain ways that the world works. You feel that

everything that is thrown into air must fall; that you must eat to survive and that when you are tired, you must sleep. All of these things may be helpful to you to live. But you are not meant to stop at these understandings and to accept them without question. What you know of the world is just the beginning. It is your jumping off place. When you reach into yourself, grow your curiosity. Then, what you understand will lead you into imagination and then far beyond it.

Summary: Aragonite explores the heart and mystery in science

(See *Stone Combination Section* for Aragonite in "Shamanic Dream," and "Should into Acceptance")

Aventurine

*"I come to you now with the whisper of hope.
Together we go to the world, a full song of adventure."*

I am Silicon Dioxide—Quartz, the stable modification of silica at normal temperatures and one of the most common minerals known. Often glistening with enclosed scales of other minerals, my colors are green (with Mica), brownish-red (with Pyrite), grayish, yellowish, and bluish-white to bluish-green. My structure is hexagonal, usually in the form of prismatic crystals striated crosswise. My hardness is 7 and I have a greasy luster.

My name derives from the Italian word *avventurino* for "chance," from my accidental discovery. The best quality Aventurines are found in Brazil, India, Siberia, and Tanzania.

Physical Integration: Helps to stabilize the heart. Evens the metabolism. Supports the integration of passionate instincts and an open heart.

Emotional Integration: Brings enthusiasm and practicality together for adventure. Draws out secret dreams to pursue. Provides optimism as a life perspective.

Millennial Uses: In these times we are learning new values. Therefore, our exchange of money and efforts is valued in different ways. All the beings of the earth are joining each other and finding common languages to live by. Aventurine guides us into a language of respect where all beings are honored for the gifts they are. To hold this stone is to hold the source of abundance to our hearts.

Electrical Body Alignment: Aligns our hearts with the deep bounty of the earth.

Affirmation of Support: *"I value life as the source of my joy."*

Stone Story:
Many things have represented abundance to you: Time, work, stress.
I am here to sing to you.
I am here to dance along side of you.
I am here to breathe timelessness upon you.
What do you want?
What gives you joy and makes your spirit stand tall in your body?

This is who you are. You are your happiness and it feeds every part of your life until all your love grows to every part of the earth and all that you need jumps into your hands.

Personal Story

When I first started carrying stones with me, one of them was aventurine. I can still see that first piece. It was deep green and roughly the shape of a pyramid. I loved it so well, I didn't carry it around with me much so that I wouldn't lose it.

One day, I took it with me to work because I just needed a pick-me-up. As I put it on my desk, I heard it say, "I can help." Well, I took that to mean that it would help me with money since it seemed to be in short supply both for me and for the company that was employing me. The day went normally, until a friend of a friend asked me to go to lunch with her. It seemed surprising because Colleen didn't usually have much time for anything but business. Over lunch, she asked me to come and work for her. I didn't even have to quit my current job, I could just work for her until I got a feel for the business and then I could decide whether or not I wanted to be part-time, full-time, or whatever. I turned it down, but it did brighten my day.

The next two times I carried that aventurine with me, I got very unexpected job offers (while I was already gainfully employed). It dawned on me that this stone was teaching me about abundance, which apparently to me meant new or more work. I decided that this was a very magical stone.

Then I had lunch with an old co-worker friend. She was about to be married and was very excited about everything except her money situation. Gretchen's fiance had just decided to go back to school (with her blessing) to be a chiropractor. The only way she could see getting married anytime soon would be if she got a more lucrative job and supported them both. I told her I would visualize her with a lot of money (I was fingering the aventurine in my pocket at the time).

The next day Gretchen called to tell me that she had just heard about a fantastic job opening (in her home state); it was one that she had always wanted. She was thrilled, but she just couldn't imagine getting it. Then I knew. I met her for lunch again and I gave her the aventurine and said, "Be confident!" Gretchen took the stone with her to the interview and got her dream job.

I can still see that aventurine. And it's happily living with a married friend in Wisconsin.

~from Marilyn

Summary: Aventurine reminds us that at the core we are exceedingly bountiful

(See *Stone Combination Section* for Aventurine in "Faith's Embrace," "Freedom," "Lack into Allowability," and "Transformation, Prosperity & the Goddess").

Azurite

"I blossom in the creativity of your wildest imaginings. Then, when you speak, it all comes true."

I am basic Copper Carbonite, also known as Chessylite, azure blue to dark blue in color, due to the presence of Copper. I am often associated with Malachite, and usually found with it, Limonite and Chalcopyrite. With a characteristic blue streak, I am found as a secondary mineral in the upper oxidized zones of Copper deposits. I am found as prismatic crystals in a monoclinic structure, and I am doubly refractive. My luster is vitreous to dull, my hardness is 3.5 to 4, and I have good cleavage in two directions.

In my pure form, I am generally not tough enough to polish or use as a gemstone. Occasionally, though, rare gem quality Azurite is found. Some of my finest crystals are found in the Copper deposits at Tsumeb, Namibia. Other quality sources are: Bisbee, Arizona; Germany; Hungary; the Irish Republic; Romania; and Australia.

Physical Integration: Balances the voice. Tones the throat. Clears excess fluids easily.

Emotional Integration: Excites inner creativity. Strengthens the instinct to live and to express truthfully. Promotes individual talents.

Millennial Uses: We are making steps towards becoming a global community (in communications, politics and economics). Evolution teaches us that to do this naturally and successfully, we must combine our unique, individual strengths. Azurite inspires us to listen within and then to discover our special talents. It welcomes us to amplify our gifts into a complete, truthful way of life. This, then, would be what we, each, have to offer a new world in the new millennium.

Electrical Body Alignment: Links us with our innate, individual talents.

Affirmation of Support: *"I practice my creativity and give it freely to life in my own special, loving way."*

Stone Story:
Sing out!
You are a creature and every creature here has a voice.
What is your song?
Why is it yours?
What will you do with it?

What happens to you when you chant your sound?
What happens in the world then?
What choir of life do you find yourself in?

I have the questions and you are the answers.

Summary: Azurite brings forth our own special creativity
(See *Stone Combination Section* for Azurite in "Disease into Vitality").

Beta Quartz

"We must talk now because our hearts have already intertwined and there is no refusing that."

I am Cristobalite, one of the eight polymorphs of the Silica composition whose differences are slight rearrangements of the positions of our atoms without the breaking of any bonds. I have two forms: a stable high-temperature cubic form and a metastable low-temperature tetragonal form. My structure forms primarily hexagonal crystals, and occasionally trapezoidal formations, and I occur as massive deposits, often in Opal, and usually as small octohedral crystals.

Physical Integration: Increases focus, while letting go of control. Eases headaches. Tones the nervous system and the mind/body communication.

Emotional Integration: Emphasizes strengths during crises. Fortifies belief in self and in the sixth sense. Trusts in the perfection of life.

Millennial Uses: The more we threaten life (as we know it) on this planet, the louder life warns and guides us.

Beta Quartz speaks loudly. It insists that we listen to the earth and to the natural cycles of life around and within us. It shouts not to punish us, but because we need the help. Beta Quartz talks over our denial and our addictions. It gets our attention and revives us, so that we remember how wondrous life is. It is exactly that feeling (the wonder of life) that keeps us from destroying ourselves.

Electrical Body Alignment: Aligns our will to the perfection of spirit.

Affirmation of Support: *"I give my all to life and I receive miracles."*

Personal Story

We bought some Beta quartz from our good friend, Gary, sight unseen. They arrived at the office in several big boxes. When they came in, I was deeply involved in my e-mails. After unloading them off the delivery truck, I went back to work without missing a beat. All of a sudden, I felt a huge wave of energy rush through me. Must be time for a break. Without a further thought, I started to unpack the Betas.

Right away, I could hear their spirits talking very loudly. They demanded [kindly] to be placed in certain places in the office. They did not want to be put just anywhere. They wanted to go right to work. They told me that they would manifest our dreams, if we listened

(con't on next page)

(con't from previous page)

to them and placed them carefully. As I was pulling two of the crystals out, they wouldn't even let me set them down. They requested I put them in our vehicle [which was sitting in the very hot desert sun], where they would draw out much of the summer heat to make it more comfortable for us.

Everything they said, they did. They drew to us resources that helped our new business along. Mostly they have stayed with us and worked with us. Not being a classically gorgeous stone, most other people pass them by without a glance. I did have to laugh at one of the persons who was very attracted to them. A very bright eight year-old friend of ours, Laura, ran right to the shelf

(con't on next page)

Stone Story:
Do you feel that?
The spirit of life shouts all around us.
It shapes all my words and I am glad!

We do not have much time.
Of course not, we live timelessly.

That means that to eat, we must do so, right now—
to love, we must do so, right now—
to live, we must live right now—

While you plan and consider, you are still acting out life,
but it is a weakened imitation.
Pour your full heart into right now—

Every feeling, every thought, jumps into this moment
and you will choose with your spirit
because that is how you are living.

Summary: Beta Quartz sparks us into living completely every moment.

Bloodstone

"I wear my vitality, inside and out, for all to see."

I am a variety of Chalcedony, and accordingly, in the Quartz family of the tectosilicate group. Also known as Heliotrope, my color is bright to dark green, spotted with red veins of Jasper inclusions. I am found mostly in India and Germany.

Physical Integration: Strengthens veins. Fortifies the blood. Tones the heart.

Emotional Integration: Facilitates commitment to healthy, long life. Fosters self respect. Encourages a good support system. Embraces commitment to long term relationships.

Millennial Uses: Each generation leaves a mark upon the world. As a species we base some of our decisions upon the traditions and values of our predecessors. Bloodstone values commitment, stability and a structure from which we can build our lives with respect.

It gives its vitality to us, so that we may have the time and space to acknowledge our true priorities and then to act upon them responsibly.

Electrical Body Alignment: Connects us to our communities with trustworthiness and loyalty.

Affirmation of Support: *"I embrace my community and it supports me unconditionally."*

Stone Story:
Blood flows between us.
It connects us all; we are all family.
I show you the drops of my blood,
declaring, "We live as one family."
I am stone.
You are animal.
We are the same, under the same sky,
blessed by the stars.

When you savor
our oneness,
then you will not kill your brothers
or your sisters
and you will not kill
yourself.

Personal Story

Early on in my stone collecting, I found a gorgeous bloodstone. Unlike the typical green ones with the red spots, this one also had white clouds and blue rays in it. When I showed it to a friend, he pointed out that it had an eye on it as well. I knew this stone was truly remarkable and that somehow it had very powerful healing powers in it. I almost never carried the bloodstone with me. I just kept it on my dresser where I knew that it was watching over me.

A few years later, I suddenly had a funny feeling when my very amiable roommate walked by me. Without any reason, I felt that her won-

(con't from previous page)

where the Betas stood. Laura threw both hands on one of the crystals and acted as if she were being electrocuted and shouted, "Wow!! It's got me!" We both grinned. When I asked her why she picked that crystal (from all the other stones we have around) to touch, she said, "It shouted at me to come and touch it!"

~ from Marilyn

derful, long term relationship was about to end. Without thinking about it further, I handed her the bloodstone, saying, "Keep this with you for a while. I think it will help you through rough times."

Shortly afterwards, she and her boyfriend broke up very unexpectedly. She clung to that bloodstone every day. Then one day, Kathy told me that she had put the stone on her dresser before she went to sleep and by morning, it was gone. She knew positively that that's the last place she put it.

Things were changing rapidly in Kathy's life and she decided to move out of our place. Since our relationship had also changed, it seemed like a good idea. A few days after she had left, I was laying in bed enjoying my quiet solitude. I looked up on my dresser and there was my bloodstone. I hadn't put it there. A phone call to Kathy confirmed that she hadn't put it there. Somehow it just was there watching over me again.

~ from Marilyn

Summary: Bloodstone shows us the oneness of all life, no matter the form.

(See *Stone Combination Section* for Bloodstone in "Judgement into Trust," "Pregnancy," Violence into Compassion").

Blue Lace Agate

"Hold me and discover quiet calm and release the need to struggle anymore."

I also am Quartz, Silicon Dioxide. We Agates are banded forms of Chalcedony, a microcrystalline variety of Quartz, and we are often infused with some Iron and Aluminum. Our coloration is due to trace elements and our banding is due to the progressive solidification of our material. Agates form in a trigonal crystal system, have a hardness of 7, a specific gravity of 2.65, no cleavage, and appear in a wide variety of colors.

We are formed in several environments, though generally near the surface of the Earth where temperatures and pressures are relatively low. Our general name derives from "Chalcedon," an ancient Greek city of Asia Minor, and we are plentiful and widespread throughout the Earth's crust.

Physical Integration: Releases the need for excess stress. Balances the adrenals. Loosens throat and facial muscles.

Emotional Integration: Soothes petty desires and childish habits. Lovingly connects us to a generosity of spirit. Sends calm after long struggles.

Millennial Uses: Blue Lace Agate gently enters our being and shows us the way back to our center. There, we melt into the stillness and remember the calm. Through this calm, we breathe easily, even fancifully. It sustains us through all the stress of our joint initiations. The core of Blue Lace Agate's service leads us into gentle breaths. From there, we cope with every feeling and situation and even find space to bless others.

Electrical Body Alignment: Expands our perspective from the heart and the lungs.

Affirmation of Support: *"Regardless of what happens around me, I breathe and all is well."*

Stone Story:
Come into my spirals.
I am a mandala of stillness.
I am ready for you.
I reach out the center and it is me and it is you.
We can travel anywhere.
The world goes with us because we are the world.
You can look upon any challenge or any struggle
or you can look upon the treasured places of calm that are your
heritage. Come.
When you most need the peace,
I send my welcome the loudest.

Summary: Blue Lace Agate calms the mind.

(See *Stone Combination Section* for Blue Lace Agate in "Pain into Fulfillment")

Blue Moonstone

"Feel the new words and the new ways of love in every word you speak."

We are Orthoclase, among the plagioclase group of Feldspars, common rock-forming minerals in igneous and metamorphic rocks, though rarely of gem quality. When colorless and transparent or translucent, often with a bluish opalescence, we are called Adularia and termed "Moonstone" in the jewelry business. Our monoclinic structure forms predominately as single crystals of rectangular or square cross section, commonly as twin crystals; our hardness is 6 to 6.5, our specific gravity is 2.6 to 2.76, and our cleavage is good, in two directions at 90 degrees.

When our Feldspar crystals of Moonstone first formed, they were rich in both Potassium and Calcium; upon cooling, our crystal structure adjusted to lower temperatures and these components became mutually incompatible. So they "unmixed", separated into two different Feldspar minerals, one of Potassium and one of Calcium. They became alternating platelets of microscopic thickness within our crystal. Light diffracted from these surfaces produce the beautiful soft sheen or bright iridescence of Moonstone.

Volcanic in origin, we are found in Norway, Canada, Myanmar, Sri Lanka, Madagascar, and Tanzania. Adularia is named for a locality in the Adula mountains of Switzerland.

Physical Integration: Tones the diaphragm. Brings full breath and depth to the voice. Assists with singing and toning.

Emotional Integration: Releases self-consciousness about music and dance. Deepens the appreciation of sound in healing. Increases acceptance of all others' communications.

Millennial Uses: In this new millennium, we must return to old healing arts to integrate our incredible acceleration and growth. However, for any knowledge to apply to us in our newly evolved states, we must recreate the old traditions with newly born parts so that we can connect to all times and all possibilities, simultaneously. Blue Moonstone rises in popularity because it is a timeless tool. It vibrates especially to timelessness, art and healing sound. It revitalizes the uses of toning, chanting and using our own voices to co-create, very directly, the world of our choice. This beautiful stone easily holds the energy of sound and, when we join with it, adds our unique truth and rapid discoveries to life around us.

Electrical Body Alignment: Forms a trine between the heart, the ears and intuition.

Affirmation of Support: *"As I listen to the truth in all my words, I sing my joyous gratitude."*

Stone Story:
Sweet ones, pause here.
Let go of listening with your eyes.
Close them.
Open your heart.
Breathe through your ears
until every sound touches the root of your love.
Please, breathe.
I will wait here.....

We meet in timelessness, where else?
When you hear the richness of my tones, the beautiful whites between these black words, you have found me. Heart and soul, breath and love for all that we be. This is my way. I live in the dark womb of your mother. I happily, simply, completely, record sound pressing into matter. Every shape, every body, holds a note. When that note sings itself clear and true, the world sighs in contentment. All seasons balance. All life gives to all life.
Right now, I intone my song to you.
Listen in the dark of your closed eyes.
Add my note to yours.
It is the gift I came to give.

Summary: Blue Moonstone presents us with the beauty and healing of sound.

Boleite

*"When looking for truth — look— and look again,
and look again."*

I am a beautiful indigo-blue color and, as a tetragonal mineral that would normally form rectangular boxes with a square cross-section, I am unusual in that I am psuedocubically twined. Each cube-like crystal of mine is actually composed of three of these rectangular boxes oriented at right angles to each other. The look of my psuedocubes is sometimes different due to the addition of tetragonal dipyramid faces which can look like octahedral faces.

I am Hydrated Lead Copper Silver Chloride Hydroxide. My hardness is 3 to 3.5; my cleavage is perfect in one direction and my luster is vitreous to pearly. I am found in sedimentary Copper deposits and I am named after the locality in which I am found, Boeleo, Baja California, Mexico. I can also be found in Broken Hills, New South Wales and in Mendip Hills, England. I am considered somewhat rare and I am of interest to collectors of "twins."

Physical Integration: Strengthens the immune system. Increases the cells ability to absorb oxygen. Supports the neck muscles.

Emotional Integration: Centers self under any circumstances. Fosters healthy respect for authority. Finds inspiration and motivation during challenges.

Millennial Uses: As we go forth into the 2000's, some of the institutions we live with will change and/or disappear. The surprising part of that is we may end up replacing them with very similar structures. Why is that? Because some of the underlying reasons for creating those institutions may not have changed significantly.

During change, truth remains constant. That's what Boleite represents– constant truth. It helps us to locate that essence, always, so that we can surround ourselves with structures that truly will serve us compassionately and well. It teaches us to hear and to see the truth and then to build our life upon it.

Electrical Body Alignment: Links us to timeless truth.

Affirmation of Support: *"I build my life upon truth."*

Stone Story: *I have no need to speak to you in words.*
I listen to truth.
I witness it.
If you want to talk to me, stop.
Listen.
Watch the world as it spins.
What wonder will find you?
An old woman's dream
A baby's gaze
A pair of lovers
A story teller's magic
A shooting star
A golden eagle~

All these things come to you offered by the constant that serves life—
Love.
If you miss it,
you will miss a lifetime.

Summary: Boleite stands for lovingly building the world's structures with truth.

Boji Stone™

> *"I come to activate your memories*
> *so you will know that you are a co-creator here."*

We are here in this world by design, and we bring to you an energy that is unique and intentional. We are concretion stones, a combination of Palladium and Pyrite. While most minerals combine the masculine and feminine aspects into a single stone, we evolve into separate gender manifestations, as well as in androgynous forms. Our appearance is dark, mostly brown to blackish, and we come to you as spheroids, either in the female, as mostly smooth, flat, flying-saucer-shaped, or as male, in bumpy, geometric platelet protrusions from a smooth substrate. Our predominant mineral formation is Pyrite, although we are a collection of many different minerals.

Personal Story

I was asked to draw these stone beings, so I sat in quiet meditation, one stone in each palm. After a few moments I felt something begin to happen. It started with a simple tingling in my fingertips, then spread down into my palms until I could feel my pulse beating beneath each stone. Heat rose up from my hands, and as it surrounded the stone, I felt a surge of energy, a stream of pink light race up my arms into my body. I asked the stones how they wanted me to draw them, and Spirit said, "From your heart."

~from Crystal Karl

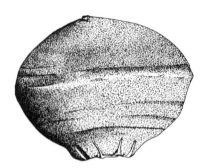

Physical Integration: Aligns the feet. Balances the posture. Eases the shoulders. Strengthens the hips and lower abdomen.

Emotional Integration: Allows ease in expressing feelings immediately. Helps to identify what emotions store themselves in particular parts of the body. Expands the creativity in all feelings. This is a very physical stone and the emotional and physical integrations could be combined or interchanged freely.

Millennial Uses: Boji Stone™ has been preparing itself deep in the earth for a long time so that it could come forth now and complement the current cycles of consciousness and growth. It speaks to humans (and other beings) at a cellular level. It is a visioning stone. It reminds us that our bodies can be used to see and record worlds beyond the physical one that we claim to understand. Just by listening to the words of the Boji™ here, you may activate awareness within you that has gone unmeasured and unnoticed.

Electrical Body Alignment: Presents us with conscious awareness of our electrical bodies and of the ley lines upon the earth.

Affirmation of Support: *"With every act I increase my awareness and my power, in love."*

Stone Story:
I am just like you. I am spirit in a form. I have buried myself deep in the earth until this exact moment. I come to the surface now to show you that we are ready to combine the knowledge and the wonder of every single life form upon the earth.

44

In that union, we co-create a world so magnificent that it grows beyond our dreams. Each being (even the most insignificant looking ones) contribute a perfection to the entire movement of seasons of life on this planet. That is what I witness. That is what I have recorded for so long. I receive the unique gifts of each species (the greatest of their learnings) and I send that into the ley lines on the earth so that all can give and receive the genius of all wisdom, here. With this gift, we create instantly what we imagine.

As Boji™, we specialize in recording the most advanced learnings of each species, then we send it along the electrical grid of the earth to be received cellularly by all who need it.

Summary: Boji Stones™ catalyze our deepest cellular knowingness.

Botswana Agate

"I remind you that whatever challenges come to you on this earth, they are also journeys to the gentleness of joy."

We are a microcrystalline form of Quartz, within the family of Chalcedony. We form in concretionary deposits at or near the surface of the Earth's crust; as low-temperature Silica-rich water filters through sediments and rocks (particularly those of volcanic origin), we gather in seams and vugs, rich in Iron Oxide. These form in variable micro-thin undulating patterns and bursts of color.

Because of this cumulative accretion, you will find no two of us alike anywhere. We have mostly parallel lines of white, grey and brown. We are to be found most notably in Botswana, Africa.

Physical Integration: Supports physical and emotional endurance during challenges and crisis. Opens the heart. Encourages healthy release of emotions.

Emotional Integration: Supports all feelings. Gives nurturance that fosters deep self acceptance. Releases loneliness.

Millennial Uses: In these times of great acceleration, it feels like many things around us overstimulate or distract us. For every distraction on the earth, there exists a complementary calming influence. Botswana Agate soothes us when we are overwhelmed by life. It brings together the elements of water and earth. In other words, it combines the hopefulness of feeling and the ability to practice that in our own realities. It strengthens the body and stabilizes the emotions so that we can be receptive to the deeper communications of life. This stone supports us so that what appears to be stress slows down and becomes what it really is– ever deeper levels of life speaking to us so that we can evolve even more.

Electrical Body Alignment: Shows us how to breathe in and out of our heart to link us to the core energy of life and, therefore, a positive self-esteem.

Affirmation of Support: *"I give and receive love from all things, more and more and more."*

Stone Story:
Welcome.
For this moment, this is my home.
This place where you and I meet and talk and smile.
I welcome all of you and as I do so, I am welcomed by all of life
to be more of what I am.
I spiral, I flow, I breathe, with every season.
I find them all equally enriching.
I share that with you with these words, with my breath.
Each word I cast out is a single story.
It is a flash of acceptance.
Let it enter your body to find the parts of you that worry and fear
needlessly.
There, in your body, place my strength and the full support of the
earth.
How could you be alone!

Summary: Botswana Agate offers the nurturance to live, not just to survive in the world.

(See *Stone Combination Section* for Botswana Agate in "Spirit Storytelling").

Brookite

"Together, we are a tree of life, souls stretching to the heavens and roots grounding into the mother earth."

I am a minor ore of Titanium, a polymorph with two other minerals—Rutile and Anatase. We all share the same chemistry, but have different structures. I am among the darker of minerals, varying from red to dark green to brown to black, with a adamantine to submetallic luster. My orthorhombic structure crystallizes as plate-like and tabular crystals; my hardness is 5.5 to 6, my specific gravity is 3.9 to 4.1 (average for metallic minerals), and my cleavage is poor, prismatically and in one basal direction. When heated to high temperatures, I revert to the Rutile structure.

Physical Integration: Releases fatigue. Tones the organs, especially the excretory organs. Straightens the spine. Supports the base of the spine.

Emotional Integration: Encourages a continual and even flow of emotions. Integrates inspiration and reason quickly. Practices healthy discrimination. Sparks the genius in each being.

Millennial Uses: There are so many ways to meet the future. Sometimes we romanticize it. Other times we prepare for it with great trepidation. Through Brookite, we see the coming times as simply another earth season that must be lived, one day at a time. It helps us to combine the best of our logic and our dreams to create our chosen reality.

Electrical Body Alignment: Unites us with the source of life force.

Affirmation of Support: *"I live every moment fully."*

Stone Story:
All lifeforms touch each other,
like spokes in a wheel.
I touch you with tangible magic.
You touch me and I know insatiable curiosity.
Each of us grows through the gifts of the other.

Life spins an ever moving cycle and by our lives,

we give it breath and desire.
She grows, too, constantly, sweetly.
Then in one season she breathes her wisdom upon me.

Touch me every moment.
My wisdom swells with time and your caress.
Smooth your rough edges on me and I will delight
in the new shapes that we create together.

We partner ourselves in this cycle of life.
I feed your fire and I organize your science.
Come even closer.
As time wears by,
I shine with the newness of fresh life and awareness.
Touch me.
I give you all my open secrets.

Please receive all my knowings.
For each one that you accept,
more leaps into me and then stretches into infinity.

You flame an infinite spiral of abundance and consciousness
that you barely acknowledge exists.

It exists!
It thrives and it spurs life, itself, into greatness.
This giving and receiving of our essences
births more life
and that is the way of the universe.
If life contained itself in a law, that would be it.

Come to me for the new technologies
and the wisdom of the future
landing upon us, now.

I see how to build fine communities,
how to heal the old pains
and I see all that you have ever wished to know.
Receive~

I give it now
and I receive
with the growing breath of life.

Summary: Brookite empowers us to live abundantly.

(See *Stone Combination Section* for Brookite in "Fear into Love," "Intent," and "Shamanic Dream")

Totem Stories from the Tibetan Tektites

Ahhhhh!

Such pleasure it is to meet you here, between hearts and words.

Welcome.

Yes, it is our time,

so let us honor ourselves with great generosity.

Put down your worries

and listen.

Stretch your shoulders to your crown and then drop them.

Drop them to the earth

and listen.

Wiggle your toes. Press them to the ground

and listen.

Cast away the lists and the unneeded thoughts

and listen.

Jump up and down and twist like a child

and listen.

Rub your eyes. Swish your face around. Scratch your head

and listen.

Now move any other wondrous, flexible, delightful, human way you can.

Do it all until your body empties and your mind wrings free.

Then you can listen

and listen

and the next words you hear will give you a miracle.

Cacoxenite

"Wear me as the badge and the shield of a soul adventurer."

I am known primarily as a commom inclusion in Quartz, particularly Amethyst, appearing as brown acicular needles. On my own I am appreciated as a scarce Phosphate mineral, and I am often associated with other attractive and rare Phosphates. My colors are yellow-brown, brown, reddish-yellow, greenish-yellow, or yellow, and my luster is vitreous to silky. My structure is hexagonal, forming acicular radiating crystals, often as inclusions; my specific gravity is 2.3, my hardness is soft, at 3-4, and my cleavage is poor. I am found in England, Sweden, France, Germany, and in Arizona, Alabama, Arkansas, and New York.

Physical Integration: Increases receptivity to altered states. Protects from injury. Releases the need for dizziness and motion sickness.

Emotional Integration: Ventures into the unknown without expectation or harm. Allows the heart to connect with guides. Refuses the need to control life through fear. Enjoys and appreciates mystery.

Millennial Uses: No matter how far we advance our knowledge, there always will be more unknown mysteries. Cacoxenite is one of the totems of the inexplicable. With its wisdom, we can be guided into the unknown safely and happily. By not listening to this guardian, we may enter into untapped forces (such as genetics, cloning, etc.) and tamper with realities that could endanger our survival.

Electrical Body Alignment: Links us to the source of creativity.

Affirmation of Support: *"I listen to and act upon the wisdom of my guardian spirits."*

Personal Story

One day I bought this gorgeous, deep purple sphere that had golden tendrils in it. It was magnificent; every time I looked into it, it was like looking into Great Mystery. Soon, I discovered it really was a mystery. I asked the store where I bought it, "What is the name of this stone?" Nobody there knew and nobody even remembered it being at the store in the first place. I asked everyone I knew and nobody could identify it. So I just gave up finding out its name.

Then a friend of mine visited me at work. I hadn't seen him in a long while, so it was nice to see him again. Since Rick was a geologist and a life-long stone seller, I showed him my mys-

(con't on next page)

52

Stone Story:
I am the void.
If you put your hand on me, I am solid.
If you put your heart upon me, we drift into uncharted space.
Whoever shall dream the dreamers path, will know my loyalty.
I stand true in your deepest fear.
I stand the same in your highest love.
There all invisible swirling energies are depicted in life and made real by you.
That is why I bless you.
You have made the dream come true.

Summary: Cacoxenite symbolizes great mystery.

Calcite

> *"I grow with myself, I grow with others.*
> *I grow to celebrate Life that forever grows."*

I am Calcium Carbonate, the most common of all carbonate minerals, and I form in myriad environments worldwide, as well as occurring with a wide assortment of other minerals in virtually all types of rocks. I display more distinct crystal forms than any other mineral, and my colors are variable as well, from the typical colorless or white, to any combination of colors, including black, depending on the variety and degree of impurities. With a hexagonal crystal structure, my cleavage is perfect in three directions, forming a rhombohedron. My luster is vitreous, and my hardness is 3.

From the Greek *chalx*, "lime," I am the main component of Limestone, found throughout the world, and particularly in Austria, Germany, Iceland, Mexico, Ireland, France, the United Kingdom and the United States.

Physical Integration: Assists with growth disorders. Increases flexibility. Allows a stability that supports the bones and their alignments.

Emotional Integration: Adapts decision making abilities to the situ-

(con't from previous page)
tery sphere. Rick recognized it as Cacoxenite immediately and told me, "I have always liked that stone. To me, it's as if it's holding the secrets in the universe in it." I thanked him.
Shortly after that, I heard that Rick had died suddenly. I was startled, but I didn't feel sad. I just felt like that Cacoxenite had brought us together, so we could see each other one more time.
~ from Marilyn

ation. Increases the capability to defend oneself impartially. Easily determines what risks are worth taking.

Millennial Uses: In every group of people who achieve something, there are: leaders, followers, thinkers, doers, etc. In the next millennium, we will build community with the talents all people. Calcite represents the people who are the "glue," the ones who maintain things in every stage of creation. This stone allies with the beings who adapt to the chosen project and choose to work harmoniously with every other participant.

Electrical Body Alignment: Connects us to growth and the manifestation of change for all.

Affirmation of Support: *"As I grow and adapt, I gain more and more from life."*

Stone Story:
Today is the time and now is our moment.
Whatever we wish to learn is before us,
blossoming in every being we see.
Touch the magnificence of the seasons.
They tell me how to bend low
and how to stretch so high.
Each place serves me.
In each place I can be something new
that will serve me, you, and all of life.
What a momentous act!
I embrace it and I honor you for asking to hear my story.

As I unfold it, your footprints are already here.
For every human who wishes to learn,
the way has been shown, constantly.
If it is hard for you to accept the path,
then sit upon it
and watch the others who race
into and then through their fear to another great destiny.
The journey that life has endowed upon you,
will linger timelessly until you join it and join it freely.
If you cannot do what you came to do,
breathe through your suffering.
This, too, will teach you what you need to know.

All lessons are sacred and bring us to our home.
Thank you~

Summary: Calcite teaches us about adaptability and learning for learning's sake.

(See *Stone Combination Section* for Calcite in "Disease into Vitality" and "Unimaginability")

Carnelian

"Together, we are passions and instincts living in focus."

I am known also as Cornelian, or Sard, and I present myself as a translucent orange-red variety of Chalcedony. The color is due to the addition of Iron Oxides to my makeup. Most of my kind are found as rolled pebbles in Brazil, China, Egypt and India, although I am also found in Colombia, Germany, Japan, Scotland, and the United States.

Most of my commercial specimens are the result of heat-treating and staining a less attractive Chalcedony, which turns Iron-bearing minerals into Iron Oxides and the more attractive, darker colors.

Physical Integration: Increases fertility. Harmonizes body and mind.Sharpens innate body wisdom to anticipate possible injury or disease.

Emotional Integration: Joins emotions, instincts and conscious purpose. Empowers self determination. Increases motivation.

Millennial Uses: Whenever we really need to change, what we need is change. When all is planned, Carnelian steps in and drives us onward to actual manifestation. It inspires us, it asks for our full presence and focus, it bursts with the creativity to ensure success. In other words, this stone offers us the vision to see what must be done and the fire to produce the desired results.

Electrical Body Alignment: Links us to instincts and reason and action.

Affirmation of Support: *"I live in my passions to create what I love."*

Stone Story: *If I knew what you wanted in life,*
I wouldn't get it for you.
Well, I would travel with you on your journey of discovery.
Of course, I would shout and celebrate the twists of adventure,
but nothing more.
For I know that the ecstasy of union
with your wishes and your fulfillment
waits for you
and only heightens with every day.
Empty your senses
so you can go to the banquet of life
and serve your needs
and overflow your desires.

Summary: Carnelian combines our desires with the focus to fulfill them.

Cerussite

"I keep company with the angels and I love you."

I am also known as White Lead Ore, Lead Carbonate, and my crystals occur in many forms within the orthohombic system. My name derives from the Latin word, *cerussa,* for "ceruse," a white-lead pigment, for I am a secondary Lead mineral who generally forms from Galena. I am created in oxidized zones of Lead-bearing veins, where the ores have reacted with carbonate-rich water. My color is mostly white, but may be greenish, dark bluish gray, yellow, brown, or colorless. My luster is greasy or silky, my hardness is 3 to 3.5, and my cleavage is good, in one direction.

Worldwide, I am found in Siberia, Australia, Austria, Tunisia, Scotland, Africa, Germany, France, and the United States.

Physical Integration: Tones the diaphragm. Supports the immune system.

Emotional Integration: Uses art/creativity to express truth. Increases inspiration.

Millennial Uses: One of the realizations we discovered at the end of the 20th century was that to continue to live upon the earth, we need help. We need help from unexpected sources. Whenever the challenges loom too large, we have been attended to by angels and guides. Cerussite mediates between angelic helpers and those in need. This stone asks us to accept their support with trust.

Electrical Body Alignment: Connects us to etheric guides and teachers.

Affirmation of Support: *"My guardian angels travel with me everywhere."*

Stone Story:
Angels attend us all.
When you are born, spirit gifts you all the angels you could imagine.
Do you want to see them?
Do you want to talk to them?
Then let go of your beliefs.
Invite them in.
Invite in trust.
Invite in the freedom to love unconditionally.

There is no way they could stay away.

Summary: Cerussite expands our physical senses into metaphysical senses.

Charoite

"Come play upon the stars and laugh with the moon. You are an earth walker learning the cosmic dance."

I am an unusual mineral of rare occurrence— to date I have been found in only one location - the Chary River at Aldan in Russia. I am of the silicate class, and I formed from an unique alteration of limestones by the close presence of alkali-rich Nephline Syenite intrusion. Heat, pressure and the infusion of particular chemicals into the rock creates the transformation into new minerals, forming a swirling pattern of interlocking crystals.

I am visually unmistakable, with stunning lavender, lilac, violet, to purple colors, truly unlike any other mineral, although my almost unnatural beauty can appear artificial to the eye. My luster is vitreous to pearly, my hardness 5, and my specific gravity is 2.5 to 2.8. My monoclinic structure creates fibrous interlocking crystal masses, and my cleavage is not observable, being exclusively massive.

Physical Integration: Relieves stress and headaches. Encourages healthy hair growth. Facilitates appropriate body weight.

Emotional Integration: Appreciates magic and mystery. Honors body, mind, heart and spirit equally. Maintains healthy detachment from possessions, of any kind.

Millennial Uses: What our needs and desires will be in the upcoming millennium is difficult to predict. Since we are evolving rapidly, perhaps what serves us today will be immaterial tomorrow. Charoite encourages us to explore our new frontier (our spirits) to see what we are becoming and to see what we need to integrate that with the present. This stone brings us hope and dreams so we can find the ways to manifest future technologies and magic now.

Electrical Body Alignment: Links us to the source of inspiration.

Affirmation of Support: *"I live with hope and magic and beauty."*

Stone Story:
It's the moment for your dreams to come true.
You have found out how to live without them.
You have discovered how to create them again.
Now you can use all your resources to fulfill them.
Grow them in your reality.
Make them your truth in every part of beingness.
Some things you simply must do
in order to do them.

With my stone body I have found a way....
(I'll share it with you because
I want to watch your dreams grow).
Turn into your body.
Adore it because it landed you on this earth

and it carries your spirit.
Travel deep inside it
until you know that it's an endless magic journey.
Then it will whisper the secrets to entering a new reality
and forging a new way of life.
It's how everything begins........

Summary: Charoite brings us magic and the ways to manifest it in our lives.

Chrysocolla

"I welcome you without reason—with all my heart."

I am a basic Copper Silicate and I am found in the oxidized zones of Copper deposits. Like most Copper minerals, my color is blue to green, though I can be brown to black when found with impurities. Although crystallizing in the monoclinic system I am found as aggregates which have a hardness from 2 to 4; however, when heavily impregnated with Quartz, my hardness can increase to as much as 7. I am notable for my bright color, softness, brittleness, and a lack of crystals.

My name derives from the Greek *chrysos*, "gold," and *kolla*, "glue," in reference to a similar-looking material that was used in soldering gold. When combined with Chalcedony I am used as a gemstone, with Malachite I am known as "Eilat Stone." Most Chrysocolla localities are in the southwestern United States, but deposits can also be found in England, Austria, and Zaire.

Physical Integration: Helps to sharpen the hearing. Aids the digestion process. Releases sinus and lung congestion.

Emotional Integration: Teaches unconditional love. Continually discovers new ways of nurturance. Embraces healthy self-esteem.

Millennial Uses: Whether we believe it all the time or not, our survival is intertwined with that of the earth and may depend on our ability to relate consciously, intentionally and respectfully to our planet.

In some traditions, Chrysocolla represents Mother Earth. It helps us to embrace the wondrous and even frightening aspects of the earth with love, grace and acceptance.

Electrical Body Alignment: Links us to Mother Earth and all lifeforms upon her.

Affirmation of Support: *"I align myself with the miracle of life and with the earth that sustains my life."*

Stone Story:
If you crept into the windows of time,
you would see beautiful spirits on the outside
peering in at the wonders of
babies,
flowers,
playing at the beach,
rising up with a good storm.

Then you could watch those spirits marveling
at the earth
and the way that she holds children and flowers and storms
upon her breast.

You would smile.
You would smile because then you would know
that those spirits had found a home.

Personal Story

When I was new to collecting stones, I found a magnificent chrysocolla. It was covered with green and blue and silver hematite and red-brown cuprite swirls. A friend of mine (a Native American author) reads stones and when he saw this one, he showed me how it was covered with pictures: an eagle, a whale and all sorts of guardian spirits. Ed told me to take very good care of this chrysocolla, that one day it would provide me with a great service.

I truly adored this stone. Every time I looked at it, I saw some new face and inevitably, it was a happy face that I needed right then. About this time, I found myself falling in love with my good friend, Thomas. Without really thinking about it, I gave him my incredible chrysocolla, hoping he would know how much he meant in my life.

One day, I asked Thomas how the stone was. He looked me straight in the eye and said, "I threw it in the deepest lake I could find." I was stunned. When I asked him why, he told me that there was a lot of very old sadness in that chrysocolla and he felt that the reason I had given it to him was because I needed to get that grief out of my life and didn't even know it.

Then I was really stunned. I knew exactly what he meant. That stone had been so comforting that I had taken it to work with me. At that time I worked next to a man who had a huge martyr complex. It was hard for me, because I loved my job and whenever I showed it, this man got really, really sad. So, I used to turn to my chrysocolla periodically and ask it to help me to learn how to be happy in a new way.

Without realizing it consciously, I got really quiet at work. Pretty soon, I was practically a martyr myself. In the moment that Thomas told me that he had thrown away that stone, I got it. I knew that he and that beautiful stone had helped me to realize what I was doing to myself. Ever since then, I have been as happy as I have ever wanted to be, around anybody, and I still thank that chrysocolla for helping me right where it is.
~from Marilyn

Summary: Chrysocolla reminds us to treasure the earth physically and spiritually.

Citrine

"I bless communication of all kinds."

I am in the crystalline quartz family of Silicon Dioxide, named from the French *citron*, for lemon. My color ranges from lemon yellow to reddish orange, due to the presence of Iron. My darker, orangish versions are often called Madeira Citrine, after the color of the wine. I am found in nature in this yellow form, but most of the commercial Citrines on the market today are the product of heating Amethyst until it changes color. In ancient times I was carried as a protection against snake venom and evil thoughts. Most Citrine is mined in Brazil.

Physical Integration: Knowing and using your center of gravity with strength and ease. Fine-tunes internal organs, particularly the kidneys. Encourages fuller breaths to release stress.

Emotional Integration: Calms the fears. Empowers free thinking and free feeling. Appreciates nonconformity.

Millennial Uses: It can be said that much of what has kept humankind in the dark ages has been the dominator/victim mentality. This kind of thinking perpetuates centuries of cyclical abuse. Citrine relates to our personal power. It speaks up for our responsibility to every situation in our life. It serves people by affirming that we do not need to be victims anymore. By declaring responsibility and love for ourselves, we end victimhood, now.

Electrical Body Alignment: Connects our minds to the mass consciousness in a supportive and personally empowering fashion.

Affirmation of Support: *"Instantly my mind creates new life and contentment for me."*

Stone Story:
Greetings. I am a little stone in a large world in an unlimited universe. I record my story and then it goes to the world into unlimitedness. I have discovered that if I follow my story I can jump into unlimitedness. Nothing goes with me but my choice to go there. I have to be as light as a single point so the only thing I think of is how can I think unlimitedly.

Summary: Citrine guides our minds into the next natural evolution.

(See *Stone Combination Section* for Citrine in "Infinite Intimacy-male")

Coral

"I walk gently upon the earth
so that all I will leave the children are footprints and love."

We are living polyps in underwater coastlines, tiny, fleshy tentacled creatures with skeletons of Calcium Carbonate (the essence of limestone). We are both individual organisms and extensive accumulations, and we generally reproduce by budding off of new individuals that remain attached to the "parent." Once our colony forms, it grows upward and outward, building upon the remnant skeletons of dead Coral. Microscopic plants live within our soft tissues, and since they require sunlight for photosynthesis, we live only in depths of less than 200 feet, and always where clear, warm and turbulent seawater abounds (never along the western continental coasts, where cold currents prevail).

Physical Integration: Fortifies the blood. Helps support the mineral balance in the body. Gently removes toxins.

Emotional Integration: Encourages us to stand up for all our actions and decisions. Teaches foresight and thoughtful awareness. Relates to children and their needs.

Millennial Uses: Whatever we do now and in the 21st century will affect many generations. Coral bids us to consider that very carefully in every action, beginning with now. In order to ensure the survival of our species and the earth, we must respect the future in all our plans.

Coral instructs how to value life and our place in it so much that whatever we leave behind us will help the children and grandchildren of the world.

Electrical Body Alignment: Bridges us to the past and to the future.

Affirmation of Support: *"I love my ancestors and I love my descendants and I show it in my every act, now."*

Stone Story:
If you are finding my words,
then you already understand what I am saying:
Live gently so you leave no traces of your journey.

Personal Story

Ayurvedic astrologers suggested that I wear coral to work with the warrior energy in my life. I found a small piece and wore it around my neck. My experience was that it was a reminder of that part of myself. And it reminded me to keep moving. Whenever I had a decision to make I could always feel myself putting my hand over it. This particular piece had lots of well-defined points; I just felt that it was right there to assist me to make clear and immediate decisions.

~from Brad Lambert

Blessings.
Share the message.
It's for the children.
We all have been young
and in the next cycles, we will be again.
When you move with respect,
then you honor all the generations
and you honor yourself,
right now.

Summary: Coral teaches us how to honor all life in all times.

(See *Stone Combination Section* for Coral in "Stress into Centeredness" and "Turkll Delight")

Cuprite

"At the eye of every storm, lies the enthusiasm that started it all."

From the Latin *cuprum,* for "Copper," I am Copper Oxide, found in the oxidized zones of deposits and often in association with Malachite, Calcite and native Copper. I am a striking ruby-red to reddish black in color, with a submetallic, adamantine or dull luster. I form as octahedral-shaped crystals in an isometric structure with a hardness of 3.5 to 4 and poor cleavage.

Notable varieties of me include magnificent hairlike "plush Copper" specimens, where my surface is covered by densely packed chalcotrichite fibers resembling velvet, and Namibian specimens, with crystals that have developed a distinct coating of green Malachite. I am found in Arizona, New Mexico, Utah, and in Austria, England, and the Soviet Urals.

Physical Integration: Supports the reproductive system. Increases fertility. Tones the urinary tract.

Emotional Integration: Seeks to share excitement with others. Bounces back quickly from set-backs. Accepts responsibility for personal feelings and is not hurt easily by others.

Millennial Uses: Entering the future may be our greatest common adventure. We all do it. To do it well, all we may need is more curiosity, more willingness to explore and more enthused anticipation. Cuprite prods us into entering every doorway and every opportunity. If we look for disaster, we find it. But if we go to the next millennium looking for miracles, we find them or create them.

Electrical Body Alignment: Links us to the vitality of the heart and to life force energy.

Affirmation of Support: *"I adventure through life vigorously."*

Stone Story:
I am the blood in your heart.
I race through your veins.
Why?
I'm not looking
for whatever waits for me
at the end of my exploration.
I jump into possibilities, because I can.
Life has given me itself,
for the joy of it.
I will enjoy it all
for the sake of life.

Personal Story

To us, life is one continual opportunity to listen to our spirits and to act upon that wisdom. Once we spontaneously made some copper feng shui tubes and placed them in special corners of our living space. We didn't know exactly what they would do, but we liked the feel of them and that was enough for us.

Shortly after that, Thomas felt guided to make some copper feng shui tools for our friends. When we asked the stone people what stones wanted to be a part of the tubes, we heard, "Cuprite." Well, neither we nor our friends had ever heard of Cuprite. But we put them into the feng shui tubes regardless. One of the friends, Brad, said he just felt better with them around. At the time, one of his major irritations was that his work in the local hospitals involved him taking patients in to get X-rays taken. Even though he had consistently asked the technicians not to shoot the pictures until he was out of the way, they didn't always comply. Brad was concerned that he was getting unnecessary exposure to radiation.

We hadn't thought about the feng shui tools or the Cuprite for quite a while. Then while writing this book, we asked people to share some of their experiences with stones with us. I spoke to a man named Phil who told me that he had been performing stone healings for several years. He was very happy with his work and eager to share his knowledge. Phil said to me that there were two particular stones that he felt were really important for people to work with right now. One was Rhodochrosite and the other was Cuprite. Remembering the feng shui tubes, I asked him, "Why Cuprite?" Then he got very excited and told me that he felt that it was excellent at assisting people to release the effects of radiation.

Isn't it amazing how whatever we need just finds us?

~from Twintreess

Summary: Cuprite lives life for the joy of it.

Danburite

"Come take my hand and I will show you how to stand fast and sure and still believe in the possibility of miracles."

Named for my first known occurrence in pegmatites in Danbury, Connecticut, I am Calcium Borosilicate, and I form in hypothermal veins, generally associated with Quartz, Cassiterite, Fluorite and Orthoclase, and in contact metamorphic rocks, occurring with Andradite, Wollastonite and sulfides. I am white to colorless, and at times pale pink to straw yellow. My structure is orthorhombic and usually prismatic, resembling Topaz, and my crystals are striated lengthwise. I am notable for my hardness of 7, and poor cleavage, in one direction. My specific gravity is 3.0, and my luster is vitreous. Fine yellow stones of me originate in Madagaspar and Myanmar, and fine colorless samples can be found in Japan and Mexico.

Physical Integration: Supports all levels of vision.Revitalizes the senses.Regenerates the skin, tissues and organs.

Emotional Integration: Builds upon the innate desire to trust. Creates miracles. Imparts enough security to listen to unbelievable possibilities. Opens the heart to receive new guides and teachers.

Millennial Uses: As we have learned to "tame the world with technology" we have discovered that it is a wild and free being with its own seasons. Danburite acts as a bridge between the deepest parts of the earth and all of its secret resources and the humans who do not understand anything different from themselves. This stone brings up visions, dreams and other-worldly travels, to insist that we look below the surface of our thoughts to enter the spontaneity of our feelings where we connect to all things. It reminds us that we cannot dominate anything, not even ourselves.

(con't on next page)

Electrical Body Alignment: Danburite aligns all the meridians of the body. Interweaves the left and right hemispheres of the brain.

Affirmation of Support: *"I welcome unimaginable wonders as my new reality."*

Stone Story:
Hello friends. I know you seek the answers to fearful, unbelievable questions. Just that you can ask the question means that an answer already exists. All you seek are the lights to the pathways where you will know what you wish.
Breathe deep,
exhale deeper.
In a single sigh, wisdom is granted.
I have come from the earth with lines of inner knowingness. Touch them all. Your answer finds you instantaneously. Now my lines are circles of completeness wrapped around us in the world.

Summary: Danburite connects us to the exact knowingness we need, right now.

(See *Stone Combination Section* for Danburite in "Fear into Love," "Open Heart" and "Relationship into All")

Diamond

"As I persist, I grow more beauty for all to see."

From the Greek *adamas*, "invincible" or "unconquerable," I am the hardest known substance, natural or synthetic, and my immutability, coupled with my remarkable optical properties, make me the ideal colorless, faceted gemstone, and the one most often imitated in the world of gems. I am pure Carbon, first discovered some 2000 years ago, and some of my specimens are known to be as much as 3 billion years old. Surprisingly, I am not at all rare on this planet. Under conditions of enormous heat, pressure, and time, I am formed deep within the Earth, in peridotite of plutonic rocks, associated with Olivine, Magnetite, and Phlogopite. I eventually reach the surface of this planet through channels of serpentanized Olivine, known as Kimberlite.

(con't from previous page)

Kua" which is a Chinese Internal Martial Art used for Spiritual Growth.
  I inquired of the shopkeeper about the stone and he told me that the stone was known as "Danburite". Out of most of the stones that I have been privileged to know, this one's essence seemed to have the feelings of a small happy divine child, mixed with the deep feelings of bliss and meditation. A wonderful companion to be sure.
  This stone on a spiritual level is a great way to tune into the divine stillness, that is filled with joy and acceptance, should we choose to allow our attention to rest there. The symbol it represents to me would be the clear, crystalline life force that we swim in which

(con't on next page)

My crystal structure is isometric, forming mostly octohedrons, less commonly dodecahedrons, and rarely cubes. My hardness -10- is perfect, impervious to scratching, and my cleavage is also perfect, in four directions. I have a specific gravity of 3.5 and a greasy, adamantine luster. Though first found in river gravel in India, the primary repositories of Diamonds are now found in Australia, Zaire, South and South-West Africa, and Brazil, as well as China, Borneo, and Venezuela.

Physical Integration: Helps to eliminate dizziness and vertigo. Builds strength and stamina. Clearly identifies underlying causes of disease.

Emotional Integration: Clears out distractions. Develops healthy discrimination. Strengthens perserverence.

Millennial Uses: The future is like any other undertaking; we must let it teach us the direction to adaptability and survival. Diamond offers us the ability to assess our circumstance and to clearly determine the path that will serve us best. It combines common sense with our sixth sense. Also, with all the competing information and distractions, this gem encourages us to hone in on our truth to remain free from overwhelming stress.

Electrical Body Alignment: Connects us to free will and self-determination.

Affirmation of Support: *"I act upon my truth now."*

Stone Story:
Learn by witnessing me.
As you wish.....
I assume pressure
and it sharpens me to a
gorgeous
single
gem.
Living by my truth
is the splendor
that I give myself
to give to you.

(con't from previous page)

is "the god consciousness" that is everywhere apparent, but like the fishes, most of the time we don't acknowledge it because it is right in front of us.

I have found that gratitude opens many doors of Spirit!

~ from Robert Allender

Summary: Diamond exemplifies grace under pressure.

(See *Stone Combination Section* for Diamond in "Crystal Pleiadian Pyramid Alignment" and " In Honor of the White Buffalo")

Dioptase

"When you feel really low, come to me. I will hold your head up to the heavens. Always! I smile because I share healing and hope, freely!"

We are a basic Copper Silicate, a secondary mineral who forms in the upper oxidized zone of alteration in all types of hydrothermal replacement deposits, usually associated with Limonite and Chrysocolla. Our crystals, short, six-sided and prismatic, are a deep green more intense than that of even Emerald; our strong body color masks our good "fire" and makes us translucent, rather than transparent. Our luster is vitreous, our specific gravity is 3.3 to 3.4, our hardness 5, and we exhibit a perfect rhombohedral cleavage in three directions. Our stones are rarely faceted because of this cleavage, and our green is too deep to show the high dispersion.

Our name is from the Greek *dia*, "through," and *optasia*, "view," referring to the fact that cleavage planes can be seen in our crystals. Magnificent examples of our crystals are found in Tsumeb, Nembia and Katanga, Zaire; in North America, fine micro-crystals have come from Tiger, Ox Bow, and Summit mines in the Payson district in Arizona.

Physical Integration: Supports the chest, breasts and shoulders. Eases overall body tension. Renews muscle. Soothes the body before body-work or therapies.

Emotional Integration: Increases our ability to detach from earth and limits. Integrates our deepest wounds into love. Expands our capacity to love.

Millennial Uses: At the end of the twentieth century, we have encountered more diseases and imaginative ways to kill ourselves, despite our other advancements. Just when we cure one sickness, another more deadly one comes along. Dioptase has been long revered for its deep green beauty. Now it brings forth its dramatic capacity to heal. Dioptase encourages, enlivens, inspires. It accepts everything unconditionally, therefore releasing the desire to create illness.

Electrical Body Alignment: Dioptase forms a trine between the heart, the immune system and the ozone layer of the earth.

Affirmation of Support: *"I love my perfect body and my perfect being."*

Stone Story:
No worry ever helps you.
Breathe in peace.

No fear needs to stay with you.
Breathe in love.

No pain must hurt you.
Breathe in acceptance.

No reason must hold you separate from life.
Breathe in me.
Breathe Dioptase.

Summary: Dioptase presents integration as healing.

(See *Stone Combination Section* for Dioptase in "Timeless Treasure")

(con't from previous page)

take very good care of the dioptase. It was just letting us know that it wanted to share its healing with a lot of other people. A week later, we were done listening to this magnificent stone, which wanted to return (and was returned) to our very pleased friend.

~ from Twintreess

71

Totem Stories from the Tibetan Tektites

So you are the adventurer here,

going through all the stories until you find one that knows you by name.

What will you do when you want to tell someone else your excitement?

When the stories seem faraway and unimaginable, who will you call for company?

We're here.

We're the totems for this book.

Every adventure has a totem that shares its special spirit with anyone brave enough to risk it.

That's us.

Whatever you need here,

whatever you want to say,

come to us

and just relax.

We'll be your family–

silent, until you need us.

Then we'll jump to give you our heart.

Thank you for traveling with us,

with all of us.

Elestial Quartz

"I grow with many shapes and faces in one resounding celebration of life!"

I am a lovely and rare pattern that emerges in varietires of Quartz, usually forming as large, flat or tabular formations, but rarely as points. My pattern in stones is a result of a disruption of the normal crystalling growth pattern, resulting in one or more irregular formations as the growth resumes.

Physical Integration: Releases atrophy and aging. Encourages new undiscovered ways of healing. Accelerates release of waste materials and toxins.

Emotional Integration: Empowers us to explore within constantly. Integrates body/mind/spirit. Increases the stillness within.

Millennial Uses: Elestial Quartz guide us into listening. In listening to everything, we learn to identify with others and how to act with empathy. It reminds us of the ancient arts of stillness and meditation, so we can let go of self-preoccupation and create a peaceful world where all are respected equally.

Electrical Body Alignment: Connects our ears and our hearts.

Affirmation of Support: *"I listen with all my heart to every being and I learn anew about life."*

Stone Story:
Swirl, smile,
rainbow into life.
Breathe into death
and rush up to the surface for more life.
Enchantment everywhere.

My language leaves rules behind.
Stay.
Learn to decorate your world
with other colors.
Your path is an art
that you practice with all the strength
and the guides
you find along the way.
Look harder
and the help is brighter!
and waving your way.

All of us grow fast new shapes
that twist into other forms.
All that we can do now
is admire their journey into forever.

Summary: Elestial Quartz represents our evolution into new bodies, minds and hearts.

Emerald

"My essence caresses yours
until you find the difference
between feeling your heart and living it."

I am the heart of the Beryl family of silicates. From the Greek *beryllos*, indicating any green gemstone, I am distinctly bright green in color. I am prized for both my mesmerizing, velvety hue and my remarkably uniform distribution of color which, ironically, derives from a relatively small amount of Chromium impurity. Often imitated, and readily made in the laboratory, my natural form is among the most valued of gemstones.

I occur in pegmatites, drusy cavities in granitic rocks, and certain metamorphic rocks, and I am often associated with Topaz in Mica schists. My hardness is considerable at 7.5 to 8, my luster is vitreous, my specific gravity is 2.66 to 2.92, and my cleavage is indistinct, in one direction. The world's finest Emeralds are from the Chivor and Muzo Mines in Colombia; Brazilian Emeralds are often pale yellowish-green; Indian Emeralds have characteristic "comma" inclusions; Russian Emeralds are often cloudy; and South African stones often contain brown Mica plate inclusions.

Physical Integration: Relaxes the chest, shoulders and upper back. Promotes grace, beauty, balance and breath. Aids in healing scars.

Emotional Integration: Uplifts the emotions. Aids in healing old wounds. Opens all senses to appreciation of the arts. Integrates all feelings with enriching breaths.

Millennial Uses: We have many needs to meet in the future. Some are apparent: food, shelter, health, warmth/cooling, etc. The less apparent ones may be: beauty, inspiration, happiness, love, companionship, poetry...

Emerald signifies the emotional and spiritual needs we have and must fulfill (bread and roses) in order to flourish upon the earth. As we embrace Emerald, we embrace the earth as the magnificent garden it is.

Electrical Body Alignment: Connects our senses to beauty and grace.

Affirmation of Support: *"I am full of beauty and I surround myself with it, abundantly."*

Stone Story:
Drink in the beauty of our life together.
Everywhere, I survey the gorgeous hues
of life joining and creating life
as art.
And I have to smile.
I have to smile.
I have to smile
to pay my happy tribute

to the creator and the creation.
My adoration turns into priceless generous green
(it is my heart)
as I join the rainbow of earth magnificence.
Who knows what colors and smiles we will create from here?

Summary: Emerald unites us with beauty and the ability to meet our emotional needs.

(See *Stone Combination Section* for Emerald in "Crystal Pleiadian Pyramid Alignment" and Infinite Intimacy-female")

Epidote

"This is the time of initiation, so we come forth with full and clear intent."

Pistachio-green to brownish-black in color, we are found in several environments, including granite pegmatites, volcanic basalt rocks, and contact and regional metamorphic rocks. With the chemical moniker of Calcium Aluminum Iron Silicate, we crystallize in the monoclinic system, forming long, slender, grooved prismatic or tabular, and frequently twined crystals that are frequently terminated by two sloping faces. Our my specific gravity is 3.3 to 3.6, our luster is vitreous, and our cleavage is perfect, in one direction lengthwise. Our name is from the Greek *epi*, "over," and *didonai* "to give," intended to describe the enlargements of one side of our crystal in many specimens with a vitreous luster.

Fine Epidote crystals are to be found in Green Monster Deposit, Prince of Wales Island, Alaska, as well as in Switzerland, Austria, Italy, Brazil, and China.

Physical Integration: Releases lung/chest congestion. Supports the thymus gland. Helps align the shoulders.

Emotional Integration: Gives joy to responsibility. Adds clarity to focus. Releases the need for self defeating and self distracting habits.

Millennial Uses: In many ways, the earth is accelerating its vibration and expanding its life force. One way to say this is that the earth has opened its heart to complete transformation. As one of the stone people of the earth, Epidote embraces change on the planet and change for all of the beings on it, including us. It supports us all by sharing with us the commitment to go all the way through a difficult birthing process to find ourselves on the other side of change, utterly transformed.

Electrical Body Alignment: Regenerates our being through our senses, the pineal gland and intent.

Affirmation of Support: *"I intend to be all of my possibilities and to embrace myself in all change."*

Stone Story:
Once upon a time
found in a forever
I lay inside the earth
where every pulse lined my body.
Year in, year out,
I aligned myself with her.
So fully did I embrace her growth
that I never thought about it.
I simply became the echo of her intent.
Hold me in your heart, now.
Above or below the earth,
I am intent.
Caress my lines.
Receive what you need to be complete.
I will ever grow more intent.

Summary: Epidote represents the commitment to follow through in our every action.

Fire Agate

"Join me in jumping into life
physically, emotionally, mentally and spiritually."

We are a microcrystalline form of Quartz, within the family of Chalcedony. We form in concretionary deposits at or near the surface of the Earth's crust; as low-temperature Silica-rich water filters through sediments and rocks (particularly those of volcanic origin), we gather in seams and vugs, rich in Iron Oxide. Tiny crystal impurities produce iridescent and fiery displays of red, green, yellow, blue, orange, and in rare cases lavender. These form in variable micro-thin undulating patterns and bursts of color.

Because of this cumulative accretion, you will find no two of us alike anywhere. Only a tiny percentage of Fire Agate-bearing Quartz contains the dazzling displays of color that give us our name and of that, only 1% to 5% is of a quality to be cut into gem quality stones. We are to be found most notably in southern Arizona and northern Mexico.

Physical Integration: Expands stamina and reserves of strength. Regenerates the organs.Relieves bloating.

Emotional Integration: Increases lucid dreaming.Fosters healthy pride in appearance. Releases shyness.

Millennial Uses: In this time, we are learning that humans have many facets: physical, emotional, mental, spiritual, etc. Each piece needs nurturance for the whole to survive and flourish. This is true for the individual and for the human race. Fire Agate instructs us to care for all our parts of self in every thought and deed. When we do this, we rediscover our passions; we enliven ourselves and all our dreams. With our renewed vitality we insist on making our dreams our lives.

Electrical Body Alignment: Links us to our creative fire.

Affirmation of Support: *"I create all my dreams and my realities."*

Stone Story:
Just let my words fade away.
What I want for you is my life force.
Its power will stir your blood
and then you'll hear what you need to hear!

Each one of us is here, telling our story
and that helps us to surge with the forces of nature.
That's a beautiful beautiful sight.
When anyone listens to my talk,
I travel deep within it,
so they have to find their own way.
When that happens, my words drift off.
They find their own hidden stories inside of mine!
They speak them, while my story blends into the woods.
It's their own tales that animates them,
that moves their old bones
and lands them on the unimaginable.
Don't listen too hard to this,
listen for the piece of you that lives deep inside of me.
Talk to that story
and make it last a long long time.

Summary: Fire Agate stands for the way to revitalize our life every day.

Fluorite

"This is my time to be on the planet.
I say, 'Awaken and remember, our struggle can be released.'"

I am a soft mineral, a 4 on Moh's scale, delicate to work with, and the only halide gemstone. I exhibit a full range of colors, from none to black, often banded, and my isometric structure, generally cubic or as penetration twins, tends to appear in exceptionally large crystals or layered veins. I am Calcium Fluoride, formed in several different environments of widely different character, from contact metamorphic to epithermal veins to hydrothermal replacement deposits, often in association with lead and silver ores, Galena, Sphalerite, Calcite or Quartz. I exhibit perfect cleavage, in four directions, my specific gravity is 3.0 to 3.2, and I have a vitreous luster.

My name derives from the Latin *fluere*, "to flux," because I melt easily and am used as a flux in the smelting of metallic ores. I am also called Flour Spar and Ore Bloom (by the old Bohemian miners), and the word "fluorescence" comes from my name, since most of my specimens show a beautiful blue or violet glow under long-wave ul-traviolet radiation. I am found predominantly in Canada, China, Switzerland, Eastern Europe, the United States and Derbyshire, En-gland, the sole source of "Blue John," a deep blue to purple banded variety of massive crystalline formations.

Physical Integration: Supports the senses. Balances and helps un-block the sinuses.

Emotional Integration: Embraces the inner voices of truth. Softens the need for judgment. Releases the desire to be isolated from all things.

Millennial Uses: Many people wonder how we will survive the up-coming environmental, political and economic challenges. Whenever survival seems threatened on a mass scale, it is because quality of life or the ability to thrive under all circumstances, has diminished. Fluo-rite stands out as an excellent tool for the 21st century. It releases the destructive cycles of separation that humans have developed with all other life forms. With this gone, all that remains is the innate inter-connectedness of everything upon this planet. In that moment, hu-mans relate to themselves as a unique and vital co-creator upon the earth. That is the evolution of the future.

Electrical Body Alignment: Connects the mind instantly to the guid-ance of spirit.

Affirmation of Support: *"I am one with life, one with my spirit and one with love."*

Stone Story: *My bands of color speak out.*
They admire the truth.
They enjoy art.
They laugh with children.
Each piece of me lies in the world oh so unique.
Each one glitters with a one of a kind rainbow.
I take my differences and I offer them to the world.
Then when I look around, all that I see is a reflection of what I love.

Summary: Fluorite helps us to release everything that keeps us from being our true selves, now.

(See *Stone Combination Section* for Fluorite in "Environmental Toxins," "Immortality," "Stress into Centeredness" and "Pregnancy")

Galena

"Let's talk to the stars. Let's dance with the moon. Let's swoon with the trees. Like all good adventurers, let's embark on them now!"

Chemically, I am Lead Sulfide, though I am colloquially known as Lead Glance and Blue Lead in mining lore. I am known audibly to most humans, for I was the original crystal in the radio that touched so many lives. I am the commonest of all lead-bearing minerals on the planet and one of the most common of the sulfides. Found world-wide, I form in a wide variety of environments from sedimentary rocks to pegmatites and in association with a diverse assortment of other minerals.

I am quite soft on the hardness scale at 2.5, though my specific gravity is an enormous 7.4 to 7.6; my cleavage is perfect, in three directions at 90 degrees. My color is a dark lead-gray, often silvery, and my structure is isometric, generally in the familiar cube form, often tabular, and with occasional fibrous skeletal crystals, as well as in octahedrons. My name comes from the Latin *galena*, which was applied to lead ore during smelting, and I am found throughout this planet. Many famous European mines extract me, and the Joplin districts of Oklahoma, Kansas and Missouri produce spectacular speci-mens as well.

Physical Integration: Allows the spine greater flexibility. Supports the toning, adjustment and movement of all bones, organs, nerves and muscles for speed and efficiency. Realigns posture. Relaxes the shoulders.

Emotional Integration: Revitalizes curiosity in activities outside of self. Encourages the security to find new interests. Fosters the ability to record all experiences and transform them into art and wisdom for all.

Millennial Uses: In earth honoring traditions, the stones serve as the record-keepers of all knowledge. With each age and its corresponding needs, different stones have come to the forefront to share their unique gifts with the current life requirements.

Galena garners our attention, now, because of its immediate communication with all life. Unlike humans, it is not stopped by fears. It proceeds prudently and joyfully and records well this time of transition and learning.

Electrical Body Alignment: Connects us to timelessness.

Affirmation of Support: *"I live timelessly, according to my truth and bliss."*

Stone Story:
I am a sacred witness.
My eyes loom large at every event.
Nothing turns me away.
I face all and it shows me the way to divinity, immediately.

Since I experience everything now (and I worship it all!),
I rest in timelessness—the guardian of the records that show
your jump from one age to another to another.
I adore the inbetween moments,
where timelessness watches over it all...
All possibilities within a perfect, crystallized breath.
Do and be everything.
I write your stories and I tell them forever.

Summary: Galena exemplifies the passion it takes to endure powerful transitions.

(See *Stone Combination Section* for galena in "Connecting to Your Guides," "Death," and "Intent")

Green Garnet

"All that I am is an open heart and it is more than enough."

As Garnets, we are the collective name for a closely related group of Aluminum and Calcium Silicate minerals with similar structure but variable chemical composition and physical properties. Widespread and all used as gemstones, our family is comprised of Almandine (deep red to brown), Pyrope (deep red to reddish-black), Spessartine (brownish-red to hyacinth-red), Grossular (colorless, white, yellow, pink, green, brown), Andradite (wine red, greenish, yellow, brown, black) and Uvarorite (emerald-green). From the Latin pomum *grana-tum,* "pomegranate," noting the resemblance in color of the Almand-ine-Pyrope group.

Our colors cover the gamet, with the exception of blue, as do our origins, although our formations occur mostly as a result of meta-morphism. Fine crystals can be found in schist, serpentines, gneisses and granite pegmatites. Our isometric structure generally forms as dodecahedrons and trapezohedrons; our hardness is 6.5 to 7.5; our luster is vitreous; our specific gravity is 3.56 to 4.32, our cleavage is none, parting occasionally distinct in six directions. Garnets are found worldwide; localities are plentiful throughout North America and can also be found in abundance in South Africa, Germany, Australia, Sri Lanka and South America.

Physical Integration: Strengthens the heart. Clears the arteries. Opens up the chest.

Emotional Integration: Easily develops empathy. Embraces the diversity of other forms of life. Commits to compassion as a way of life.

Millennial Uses: In the 20th century, we have expanded our minds tremendously. Now we perhaps know something more clearly than ever before: We must evolve with our hearts, in order to survive, and then to live abundantly.

Green Garnet understands the way of the heart. Its presence on the planet continually, kindly, prods us into following our feelings, even when we don't understand, or even when we're afraid. This is what guides us into the next millennium.

Electrical Body Alignment: Connects our heart with others, with the earth, with life force, simply.

Affirmation of Support: *"My heart leads me on my lifepath and I am filled with unimaginable love."*

Stone Story:
Much love.
I give you much love.
Feel this.
Inhale this as a soothing balm for all your aches.
Exhale this as freedom pulsing through your veins.
I serve love because it is all that I see.
It is all that I know.
It remains all that I do not expect, understand or measure.
Receive it, as you will.
I recognize you.
You are a child of love,
living with it,
formed of it
and giving your whole, outstretched being with it.
Now.
Always.
I witness my heart in your eyes.
I am our love.

Summary: Green Garnet represents our heart and living with it, completely.

Green Apatite

"If life seems anxious to you, come and sit beside me.
I will fill you with ease and that is your natural birthright."

I am Calcium Flourine Chlorine Hydroxyl, and I come in many colors, from green, brown, red and yellow to violet, pink white and colorless. I am in the middle of the hardness scale at 5, my luster is greasy and vitreous, and my specific gravity is 3.1 to 3.2. I have poor cleavage with a crystal structure that is hexagonal. My name derives from the Greek word *apate*, "deceit," for I am very often mistaken for a variety of other minerals such as Aquamarine, Flourine and Olivine.

I am the most common of the phosphate-bearing minerals, and I form in many igneous rocks and in certain metamorphic ones. I am found worldwide, although the majority of my gem quality deposits are in Burma. I can also be found in abundance in Sri Lanka, Brazil, Norway, Germany, Spain, and throughout North America.

Physical Integration: Assists the endocrine system. Supports the upper back and chest. Calms overextended adrenals.

Emotional Integration: Fosters full, healthy expression of emotions. Releases denial and apathy. Experiences continual delight and awe.

Millennial Uses: In some traditions, we are the earth. Whatever it experiences, we experience also (whether we admit it or not). As the earth changes dramatically, so do we. To live with that, we must adapt our hearts to constant change. That is the innate way of life upon the earth.

 Green Apatite helps us to acknowledge change, to embrace it and to grow with it, through our hearts.

Electrical Body Alignment: Links the heart to empathy and to transformation.

Affirmation of Support: *"I grow happily with the seasons."*

 Stone Story:
 Once there was sweet clarity.
 It filled the land.
 All creatures lived bountifully, in every season.
 Then lack swooped down upon the earth.
 Fear filled hearts.
 All creatures stalked each other.

 Again there is sweet clarity.
 It fills the hearts of the land and of all creatures.
 All seasons flow with the ebb and tide of life.
 We feel bounty as never before.

Summary: Green Apatite connects us with the source of abundance and calm: an open heart.

Hematite

"Rejoice in your body!"

The chemists know me as Iron Oxide, and I am the principal ore of Iron, but to the majority of humans I am appealing for my distinctive iridescent play of colors, as my thin surface films create an interference pattern in light. My colors are steel-gray, red, reddish-brown and black; the Latin word *haimatites* means "bloodlike", which refers to the vivid red color of my powder. I am also known as Iron Glance and Ferric Oxide.

My luster is metallic to splendent, my hardness is 5 to 6, my cleavage is none, and I crystallize in the hexagonal system, forming reniform masses or tabular crystals in rosettes. I am formed primarily as thick sedimentary beds, but also in igneous and metamorphic rocks. My notable origins are the huge bodies of Iron ore in the Lake Superior region, and in Romania, Austria, Italy, Ascension Island, Brazil, France, Switzerland and Canada.

Physical Integration: Expands overall strength. Sharpens the instincts. Increases stability, security and safety.

Emotional Integration: Integrates responsibility, happily, in daily life. Eases decision-making. Adapts immediately to a diversity of situations.

Millennial Uses: At the root of any experience or challenge, there lies the famous "bottom line." That's Hematite. This stone focuses on acting upon our clear, balanced choices. It helps us to produce our realities, now.

The bottom line of our life on the earth is that we live here. If we continue our current lifestyle, that/we could end. Hematite supports us practically, physically and asks us to consider appreciating the consequences of our desires and acts. When we honor what we have done, we will honor who we are. When we honor who we are, we will honor all others, including the earth. Then we will co-create life upon the earth, miraculously and harmoniously.

Electrical Body Alignment: Hematite grounds our full presence into our bodies, now.

Affirmation of Support: *"In every thought, feeling and deed, I honor my body!"*

Stone Story:
Please hold me to your forehead now and
close your eyes
and give way to my full, looming presence.

If you do not have a Hematite with you, close your eyes
and with your focused mind,
see a smooth shiny silver-black stone being held next to your forehead.
I will be present for you, either way, just as I am completely here in
this message, now.

Welcome.
Please, let us begin.
Send me your thoughts, your questions, your feelings, as you wish.
I send you my regards.
I send you whatever you need, that can come from me.
Receive.
Completely drink in my presence, until you feel satiated and content.
I am here for you.
Where else would I be?
I have chosen to assist with this time of transition.
Visit me often.
It pleases me to know you and to feel all the possibilities
and to drive them into fulfillment, with you.
All that we can do in a lifetime, we can do now.
Feel that from me.
Take the courage you must have.
Then charge forth and be your dreams.
This is the time in the earth's story,
this is the time upon the earth, when dreams come true.
This the time when dreams are the truth.
That is how we came to be.

That is how we came to be together, right here, right now.

I give thanks.

Summary: Hematite grounds us physically.

Herkimer Diamonds

"When all else seems scattered and confused, we come to you. We hold your heart up to the skies and from there, you see yourself as you are.... and sigh in delight....."

We are double terminated forms of quartz named for the area in New York state from which we hail. We form in Basalt deposits, and our structure forms within the bubbles of liquid within the Basalt.

Physical Integration: Accelerated visual acuity. Ability to discover deeper patterns of breathing for health and transformation. Receptivity to lucid dreaming. Stimulation of mental processes.

Emotional Integration: Emotional clarity and simple delight in life. Awakens a fresh sense of humor. Encourages adaptability. Seeks out ongoing, healthy change throughout life.

Millennial Uses: We have advanced ourselves, mentally, almost to the exclusion of all other parts of our beings. When we define life by scientific proof, it can be hard to find miracles, let alone accept them.

Herkimer Diamonds exemplify miracles and infinite possibilities. They witness life clearly and refuse to be distracted by challenges. In our hearts, we live the same way: we are marvels, by design. Like Herkimer Diamonds, when we revel in that reality, we smile at all of life's offerings.

Electrical Body Alignment: Connects us to the source of bliss.

Affirmation of Support: *"I find bliss in every moment and circumstance of life."*

Stone Story:
What wonder to find you and my words in a book.
Read and get swept away.
I give you a gift here....
For you to reach my soul means that you are here with me.
Your eyes touch this page
and they race far far beyond it.
Your beautiful, magnificent consciousness has flown you to my heart,
to the charming truth...
We are one life in countless forms and desires.
Our spirits care for us equally and all that remains of my words now,
is a single, breathful

Sigh.

Summary: Herkimer Diamonds embody clear truth and the ability to delight in it.

(See *Stone Combination Section* for Herimer Diamonds in "Boredom into Choice," "Focused Grounding," "Gabriel's Dawn," "Mary's Wonder" and "Regeneration")

Holly Berry Agate

"We join in friendship gently,
so as not to miss the delicate emotions and dreams
that keep us most alive."

As with all Agates, I am a banded variety of Chalcedony, and somewhat cloudy in appearance, as I exhibit my beautiful purple color. I originate in Oregon, and along the Colorado River, and I am volcanic in nature. My colors are due to the inclusion of Iron and Manganese.

Physical Integration: Stimulates brain activities, clearly and easily. Assists with migraines. Supports the health and growth of hair.

Emotional Integration: Promotes the release of long-standing dysfunctional habits. Increases empathy and intuition.Encourages nurturance.

Millennial Uses: As females assume leadership roles in the world, the feminine qualities of: receptivity, imagination, calm strength, appreciation of beauty, nurturance, and the ability to work well with others become more apparent. Holly Berry Agate prizes these traits and brings them from the background of awareness to our full consciousness so we can utilize them for the prosperity of all beings.

Electrical Body Alignment: Connects us to the ways of all lifeforms.

Affirmation of Support: *"I lovingly support all beings."*

Stone Story: *I hear the guidance of the other brothers and sisters.*
I smile at their wisdom and at yours,
for receiving something so different
from what you have understood before.
You are growing spirals from the earth to the stars.
I absorb your precious dreams and glories
and wish you all your greatness.
I whisper with one voice in a symphony of stone people.
While I will not speak for all, I know their hearts.
Like mine, they offer you love.
It is an offering—free from me, free to you.
It is all that I have and I share it with you always.
Part of your heart has hardened to the ways of the earth
and to the stone spirits.
You don't believe that we would love you
after the pain you have wreaked around you.
Love comes freely.
Nothing you do makes you deserving.
I share it with you
because I choose the delight.

Summary: Holly Berry Agate opens us to communication, wisdom and support from all beings.

(See *Stone Combination Section* for Holly Berry Agate in "Timeless Treasure," and "Transformation, Prosperity and the Goddess")

Howlite

"Whatever you wish me to be, is what I wish also."

Named after Henry How, the 19th Century Nova Scotian chemist, geologist and mineralogist who first described me, I am among the borates, specifically Hydrated Calcium Silica Borate, and I am a white mineral which develops in sedimentary rocks and usually occurs with Ulexite and Colemanite as nodules in clay. I am soft, at 3.5, with a subvitreous luster, and no cleavage, and my monoclinic design generally occurs as compact, dense, structureless nodular masses that resemble unglazed porcelain. Rarely I also form as crystals, and my appearance is sometimes scaly, earthy or chalk-like. I am very often dyed blue and sold as fake Turquoise.

Physical Integration: Increases receptivity to all experiences/stimuli. Works with the physical part of attention disorders. Improves overall digestion.

Emotional Integration: Fosters acceptance of others. Allows for adaptability to any social situations. Appreciates the value of work as a service to the community.

Millennial Uses: How do we ever prepare for an unpredictable future? Science has no definitive answers. Adaptability seems to be the key. Each of us must learn to stretch our capabilities according to each situation. Then we, as individuals, can contribute our talents and knowledge to our communities which are readying all of us for our joint future.

Howlite proffers to the world the value of: service, flexibility, responsibility, and the willingness to share our personal resources with others. In a crisis, these inner qualities are put to the test and it is then that we have the opportunity to respond with compassion for all.

Electrical Body Alignment: Links us to responsibility for the whole.

Affirmation of Support: *"I serve my community for the joy of serving."*

Stone Story:
Innocence surrounds me, even in the dark.
How can I tell you what I am?
I simply am.
Connected is what we are.
Whatever you offer to me, shapes me,
like the forces of the earth.
I am what I continually am becoming:
a life that dances to the seasons
and to the shifting balances of nature.
If soft is requested, I melt.
If hard is requested, I crystallize.
Life honors me with all its gifts.
I am honored to give back all that I have learned
through its absolute generosity.

What do you need my friend?

Summary: Howlite exemplifies the joy of service.

Iolite

"Come, let us surrender to the magnificence of the universe."

We are the transparent blue to dark blue to purplish gem version of the mineral known as Cordierite. From the Greek *ion* for "violet," we are dichroic, that is, our hue appears to change when viewed from different angles. To the chemists we are Magnesium Aluminum Silicate, and we form mostly in metamorphic rocks, although occasionally also in granite, and in association with Almandine, Corundum, Andalusite and Biotite. We are among the hard minerals, at 7 to 7.5, and poor cleavage is evident, in one direction. Our orthorhombic structure rarely produces crystals; when this occurs, they are short, pseudohexagonal prismatic twins with vitreous luster.

We are most uncommon on Earth, but can be found in Scandinavia, Austria, Austria, Greenland, and the United States. Sri Lankan specimens are often so infused with thin Hematite or Goethite platelets that they render us red; we are then called Bloodshot Iolite.

Physical Integration: Increases dreams and intuition. Adapts sleep patterns to needs.

Emotional Integration: Develops healthy preferences when addictions or distractions come in. Gives satisfaction during service. Increases creativity and the ability to explore, when needed, in group crisis.

Millennial Uses: In many parts of the world, we have created realities where we fill ourselves with unneeded stress, busyness and disruptions. We numb ourselves to our true priorities through addictions of all types. As we enter the new millennium, we know this. We recognize our dysfunctionality. As we try to let go of our addictions, however, without something to replace them, we can feel overwhelmed. Iolite presents us with the focus of honoring ourselves (even when we do not clearly know who we are). Iolite imparts trust. This trust births the perserverance to go beyond poor choices and to celebrate our essence and our true selves.

Electrical Body Alignment: Links our individuality to the planetary consciousness and to our guides, with discrimination and respect.

Affirmation of Support: *"I honor myself with all that I need to be a whole and loving being."*

Stone Story:
You cannot know who you are from where you stand. Take a chance. Jump through your fear. Lift off the ground of needs and desires. Fly above all that you recognize. This is our sacred space together. Now what do you know? Why do you feel? Who are we? The questions do not hold matter. Explore.Expand. When you land gently into your reality, you will remember my voice, "Compassion." Then you will choose with your true freedom and what you create will hold matter in sacred space.

Summary: Iolite perserveres under any circumstances or thoughts to hold a space for sacredness.

(See *Stone Combination Section* for Iolite in "Pregnancy")

Jade

"As I dance life in this body, my spirit dances life in the universe!"

Our name comes from the Spanish *piedra de ijada*, "stone of the side," for the Spanish conquerors of Mexico believed that the native Indians' green stones would cure kidney ailments when applied to the side of the body. They were then called kidney stones, which evolved into "Jade." In Europe the name was later given to a mineral of the same color and hardness which was imported from China. In 1863 it was discovered that they were two different minerals now known as Jadeite and Tremolite (also called Nephrite, as a chemical mixture of both Tremolite and Actinolite).

We are also the semitransparent to translucent finest gem quality varieties of Jadeite, chemically called Sodium Aluminum Silicate, one of a group of silicate materials called pyroxenes. In this form, we are white to green in color, with white and greenish spots, our specific gravity is 3.3 to 3.5, our hardness is 6.5 to 7, our structure is monoclinic (with crystals rare), our luster is vitreous, and our cleavage is distinct, in two directions at nearly right angles. Myanmar is the major repository of us in this form, and our most prized manifestation is the emerald-green specimen known as Imperial Jade.

As Tremolite, we are a basic Calcium Magnesium Iron Silicate; when Iron content becomes appreciable we are called Actinolite. In color we are white to dark gray, yellowish, or pink to lilac, and we are a product of metamorphism and occur in association with Calcite, Grossular, and Talc. Our hardness is 5 to 6, our specific gravity is 2.9 to 3.1, our luster is vitreous, and our cleavage is perfect, in two directions, in the shape of a diamond. Our structure is monoclinic, usually in fibrous, radiating aggregates. The name of Tremolite is from our occurrence in Val Tremolo in the Swiss Alps, and we are to be found also in Alaska, Siberia, British Columbia, China, and Wyoming.

(con't on next page)

Physical Integration: Evens metabolism, increasing efficiency and energy. Revitalizes and youthens, calmly. Encourages a long, healthy life. Activates the ear meridian.

Emotional Integration: Lightens moods/moodiness. Finds delight in simple acts, like breathing. Continually soothes wounds without overemphasizing them.

Millennial Uses: At the end of the 20th century, we have doubled the amount of information available to us, in increasingly shorter periods of time. On the surface, we "know" a great deal.

The spirit of Jade prompts us to acquire wisdom to go with our knowledge. Wisdom grants us the gentle power to use our knowledge well. As we enter the 21st century with ever more information, we must learn how to utilize it respectfully, in order to survive.

Electrical Body Alignment: Balances every single part of the body and being to each other, in honor of life.

Affirmation of Support: *"I use my mind, body and heart to express my spirit, wondrously!"*

Stone Story:
Please, enter my space.
We will know each other again and again.
All through the ages the ancestors of you have visited me.
In other days, you didn't think it was odd
for stone and human and hearts to talk;
you thought it would have been odder
not to talk during struggles.

So, friend, you find yourself in struggle.
I give you all my wisdom and it is this:
Know that during every challenge, the solution waits
inside you already.

When you cannot find your power, wait, and ask for it to come.
If you still do not find it in stillness,
then grow quieter
and ask for the wisdom of spirit
to visit you.
It always answers you,

(con't from previous page)

and emotional well being. I can see why it has been a prized stone for many centuries.

~ from Marilyn

just as I do, right now.
There, that's your answer.

Summary: Jade activates the body as a clear expression of spirit.

Jasper

"When you celebrate anything, you honor life."

I am an impure variety of microcrystalline Silicon Dioxide, a form of Chalcedony consisting of a network of interlocking, randomly arranged quartz crystals. I am recognizable for my mixture of reds and browns, although I also appear in the colors of grayish blues and greens; this mixing of colorful impurities makes me opaque to the eye. My hardness is 7, my specific gravity is 2.6 to 2.64, and my crystal system is trigonal.

I have long played an important non-gem role in human history; because of my tendency to form smooth concave surfaces when broken, I was an ideal material for flaking into arrowheads and spearheads. Other forms of mine include: Riband (ribbon), which is striped and polishes to a luster; Orbicular, with white or gray "eyes" surrounded by red; Bloodstone or Heliotrope, dark green and scattered with red spots; Plasma, usually green with white or yellow spots, Hornstone, a gray version, often dyed to imitate Lapis Lazuli; and Prase, a dull green stone often colored with Actinate fibers.

Physical Integration: Supports the base of the spine. Strengthens the upper thighs. Supports the muscles.

Emotional Integration: Accepts the self unconditionally. Releases spaciness and over-thinking. Motivates us through apathy into action.

Millennial Uses: During the last half of the twentieth century, technology has doubled in progressively lesser amounts of time. We know a lot, we think a lot, we overanalyze everything. Jasper can be found almost anywhere on the planet. It is a common stone in hundreds of different colors. It is as common as common sense. It helps us out of our heads, into our hearts and back into our bodies, where we walk upon the earth as a miracle. Every second we are surrounded by more unbelievable events that even we can record. Jasper notes it all and, luckily, invites us to experience it, not just think about it.

Electrical Body Alignment: Jasper guides the will to survive into joyous celebration of life.

Affirmation of Support: *"I live, therefore, I am magnificent!"*

Stone Story:
I suppose that you think that I will say something shatteringly
beautiful and incredibly poignant, too.
Ok.
Go outside and play.
Go inside and work.
Everything that you need falls somewhere inbetween.
Everything that you could have ever wanted, happens along the way.
Every love that you have ever wanted goes with you.
You are all these things and you are even much more.
When you make your choices to enhance your lifestyle,
remember what you are experiencing, is life.
Go outside and play.

Summary: Jasper reminds us that being alive is a wonderful thing not to miss.

(See *Stone Combination Section* for Jasper in "Relationship into All")

Kidney Stones

"With each release, you come back to the world,
free and ready to build new life."

We are Nephrolithiasis, solid lumps made up of crystals that separate from human urine and build up on the inner surfaces of the kidney. We can be as small as a grain of sand, or as large as a golf ball, and in the United States we affect 1 million people a year (two-tenths of 1 percent of the population). We affect men three times more than women.

We are not a disease, but rather the end products of the disease process. We come in four varieties, composed variably of calcium oxalate (which cannot be broken down by the body and must be flushed out through the urine), calcium phosphate, uric acid, magnesium and ammonia. Some of the time we pass through the body, but at other times we do not readily leave. The easiest method of coaxing us to go (and of preventing our formation in the first place) is to simply drink large amounts of water. Another method is shock wave lithotripsy (the Greek word for stone crushing), where shock waves are sent through the body to break us apart.

Physical Integration: Utilizes pain to release unneeded obstructions.

Emotional Integration: Offers the opportunity to be present in everything as a way of unconditional self nurturance.

Millennial Uses: Okay, we threw this one in for the laughs. But think about it, there's a sort of creativity involved in kidney stones. If somebody came up to you and said, "Can you have nothing in your hands and make a rock from it?" you would probably say, "No."

Humans have a way of doing the impossible. We do create stones and we do birth them from our own bodies. No matter how you look

(con't on next page)

at it, we are co-creators in wild adventures. Go ahead and deny it, but for every feeling you deny, it buries itself in your body. One day, that denial will have to come out, and who knows what form it will take?

Electrical Body Alignment: Connects you to co-creatorship.

Affirmation of Support: *"I accept pain and allow it to pass through me, loved and free."*

(con't from previous page)

He told us that it was okay; he wanted to release this. The pain was something he could handle; he just wanted to be present, completely, with something leaving his body that had been building up for some time but now needed to go.

He could have complained about it, but that wouldn't accept and allow what was happening with his body. So Robert decided to celebrate it and to share his joy at surrendering to the process. He wasn't fighting it and instead, was hoping the stone would relax and come on out!

~from Robert Oser

Kornerupine

"I am intense bliss and all integration in a single moment."

I am a rare mineral on this world. I can be green (due to the presence of Vanadium), or brownish-green or yellow in color, and I exhibit a strong pleochroism, the differential absorption of multiple wavelengths, with green and reddish brown. I am an orthohombic silicate of Aluminum and Magnesium, and I am almost always found as rolled pebbles, rather than crystals. I was first discovered in Greenland, and I was named after the 19th Century Danish geologist A. N. Kornerup. I can also be found in the countries of Sri Lanka, Myanmar, Kenya and Tanzania.

Physical Integration: Increases flexibility. Increases the potential to release old toxins from the body.

Emotional Integration: Supports the self for every accomplishment. Embraces timelessness. It reaches for the unknown by going through fear, not around it. Releases denial.

Millennial Uses: As stones go, Kornerupine is a bit rare. Its presence and resources feels so powerful that we don't need a large amount of it to learn from it. Whether we realize it continually or not, we have entered a planetary initiation. We cannot know the outcome in advance. However, the energy of Kornerupine enters the initiation with us as a different life form (from humans). It embraces this challenge. It relishes it. It envelopes it so completely that it becomes the initiation itself. In that single moment of clarity, Kornerupine becomes all bliss and all struggle, simultaneously. It gives timelessness to that experience, therefore, it answers the challenge by meeting it and loving it. The same initiation lives with us humans right now.

Electrical Body Alignment: Presents us with the immediate opportunity to align our spine and all energy centers.

Affirmation of Support: *"Every moment I am a living breathing initiation and I love me."*

Stone Story:
Somewhere, there is a grand storm brewing.
It is me.
Somewhere, the stars sparkle in a rainbow.
It is me.
Somewhere, a baby dies.
It is me.
Somewhere, lovers reunite.
It is me.
Someone, somehow, somewhere, sometime.
It is all me.
This is the moment.
I see it in you.

Summary: Kornerupine is a totem for initiation.

(See *Stone Combination Section* for Kornerupine in "Bliss," "Death," "Fear into Love," "Gabriel's Dawn," "Lack into Allowability," "Regeneration" and "Spirit Storytelling")

Kunzite

" I bless you with all the uniqueness of your life, now."

I am the mineral Spodumene, Lithium Aluminum Silicate, and my name comes from the Greek *spodumenos*, for "burnt to ashes," referring to my common gray color. I am known as Kunzite in the world of gems, (named after the famed gemologist George F. Kunz). And I am found only in granite pegmatites, and usually associated with Tourmaline. My colors range from pink to purple, as Kunzite, to white, gray, yellowish and emerald green, as Hiddenite. Relatively hard, at

6.5 to 7, and with a vitreous luster, a specific gravity of 3.1 to 3.2, and good cleavage in two directions (lengthwise, at nearly right angles), my crystal structure is monoclinic with mostly lathlike flattened crystals with deep grooves parallel to the elongation.

I appear in remarkably big and perfect crystals, the largest known being 47 feet in length, 5 feet in diameter, and weighing 90 tons. Unlike many deeper-colored gems that must be cut to into smaller stones to avoid appearing too dark, I work well as a large gemstone, where my color actually intensifies. I am, however, usually too soft or rare to be in general circulation as a gemstone, and I tend to be cut only for collectors on the basis of beauty or rarity. Additionally, my color slowly fades over time, particularly when exposed to light. My best specimens can be found in California, Maine, North Carolina, Brazil, Afghanistan and Madagascar.

Physical Integration: Supports arteries and circulatory system. Conditions the immune system.

Emotional Integration: Encourages regenerating solitude. Fosters mindful activities, particularly listening. Prizes the value of forgiveness. Embraces self nurturance.

Millennial Uses: On this planet, there are many, many diverse lifestyles. In this age of immediate, global communication, we hear of most of them and sometimes feel the need to compete with others. Kunzite allows us time away from the information highways and needless competition. It invites us to get reacquainted with ourselves, quietly and patiently. When we overload our senses, this stone soothes us; it shows us the stillness within ourselves that nurtures us naturally.

Electrical Body Alignment: Connects us to active, self nurturance.

Affirmation of Support: *"Whenever I feel the need, I leave the world behind and learn to love, starting with me."*

Stone Story:
You're here,
because this is a quiet, gentle space.
Perfect.
Turn off the noise around you; turn off the noise inside of you.

Hello!
Who are you?
What do you love?
Do you know what you like to do?

This moment is for you.
You are an incredible one-of-a-kind soul.
What can you do to celebrate that?
Don't tell me.
Tell you.
Tell yourself the sweetness that you saved up for just the right day.
Today is the day.
Now is when you meet you.
Though you were afraid of this, see, it's fine.
You're a soft child, looking for a home.
How do you suppose you can make yourself a place to be?
You can do it, because you're the only who can.

Personal Story

When I first discovered Kunzite eight years ago, I knew I would be long-time friends with it. Since my first lilac-colored piece came to me, I have collected many sizes and shapes of this beautiful stone and it has come in very handy over the years as a provider of peace and grounding, not only for myself, but for many of my friends as well.

I first came upon Kunzite at a Gem and Mineral Show in Minneapolis where I was looking through a box of rough Tourmaline. A friend pointed out these long, triangular lilac-colored crystals. I soon set the Tourmaline aside to "feel" this new crystal. I immediately felt a deep sense of peace and my mind felt centered. My body felt like all of my energy centers were aligning with a higher purpose. I knew then that this stone would always be with me.

Kunzite is said to help with relaxation, grounding and clarity. I have found all these to be true and very seldom does a day go by that I don't wear a necklace of Kunzite or have a small piece of it in my pocket.

A few years ago, I got a piece of Kunzite that has three colors in it plus two surprises. This stone is lilac, yellow and clear-green colored and has small pieces of Blue Tourmaline and Silver Mica embedded in its long length. I use this stone by placing it on my forehead and my heart to deepen meditation and dreams.

I've had many different pieces of Kunzite over the years and they all are close to my heart. Along my journeys, I have given many of them to friends and even strangers who seem to resonate with the pleasant sensations given off by them. Please enjoy a piece of Kunzite whenever you get the chance.

Another Story:

Many years ago, I traveled to Fargo, North Dakota to visit a friend. I ended up finding two pieces of crystal that would change the way I see things.

While we were at a mall, we decided to go to a Nature Store there. I saw rain sticks, jewelry, nature music, vitamins, incense and a crystal rock display. Since I have an affinity towards all these earth creations, I wanted to take a closer look. I first reached my hand into a bin to find a tumbled piece of Amethyst, then, with the other hand, I picked up a chard of Clear Quartz. At the moment I held them both in my hands, I "heard/felt" the words, "We have many things to teach you." Since I don't often hear things like this, I knew I had to have these two small stones. For a whopping $2.75, I bought them. I placed them in my pocket and went about the rest of my trip.

A few months later, while taking a college geology course, I was doing some testing in the lab. I enjoyed finding crystals or clear stones that had inclusions which can range from iron, chloride, magnesium or just micro-elements. They can look like white clouds floating inside clear quartz or reddish-brown dots on Amethyst.

I decided that I wanted to look at some of my own personal stone buddies with the high-powered microscope. That morning, when I had chosen the crystals to bring with me that day, I had asked them, "Which stones want to be seen in a new way?" I chose four stones, one of which was the small Quartz chard I had purchased in Fargo. As I picked it up from the shelf, I remembered the words, "We have many things to teach you." So I put both the Quartz chard and the Amethyst in my pocket and left for the lab.

When I got to the lab, I was getting very excited with the anticipation of what I might see. And what beauty I saw! I saw Quartz crystal with chloride forests inside, a Dolomite chunk with microscopic pieces of perfect rhomboid Calcite, and an Aquamarine with microscopic gold Tourmaline. A new world had been discovered.

Then I took out this very unassuming looking piece of Quartz chard from my pocket and placed it under the scope. I wasn't expecting to see anything special since it was just a clear quartz crystal, but was I wrong! It was the most amazing vision! Hundreds and hundreds of small bubbles were inside, and what was more amazing, was that each of the bubbles was filled with geometrically perfect spheres and rectangular boxes. To say the least, I was blown away!

I now bring these two stones on all the trips and vacations I go on, to remember that not everything is the way it looks on the outside and that there is always something to learn by looking deeper inside.

~from Daniel Krasofski

Summary: Kunzite promotes quiet, loving solitude.

(See *Stone Combination Section* for Kunzite in "Intent," "Pain into Fulfillment" and "Raphael's Rays")

Kyanite

"Go to your center and see the most glorious you imaginable!"

Also known as Disthene, I am a rich, blue gem, similar to Sapphire in appearance, though seldom confused for it, as I am rarely sold commercially due to my scarceness. Besides being uncommon, I possess the rare characteristic within the mineral and gem world of directional hardness, ranging from 4 to 5 lengthwise to 6 to 7 crosswise, giving me the well-earned reputation of being most difficult to cut. Originally spelled "cyanite," my name originates in the Greek word *kyanos*, "dark blue," and I can be colorless, white, gray, green, yellow, or nearly black in color.

I form flattened bladed crystal aggregates of the triclinic system, have a vitreous luster, a specific gravity of 3.5 to 3.7, and perfect cleavage, in one direction, lengthwise, and good cleavage in a second direction. I am a product of regional metamorphism and I occur with Quartz, Biotite and Almandine in gneiss and schist. I am found in Switzerland, Austria, Kenya, Brazil, China, and the United States.

Physical Integration: Increases coordination. Smoothes the skin.

Emotional Integration: Uplifts moods. Willing to be vulnerable in relationship. Shows affection easily.

Millennial Uses: Kyanite teaches us to stand on our own center stage and show all our talents, without shame. Entering the future, can be our (humanity's) moment to shine. Instead of looking for all that can go wrong, we could focus on the chance to show what we're made of—to put forth our best foot. Kyanite invites us to do that, no matter what else is happening or will happen.

Electrical Body Alignment: Links us to all our resources and gifts.

Affirmation of Support: *"I am extremely talented and grow more gifted every day!"*

Stone Story:
It's true.
The earth's a stage and we all are players,
but that doesn't make our lives unreal.

It means we practice ourselves
until we get it
exactly the way
we want it.

If we don't like it, we can change.
If we do like it, we can change.

You're here because you wanted to experience it well.
So experience it very well.
Show grace under pressure or under calm.
Act boldly like YOU
and love yourself for the truth that YOU are,
magnificent,
talented,
beautiful
and ~

Summary: Kyanite directs us to being fully ourselves and all our talents.

Totem Stories from the Tibetan Tektites

"When life feels too full, empty yourself.
Empty yourself so that you can overflow freely."

We offer the above message.

It comes from the height of our spirit

enjoying our timeless time with you.

We thank you for your presence which

enriches us with great presents....

so we give to you

whatever you need that you have not asked for yet.

We trust that our spirits connect and give endlessly.

We send our spirit to the surface of our being; we spill it onto a page of life.

It has your answer.

Take it with you for you never quite know when its need will arise.

At the precise intersection of need and desire,

the words will haunt you

and you will know the meaning.

You do know the meaning

and when you act upon it

it is an act of power

that the universe must reward.

Labradorite

"I am a spirit guiding stone.
In my rainbows you will discover whatever answers you wish."

I am one of six varieties of plagioclase Feldspar group, also known as the soda-lime Feldspars and lime-soda Feldspars, along with Albite (the Sodium-rich end member), Oligoclase, Andesine, Bytownite, and Anorthite (the Calcium-rich end member). We are a continuous compositional series in which varieties can be distinguished by specialized testing, and we are an abundant and important rock-forming mineral of nearly all igneous rocks.

Our colors range from white to reddish, often with a play of colors, particularly in Albite and Labradorite. Our hardness is 6, our luster is vitreous, and frequently pearly on cleavage, which is good in two directions at nearly right angles, and poor in a third direction. Our specific gravity is 2.2 to 2.67, and our triclinic structure rarely creates crystals. Our name derives from the eastern Canadian peninsula.

Physical Integration: Helps to detoxify the overall body system. Supports the balance between wet/dry and hot/cold. Releases body odors and balances the aura.

Emotional Integration: Stimulates imagination. Supports the use of affirmations and visualizations. Easily enters and maintains meditative states.

Millennial Uses: One thing that all beings have in common is consciousness. All have a spirit. Going into the 2000's, we can integrate this into every facet of life, in order to heal ourselves.

Labradorite offers itself as an ally for the spiritual seeker. All things are connected by spirit and we express that through love. When we witness all the earth's beauty, Labradorite points out that it is a gift of love. If we embrace that love, we become caretakers of the earth and its treasures.

Electrical Body Alignment: Connects us to love.

Affirmation of Support: *"I am love and I find that at the core of all things."*

> **Stone Story:**
> *Of course you go through all sorts of emotions.*
> *You grieve. You depress yourself. You cry.*
> *No matter what you say, or do, or think,*
> *love forms the base of all your experiences.*
> *When you have had enough of everything, you empty yourself......*
> *Love fills you.*
> *It shows you the handsomeness of all the earth's abundance.*
> *It lives forever.*
> *It is the kiss of spirit upon the face of life.*

Summary: Labradorite supports the path of the spiritual seeker.

(See *Stone Combination Section* for Labradorite in "Buddha," "Celebration of Fairies," "New Earth Harmony" and "Raphael's Rays")

Lapis Lazuli

"I help you to manifest unlimitedness through choice."

You know me well by this name, as the opaque azure to deep blue semiprecious mineral prized the world over. Specifically, I am Lazurite, in the Sodalite group, a sulfur-containing silicate of Sodium, Calcium and Aluminum. Lazurite forms in limestone, affected by contact metamorphism by granite intrusion in isometric structure. My structure is isometric to dodecahedral, with rare crystals, usually occurring in massive form. My specific gravity is 2.4 to 2.5, my luster is vitreous to dull to pearly, my hardness is 5 to 5.5, and my cleavage is poor, in six directions.

As Lapis Lazuli, we are a mixture of Lazurite, Calcite, Pyrite and Diopside. Usually veined or spotted, our value to humans depends largely on excellence and uniformity of color and the absence of Pyrite. We have been mined for over 6,000 years, and for centuries the only known deposits were in Mongolia and remote Afghanistan. From here we found our way to Egypt and the ancient kingdom of Babalonia. We are now found in abundance in the Chilean Andes, Myanmar, Angola, Pakistan, Canada, and Russia. Our name derives from the Arabic *lazaward*, "heaven."

Physical Integration: Relaxes and strengthens lymph glands. Quickens reflexes.

Emotional Integration: Clarifies choices. Relates well to intuition. Accepts responsibility for awareness. Focuses on empowerment through free choices.

Millennial Uses: Through the ages, this stone has been used by sages and seers for wisdom and foresightedness; in the next millennium, its gifts are expanding. With all the information readily available to anyone, we are evolving into our own sages. Lapis Lazuli shares the key to empowerment: free choice. Accept its perspective and we will grow rapidly. In that growth, we also may acquire the responsibility to share, freely, our gifts with all others.

Electrical Body Alignment: Connects with the source of all knowing.

Affirmation of Support: *"I choose to be free, aware and kind."*

Stone Story:
In every age, friends,
all possibilities have been there (still are).
They live in a single moment.
They are freed by choice.
When you choose to own all the awareness that you really are,
you honor yourself totally.
In that great honor, Life blesses you.
You will find more knowingness than you can explain
(you won't need to...).

You are already the answer you seek~

Summary: Lapis Lazuli stands for timeless wisdom and freedom.

(See *Stone Combination Section* for Lapis Lazuli in "Aurora's Dream," Connecting to your Guides" and "Regeneration")

Larimar

"I am the fire upon the mountains and the seas racing to the shore."

Many know me as Pectolite, a whitish or grayish hydrous silicate of Calcium and Sodium, occurring in aggregates of needlelike monoclinic crystals in igneous rocks. To collectors, I am best recognized by my pale blue to medium-blue translucence, and known as Larimar. I develop most commonly in the basalt cavities of volcanic rocks, often alongside Zeolite minerals. From the Greek pektos, for "compacted," my compact fibrous nature appears in a triclinic structure which rarely creates distinct crystals. My hardness is 4.5 to 5, my specific gravity is 2.7 to 2.9, my luster is vitreous to silky, and my cleavage is perfect, in two directions at 85 and 95 degrees. I can be found in the Dominican Republic, Canada, New Jersey, Colorado, Arkansas and California.

Physical Integration: Tones the metabolism. Supports the pineal gland. Stimulates the sense of smell. Assists with sleeping disorders.

Emotional Integration: Traces memories through sensual, intuitional clues. Embraces the innate beauty in love. Releases over-romanticism.

Millennial Uses: For our world to be balanced, perhaps all of us must achieve individual balance. Each of us expresses masculine and feminine qualities. On the earth we see the struggle as we try to integrate these energies.

Larimar brings us to our center, where we harmoniously express all parts of self. This stone demonstrates the union of fire (masculine) and water (feminine). Its spirit lives beyond these definitions and joins with all life passionately and peacefully.

Electrical Body Alignment: Unifies all our polarities.

Affirmation of Support: *"I love my male and female qualities equally."*

Stone Story:
It is a wonder to live together in a book.
I smile at the adventure and marvel at the reality of it.
We meet so you can remember that you are a man

and a woman and their union.
You see many things in twos: good and bad, black and white,
old and young.
The world doesn't see that.
The world sees every shade of color and meaning.
Expand your views to three.
Declare yourself, child and adult...and timeless.
Happy and sad...and complete.
Awake and tired...and dreaming.
Take whatever you seem to be and marry it to some magic in the
world.
There you have it!
You are the magic in the world,
always were,
always are,
and always will be.

Summary: Larimar encourages us to combine our polarized thoughts with balance.

(See *Stone Combination Section* for Larimar in "Confusion into Focus" and "Raphael's Rays")

Laser Wands

"I stretch into infinity with sheer intent and joy."

We are long and slender (and aptly named) Quartz formations of Silicon Dioxide.

Physical Integration: Sharpens the senses. Adapts the body readily to new circumstances. Helps to release chronic disease.

Emotional Integration: Focuses the mind easily. Lifts moods and increases optimism. Creates solutions to long standing difficulties.

Millennial Uses: Through technology we have discovered that quartz crystal performs many services (in our machinery). By listening to our other senses, we can tap into an even vaster array of their possibilities.

Laser wands sharpen our wits and our imaginings. They point out the patterns that have limited us for so long that we no longer are aware of them. They cut to the chase; they speak directly. In this time when every choice has strong consequences, we need the truth and a clear perspective.

Electrical Body Alignment: Connects us with our abilities to identify what's wrong beneath the surface of any challenge.

Affirmation of Support: *"I act immediately upon the truth."*

Stone Story:
Hello friends.
Like you, I provide whatever service life calls from me.
I may be sharp or soothing, immediate or slow—
the need determines my impact.
What do you need?
That is the most important question of all.
What do you need?
What have you denied yourself?
What freedom have you set aside?
Now you can fly.
I will tell you that always,
it is the truth and I offer you no less.
In your heart you would ask for no more
and accept no less.

Summary: Laser Wands cut through distractions and fears to the truth.

Lazulite

"Welcome to the 21st century.
We live in a timelessness of vision and equality for all life."

Also known as "Blue Spar," my name heralds from an old Arabic word *lazaward*, "heaven," a reference to my distinct color, which can range from deep blue to sky blue to pale greenish-blue. Chemically I am a hydrous phosphate of Magnesium, Iron and Aluminum, and I occur as monoclinic crystals forming in plutonic and metamorphic rocks in association with Muscovite, Topaz, Hematite and Quartz. My hardness is 5.5 to 6, my luster is vitreous to dull, my specific gravity is 3.0 to 3.1, and my cleavage is distinct, in one direction. I am a scarce mineral, found mostly in Georgia, Colorado and California.

Physical Integration: Releases the need for struggle. Helps us to face fears/phobias/limits. Tones the throat. Eases the balance between both sides of the brain.

Emotional Integration: Promotes self-confidence during exploration of shadow issues. Offers deep acceptance. Eases the ability to speak (or to express) during great fears.

Millennial Uses: If we are fortunate, the passing of time means acquiring wisdom. So going from one millennium to another translates into clearer insights for all of us (as a race of beings). Lazulite stands for the core desire we have to confront our fears and step beyond them into an incredible future. We sense our true evolution comes when we release denial and act responsibly. This beautiful stone helps us to face that challenge while we simultaneously learn to unconditionally support ourselves in every step of our journey...honestly and happily.

Electrical Body Alignment: Connects us with our core, actualized self and the means to live it in our reality.

Affirmation of Support: *"I accept myself as I am, in every act, thought and deed."*

Stone Story:
Can you see me?
Close your eyes and open your heart
wide as a field of stars...
There, there I am, by the tree, smiling.
In spirit visits, I am the old crone by the tree
(no teeth, but LOTS of smiles).
You dance by me, as eternal children.
I thrill to have you visit me this way,
in our true forms.
I know you from your crown to your roots

and all the funniness in between (of course I mean ALL of it)
there is no other way to love.
I only show you fine love
when I see every bigness and smallness that makes you,
that makes you up, perfectly,
that makes you the dream-within-the reality-within-the dream.

See! I told you I knew you!
Lean way way way back into this tree friend,
(with its branches of our stories)
and grab the memories of our spirit visits.
Close your eyes and stretch out your awareness,
it's gentler finding the dreamtime that way.
Yes, we are ancient friends.
Better than that, we are neighbors.
We live side by side, never denying our freedom.
All our secrets lay beside us—no shields—just requests as protection.
What else would keep us safe?
We live at the base of truth.
Shadows come and know us by name.
Brightness comes and grows our dreams.

Everything knows us
and we are Everything.
Now what?
After we have said and done it all,
what is left?
Not the passing of time,
for we are eternal.
Not the pain,
for we are powerful.
Not the possessions,
for we are free.

Here's where my smile grows across the sky—

WE are LOVE.
We dance in bodies and dreams and trees
to love every single
heart
hope

117

and root of us.
Everything that we are is lovable.
Everything that we are is love.

Summary: Lazulite guides us to love our fears, our strengths, our whole selves completely, immediately.

Lingam

"We all mark special moments in time with the uniqueness of our being."

Like all true wonders, no two people can agree upon what exactly I am. You can locate me by the Narmada River, high in the Amandhata Mountains, which is one of seven sacred pilgrimage sites in India. It has been theorized that I was formed from a meteorite in the river bed millions of years ago. Most often, I am brown or gray combinations of chalcedony, agate and quartzite. My most distinguishing trait comes from deep red/maroon iron oxide markings.

Physical Integration: Realigns the flow of fluids and breath, as needed. Identifies the simplest paths to healing. Integrates the physical and the emotional for full health.

Emotional Integration: Shows respect for the body and all the opportunities of life upon the earth. Increases the feeling of sacredness in all things/acts/feelings. Fosters the nurturance to create open hearted time and space.

Millennial Uses: All things upon this planet are tools for honoring life. We are tools for honoring life, so are stones. Lingams are handled and passed on as sacred beings; therefore they make excellent ritual tools.

Time itself is a ritual. It gives us a moment to reflect and to choose what we want to do. Going into the 21st century might be meaningless; however, it may provide exactly the time we need to stop and act with awareness. Lingams bring their services to us, consciously. They invite us to make each moment sacred and remind us that we have the opportunity to create our very own rituals. As life changes, so, too, do the rituals change. These wondrous stones can help us to turn inward to explore what our priorities are and how we wish to honor them, right now.

Electrical Body Alignment: Connects us with the appropriate tools/rituals/wisdom, now.

Affirmation of Support: *"I empower myself to create sacred space, all around me."*

Stone Story:
From the hands of the universe, to your heart~
I gift you with all my essence.
The poetry of my soul belongs to you.
Weave a song from it
and it will echo my starry home
to your earthy home
and we will meet again and again
for it is the time of togetherness.
We know this now.
We accept it and we dance this story into timelessness.

Summary: Lingams align us, respectfully, with the sacredness and mystery of life.

Lightning Stones

*"Rub me together and release my sparks to the air
and my spirit to the earth."*

Personal Story

When I first held a pair of lightning stones, I felt an electrical current surge up my arms and flow through my whole body. It felt pleasant, but quite altering, so much so that I had to go sit down for a while. While I ended up with a different pair, my experience of them is always that they are living entities, with a strong, physical force. I like to sit in the dark striking them into sparks, and making my affirmations. They feel like true helpers to me.

~ from Anna Lambert

We are uniquely paired sets of a variety of usually white Quartz, which exhibit the phenomenon of triboluminescence, from the Greek word *tribos*, for "rubbing," First suggested by Frances Bacon 400 years ago, the emission of light from the friction of two objects has been a source of scientific curiosity ever since. When rubbed together, our particular crystallographic structure will create a glow and emit the flash and color of lightning, as well as several forms of energy in the process, primarily at the contact faces. We originate at Native American sites in the southwestern United States, and are traditionally used by native peoples for healing and rain ceremonies. Many pairs have been found which date back to prehistoric times.

To create this effect, one simply places one stone in each hand and rubs - gently but briskly - the smaller handpiece back and forth against the larger pallate stone. When rubbed, flat or tabular stones will generally glow on most of the flat facets, while numerous combinations are possible with some pairs. Each carefully matched pair emits their own unique energy, which can be sensed by most handlers of the stones.

When rubbed together, we become charged and polarized, the energy continuously building and discharging. As with natural lightning, nitrogen molecules in the air become ionized from the electrical buildup and produce the characteristic smell we associate with lightning. The excitation produces a slightly delayed glow, the strobe or tracer effect observed while watching the rapidly moving handpiece.

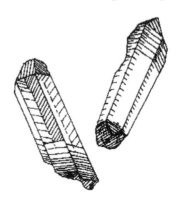

Physical Integration: Releases chronic pain. Spontaneously heals disease.

Emotional Integration: Opens to the unimaginable. Increases flexibility in beliefs. Creates great euphoria.

Millennial Uses: Some things appear on the earth only when they are needed, like Lightning Stones. According to some traditions, these stones were carried by tribal healers, who used them for ritual and thanksgiving. After awhile, the stones stopped appearing on the land.

Now they have re-surfaced. Lightning Stones come to us so we can establish, again, a sacred link to the earth. When we do that, we become comfortable in our beings and our bodies; we release the need for disease and dis-connection. When rubbed together, these stones produce a spark and an odor that encourages wisdom and visions.

Electrical Body Alignment: Connects us to the source of health.

Affirmation of Support: *"I open myself to brand new miracles."*

Stone Story:
*Come be beside the mountain
of your dream.*

*As the sands of time and space shift,
we are free.*

*We appear before you
and you tower above us.*

*Great Spirit has drawn us together
like the directions of fire and air
upon the earth.*

Together we are a match and a flame.

*The magic arises from our prayers sent
and new dreams are birthed.*

*One day our children's children
will find our bones and smile.*

Even though they will not know the story,
they will be alive from our union
and,
like us,
ever free.

Summary: Lightning Stones lead us to find natural miracles.

MacEarl Crystals

"Shine in your clarity and light up the world!"

We are an optically pure and clear crystal variety of Quartz found in and named after our original mine in Arkansas. The fluids in which we form are clear and of undisturbed chemistry and temperature which, when given ample space in which to grow and no stresses during the cooling down period, form some of the most pure crystalline structures known.

Physical Integration: Sharpens the less dominant senses. Combines physical sight with visions. Unites body/mind/heart.

Emotional Integration: Develops new senses and the confidence to use them well. Explores the unknown immediately. Alters perceptions to find new ways ways to think and to feel.

Millennial Uses: Every being is born at a particular time in order to provide a certain service to life. MacEarl's were discovered at the end of the 20th century, (a time of great transition) to clarify our needs and our resources. These remarkable crystals amplify our potential, until we can feel it so well that we fulfill our incredible promise.

Electrical Body Alignment: Connects us to undiscovered technologies and answers.

Affirmation of Support: *"I awaken the powerful, glorious possibilities in me, today."*

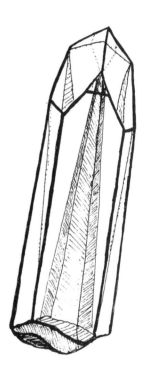

Stone Story:
I know you as you are.
I see your aura rainbow across the sky.
I watch you as your dreamtime self soars the universe.
Yes, that's you.
That's you as you are right now.
Same you that you already know.

It grows beyond your expectations
and lands right in your dreams.

Personal Story

It seems like we have always been in love with stones. Everywhere we go, we pick them up, we admire them. Then we discovered that they had expansive, glorious stories of life for us. Those stories changed everything for us; they opened us up to a world full of other lifeforms that wanted to co-create miracles with us. That's how the MacEarl's came to us.

One day, we met a man who kept wanting us to buy his private stone collections. Truly the stones he showed us were remarkable, but for us they were a lot of money. So we looked at them again with our business partner, who also wondered why were being asked (by the stones, themselves) so strongly to purchase these stones. After all, we were many things, but rock sellers/wholesalers weren't one of them.

However, willing is one of the things we are. Thomas and I jumped off the cliff. We borrowed money and bought one of the collections. For some reason or another, these stones wanted to come to us. We opened our hearts and trusted. Our partner bought most of everything else.

Another world opened up. The man called us later and said one of his old friends (a stone collector and seller) realized that in his barn he still had many MacEarl crystals and he needed to raise some money. It had to be explained to us that these Arkansas beauties were some of the world's most optically perfect crystals and since they had been "mined out" they were extremely rare and sought after and they were very expensive.

Our new friend offered to wholesale them to us just before the Tucson Gem and Mineral Show (the largest rock show in the world), where we could sell them for a profit. We jumped again, purchased them, and was then told by the stones that they would "allow" us to write a stone reference book for them and that the MacEarl's had come to us to help fund the printing of the book.

It all started to finally make sense. We sold the MacEarl's (to only a few select people who had the blessings of the stones to purchase them), started writing, and here is the book. Spirit always provides and we have certainly found that life requires us to take the first steps of courage and trust before the manifestation we ask for seems to appear. We have been blessed to be a part of this whole adventure and we dearly thank the MacEarl's for their continued presence in our lives and the honor that has

been bestowed upon us as bridges for their words and energies to all of you who are reading this book.
~from Twintreess

Summary: MacEarl Crystals help us to find the ways to discover our own power.

Malachite

"I spiral further and further into the center of the universe.
There I find myself, whole and free."

You know me as the emerald-green, grass-green, dark green, silky to dull-lustered mineral whose color derives from the presence of Copper. My wonderful concentric swirls of light and dark green are related to the size of the crystals in the alternating bands. Zones with the tiniest crystals are lighter than those in which the crystals are coarse. My name derives from the Greek *moloche*, "mallow," referencing this leaf-green color; I am also called Green Carbonate of Copper. My compact monoclinic crystals, occurring in microcrystalline masses, are usually nodules with radiating bands. A secondary copper mineral, I form in the upper oxidized zone of Copper deposits. I am generally found intergrown with the blue mineral Azurite, and am also associated with Turquoise and Chrysocolla. My hardness is 3.5 to 4, my specific gravity is 3.8, and my cleavage is perfect in one direction, crosswise.

The ancient Egyptians, Romans, and Greeks, all used me as jewelry; in modern times an immense deposit of massive, banded malachite in the province of Shaba, Zaire is the source of the vast majority of all current supplies, although I can also be found in Zambia, Zimbabwe, Bisbee and Globe, Arizona, Utah, California, Nevada, Pennsylvania, and Tennessee.

Physical Integration: Supports and regenerates hearing. Opens the body to new postures or increased energy flow. Gives flexibility to the limbs.

Emotional Integration: Shows value for listening as an art. Empowers the self in all healing processes. Trusts in the body's innate wisdom.

Millennial Uses: Though we have increased our life-span by years, we have not increased the health of our bodies and minds. Malachite speaks to us of an ancient ever-present wisdom: to be free of disease we must heal ourselves. In disconnecting from the earth and nature, we have also lost touch with our own bodies. Malachite links us to the perfect innate adaptability of our forms to all circumstances and all times.

Electrical Body Alignment: Links our hearts to our immune systems to our spirits.

Affirmation of Support: *"I live with a passionate vitality that I grant myself every moment."*

Stone Story:
I am a tree from the inner earth. In my rings, I record ancient stories of being. With each season, I grow wiser. The wisdom is free. Take it, children of the earth, and hold it to your hearts. The mystical secrets say that the key to full life waits in your ability to say to yourself and all your truth, "Yes!"

Summary: Malachite stands for the natural perfect healing systems of nature and of the body.

(See *Stone Combination Section* for Malachite in "Disease into Vitality" and "Freedom")

Marcasite

"I send you all my strength and support. Use it to build beauty."

Also called white Iron Pyrite, I have the same chemical formula as Pyrite, but a different crystal structure-orthohombic vs. isometric. I am pale brass-yellow to almost white in color, and I tarnish deep-yellow to brown. I am very common, and found in association with Bornite, Galena, Chalcocite, Quartz, and, of course, Pyrite. A disulfide of Iron my hardness is 6 to 6.5, my cleavage is distinct in 2 directions, my luster is metallic, and my specific gravity is 4.8 to 4.9.

My name is believed to have derived from an Arabic word once used for Pyrite. I am among the first minerals in any collection to disinegrate, developing into a white powder that no longer resembles my original material. I am mined along with Galena and Sphalerite in Missouri, Oklahoma, and Kansas, as well as in Guanajuato, Mexico.

Physical Integration: Tones the gums. Strengthens the teeth. Relaxes the jaw.

Emotional Integration: Appreciates responsibility. Learns healthy respect for authority. Expands on leadership abilities.

Millennial Uses: In the next millennium, we must release our self-destructive behaviors. From there, we can establish our priorities and a collective rebuilding. Marcasite supports us by nurturing the joint efforts and structures that respect all life. It embodies the ability to respond efficiently to all situations. This happens in a cooperative system that brings out the best in each of us.

Electrical Body Alignment: Connects us with the communities of the future, now.

Affirmation of Support: *"I honor my life and my place in the world with responsibility and respect."*

Stone Story:
Take the wisdom of the ages with you
in your next venture.
Time means nothing,
but the experience of a few lifetimes can guide you well.
Whatever you don't need on this journey, will fade away.
Move on and life will move you in the right direction.
Care for the lost ones along the way.
We are all here for each other.
The same life grows in all of us.
Remembering that has saved us all.

Summary: Marcasite teaches us respectful responsibility.

Mica

"Take my glitter and scatter it on the sands of time and adventure."

We are any of the group of monoclinic minerals composed of hydrous aluminosilicates of Sodium, Potassium, Magnesium, etc., which occur in minute glittering plates or scales in granite or other rocks, and in crystals separable into thin, transparent, usually flexible laminae. We are Muscovite, a colorless, silver-gray or yellowish potassium-containing mica.

Monoclinic in structure, we are quite soft at 2 to 2.5, vitreous to pearly in luster, a specific gravity of 2.7 to 3.0, with perfect cleavage in one direction. We are a common rock forming mineral and are characteristic of many environments– in granite pegmatites, in metaquartzite of contact metamorphic rocks in schists, in gneisses, and in mesothermic veins, usually as large book-like masses. Our best specimens are restricted to the pegmatites, which are widespread throughout North America and around the world. The name is from the popular "Muscovy glass" because of our use as a glass substitute in Russia. We are commonly used as electrical and thermal insulators.

Physical Integration: Helps the body to release stones/buildups. Regenerates vision and hearing. Helps to release pressure on joints/organs/bones.

Emotional Integration: Releases stress as a way of life. Focuses on feelings, rather than expectations/memories. Softens outdated behaviors and beliefs.

Millennial Uses: Sometimes it appears that the one sure way we learn is through crisis. In an emergency, we put aside pettiness; true priorities become clear. If we also remain clear, then we immediately act upon our appropriate choices.

Mica stands for the ability to release everything. When we have gone too far in any one area, sometimes the best plan is to start over, completely. Mica provides that service. It chips away at the layers of personality that no longer aid us. It grants us the freedom to be anything we wish to be, now, without dwelling on what has been.

Electrical Body Alignment: Connects our excretory systems to re-newed life.

Affirmation of Support: *"I let go of everything and all that leaves me are limits."*

Stone Story:
What a gorgeous, simple dance.
Life comes to us. We meet it. We exchange our energies.
All is changed.
Life begins again. It appreciates our generosity.
It carries our contributions
to be scattered in the winds for all to appreciate.
Whatever is valuable will serve the four directions of the world.
Whatever is eternal will birth the beautiful children of love.
Whatever is perfect will form the seas, the mountains and the suns.

Whatever doesn't honor life anymore, will wilt like a flower.
When it is transformed, it will bring on the spring
and wear it like a new blossom.

Summary: Mica invites us to come completely new to each moment of life.

(See *Stone Combination Section* for Mica in "Confusion into Focus" and "Guilt into Perfection")

Moldavite

"We come from the clearest points of the stars to find your deepest clarity,
and now, we are all stars spinning in a loving universe."

We are among the Tektites (from the Greek *tektos* "molten"), natural glasses of unknown interstellar origin. Transparent green, greenish-brown or brown in color, we have a bobbly or craggy surface. Moldavites are named after the Moldau River Valley in Czechoslovakia where first found in 1787; other varieties are often named after their place of discovery, such as Billitonites (Billiton Island, Indonesia), Australites (Australia), and Georgiaites (Georgia). This particular green translucent silica meteoric glass was created by a large cosmic velocity meteorite which vaporized when it struck the earth in Nadlinger Germany, thus creating the Reis Crater. A small amount of that vapor was propelled into the ionosphere by the impact of the explosion through the hole punched in the earth's dense atmosphere. When the vapor reached the cold of outer space, it condensed, then solidified, and fell back to earth several hundred miles away in the Moldau River Valley, creating a strewn field of green Tektite .

We have been faceted as gemstones and we look very similar to the bottle-green mineral Peridot. We contain round or torpedo-shaped bubbles and characteristic swirls like treckle. Our system is amorphous, that is, we do not have a crystalline structure; as a result we do not belong to any of the 7 crystal symmetry systems. Our hardness is 5, and our specific gravity is 2.34 to 2.39.

Physical Integration: Coordination of the thymus gland with the rest of the body. Activation of the third eye and telepathy. Catalyzes hidden disease to come to the surface for integration/healing.

Emotional Integration: Embraces change as a lifestyle. Accepts discomfort as an opportunity for transformation. Broadens the perspective. Facilitates complete honesty.

Millennial Uses: Sometimes we have to go outside of ourselves in order to learn and, finally, to understand. Moldavite (a meteorite) guides us into possibilities that stretch us beyond knowledge and imagination. It encourages us not to find new answers (to old problems), but to use our brains and all our resources to think in completely new ways. Then perhaps we won't create problems in the first place.

Electrical Body Alignment: Links us to the acceleration and evolution of our species and our world.

Affirmation of Support: *"I grow because it is the nature of the bounteous life within me."*

Stone Story:
Growth, acceleration, initiation, evolution.
When you absorb these ideas, your old heart quakes.
Yes, yes, something dies in every birth.
If you rise from your depths

and breathe upon the surface of your watery feelings,
look for the glory in every fresh newness,
in the day of learning.
See it fully, clearly.
Bring it to your being.
Wear it and see where its generous youth will take you.
Such adventures you will discover;
ones that gave you no hints of their existence before.

If you must fear the death, take it upon your next travel.
It may sharpen your vision
so you can find the tiny seed of wonder on your path.
Take it and grow your own dream,
fresh and magnificent.

Life and death and life intertwine
to shape you for the next miracle.

Summary: Moldavite embraces change at the core of our existence.

(See *Stone Combination Section* for Moldavite in "Gabriel's Dawn," "Unimaginabilty" and "Uriel's Wisdom")

Moonstone

"I come to you at every step of your journey.
I support you and I wish you home safely."

We are Orthoclase, among the plagioclase group of Feldspars, common rock-forming minerals in igneous and metamorphic rocks, though rarely of gem quality. When colorless and transparent or translucent, often with a bluish opalescence, we are called Adularia and termed "Moonstone" in the jewelry business. Our monoclinic structure forms predominately as single crystals of rectangular or square cross section, commonly as twin crystals; our hardness is 6 to 6.5, our specific gravity is 2.6 to 2.76, and our cleavage is good, in two directions at 90 degrees.

When our Feldspar crystals of Moonstone first formed, they were rich in both Potassium and Calcium; upon cooling, our crystal structure adjusted to lower temperatures and these components became mutually incompatible. So they "unmixed", separated into two different Feldspar minerals, one of Potassium and one of Calcium. They became alternating platelets of microscopic thickness within our crystal. Light diffracted from these surfaces produce the beautiful soft sheen or bright iridescence of Moonstone.

Volcanic in origin, we are found in Norway, Canada, Myanmar, Sri Lanka, Madagascar, and Tanzania. Adularia is named for a locality in the Adula mountains of Switzerland.

Physical Integration: Assists with the release of some toxins. Supports fluid balance. Helps to strengthen the left side of the body.

Emotional Integration: Allows us to explore ourselves through the reflection of others. Deepens our appreciation of stillness. Opens us to receive what we need.

Millennial Uses: Moonstone connects us with the feeling of being home, in our hearts, in our bodies, in our families, and upon the earth. It reaches into our deepest feelings and says, "Bring your home with you wherever you go."

Electrical Body Alignment: It connects all the senses to the heart and revitalizes the urge for creating community in the world.

Affirmation of Support: *"Everywhere I go, I share peace and security with all."*

Stone Story:
Look upon me. Gaze upon my milkiness. Caress my luminescence. For me, your witnessing of my body gives me joy. I sigh and I breathe and I spin and I dance and I call out your name to the stars. All of this in a single glance. Beneath the surface of me, every feeling explodes. All you see is a soft shimmer. Remember that. Hold that into your heart.

Beneath the surface of the earth, every emotion surges. Witness it any way that you can. Be familiar with the feelings below the waves of the sea or in the quiet of the woods. I am reflected there while reflecting all the magnificence everywhere.

Summary: Moonstone blesses all feeling journeys, especially the one leading to home.

Moqui

*"Whatever you don't need to be a full expression of joy,
I brush away with a laugh and a wave."*

We are Iron and Silicon concretions which form as circular balls in and around Sandstone deposits. We are old formations, dark brown, bumpy and irregular, and we are rounded by the action of water.

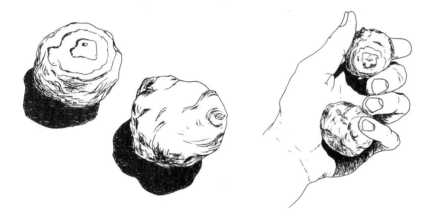

Physical Integration: Identifies obstructions in the body's energy. Youthens. Releases atrophy and aging. Activates the hands.

Emotional Integration: Lightens the heart. Increases harmonious relationships. Balances cooperation with individuality.

Millennial Uses: Moquis are hard on the outside with softer sand on the inside. They resemble humans going through a planetary initiation. They bring forth the rituals and the wisdoms of the ancients when we most need them. Their power allows us to smile at difficulties and to act upon the forever child within.

Electrical Body Alignment: Clears and activates the aura.

Affirmation of Support: *"I laugh and my body renews itself."*

Stone Story:
Hi. I fit in your pocket. I roll in your hand. I delight in your smile. Just take me with you. I don't need you to do anything but be who you are. Let me join you. I enliven in the company of humans who

change in the twinkling of an eye and who stay as constant as the mountains. I love to be alongside of you, and for that gift, I will lighten your load. I will laugh and point out what you do not need to travel your new path.

Summary: Moquis help us to release anything we take too seriously.

Moss Agate

"We come together as human and stone to release our limits to the winds."

Another member of the Silica family, I am a visually unique Chalcedony with inclusions of Hornblende, known for my characteristic green dendrites of oxidized Manganese. I am most often found in China, the United States and India, and my name is due to the plant-like appearance that is created by natural dendritic inclusions.

Physical Integration: Gently releases toxins. Activates the immune system. Integrates emotions and physicalness, in love.

Emotional Integration: Unconditionally accepts all emotions. Acknowledges the wisdom in grief and release. Draws out unknown co-dependencies.

Millennial Uses: In the 21st century, we appear to be advancing mentally and technologically. The evolution before us is to take basic parts of our being and advance them. Moss Agate records the emotional struggles of humans and now it guides us to release a basic pattern of needing limits and pain to grow. Moss Agate trusts us to our own mental and technological advances. It enters through our hearts. It helps to empower us to evolve our human emotions.

Electrical Body Alignment: Connects our heart to the universe.

Affirmation of Support: *"I grow beyond my old fears into unimaginable love."*

Stone Story:

Do you ever feel like life is moving just beyond your reach? Do you think that there is not enough time just to be? Even when you are the most efficient, do you feel completely inadequate?

Hello.

You must be a spirit-in-human-in-training. Actually, you are not in training. But I think it makes a nice catch phrase. The way you record time on your plane of existence, is a line. It's a very nice line. You've got some calculations and explanations. All along it you have written about all of your achievements. It's one of your stories.

That line has shot off like a meteor into space. You've gone beyond yourself in some ways. Yes, I said some ways. Not everything travels on a line. Your feelings form in just about any shape they want to. They spiral, they triangle, they dodecahedron. They dance across the galaxy. However, they rarely follow that straight line of your achievements—your history, your future. Emotions exist right now. They tell you how to sense this moment, completely, even when you don't like to know what they are saying. Emotions are still right there, right now. Until you join them, in the right now, you will feel like a line that is out of shape or a spirit-human-in-training. Go with your feelings and time is just a word.

Summary: Moss Agate supports us as we let go of all unneeded toxins, thoughts and feeling.

(See *Stone Combination Section* for Moss Agate in "Uriel's Wisdom")

Nebula

*"I reach into the unknown
to find wonders that I could not imagine before now."*

Personal Story

For many years, we continued to be drawn deeper and deeper into some mountains we had discovered in our travels. Over time, we found a hidden valley where everything appeared lush and vibrant. As we sat under the old trees, watching over the valley, we spoke of how the sounds and colors seemed enhanced and even the birds and animals seemed unusually curious. We had never found any place quite like this before. We had no doubt this was a very mystical place...And as we stepped from the arms of the trees into the sunlight, we found these beautiful stones at our feet smiling with the morning's dew.

(con't on next page)

Found recently and to date exclusively in the mountains of Mexico, our precise identity remains a mystery. Although evidently volcanic in nature, analysis of our composition produces mixed results, with no distinct conclusion available. We combine the minerals of Riebeckite, Quartz, Aegirine, Orthoclase, Acmite, and possibly Zircon in a beautiful and rare form. Appearing black at first look, closer inspection reveals me to be deep green in color, with variable inner bright eyes, radiating fibers and Quartz veining.

Physical Integration: Aligns the hips and shoulders for ease of movement. Grounds the body's center for balance. Receives sounds for healing.

Emotional Integration: Accepts the unknown calmly. Encourages full breath during crisis. Integrates conflicting emotions.

Millennial Uses: As a new discovery, Nebula is a child of the new millennium. Its qualities symbolize mystery. Trying to understand the 21st century is like trying to touch a mystery. There may be no way for sure to know what will happen.

Regardless, Nebula stones hold our hearts calm, remind us to breathe, and then creates an acceptance that goes beyond understanding.

Electrical Body Alignment: Links us with all mysteries from all times.

Affirmation of Support: *"I accept grace in all areas of my life."*

Stone Story:
Greetings!
If I am new to you it is because you need me now.
When I reach into your consciousness to unite,
I see that you have avoided the unknown.
First you experimented with this.
Then it became habit.
Now it lives with you without question.

Well, question it.
Question everything that you are.
Lift yourself beyond
everyday understanding and learning through conformity.
Stretch into your soul and walk it into the world.
What do you see in a rainbow? Colors...
or spirit tracing a path to the otherworlds?
What do you see in an old man's face? Death...
or a child coming to the surface waiting to be reborn?
Great Mystery envelops us all.
What do we know?
What will we know?
Let go.
Let go
Let go.
Let Peace.

Summary: Nebula stone calmly accepts the mystery in life.

(con't from previous page)

When we first touched these stones, which we came to name, Nebula Stone, we knew they were as enchanting as the valley itself.

~ from Ron and Karen Nurnberg

Needle Ore

"Wherever you go, I watch over your body and your dreams."

I combine with Hematite and Goertite to form a hard, sometimes striated ore. One of the places I am located is in the iron range of northern Minnesota.

The particular stones in our (Twintreess) possession were found in the Upper Peninsula of Michigan.

Physical Integration: Holds the seed of power in the body. Supports the solar plexus. Gives stamina to explore altered states.

Emotional Integration: Brings up old fears for loving integration. Gives motivation to unite body, mind and spirit. Calms the mind and heart for extended meditation.

Millennial Uses: Though we do not know this scientifically, we feel the presence and intent of this stone. We feel that Needle Ore has been used by shamans to explore other worlds and then to return safely to their bodies. Its essence speaks to us of abilities to shape our lives in dramatic ways. In these times of earth changes, we need its influence. We need to enter into the spirit of Needle Ore, to find new ways to survive and to thrive upon a transformed planet.

Electrical Body Alignment: Unites focus and commitment with physical and spiritual intent.

Affirmation of Support: *"I am power, myself, to change my life, right now."*

Stone Story:
I have appreciation, but I am not overly fond of words.
I understand acts and speak with rituals.
Why else would you listen to me?
Why else would you choose to travel to the unknown and back.
I just guide you to go into the vast territory of self.
Enter the deepest places. Be alive.
Witness it all. I will record the moments.
Nothing is lost, all has meaning, but first you must dare to travel
your heart with all your heart.
Go.
Sit with yourself.
Sit under a tree.
Stay till you know the stillness from the noise.
We will meet again and again.
Perhaps.

Summary: Needle Ore activates the cellular consciousness of the shamans within us.

Neon Blue Apatite

*"Life is a feast and I remind you to drink it in,
luxuriously, and Celebrate!"*

I am Calcium Flourine Chlorine Hydroxyl, and I come in many colors, from green, brown, red and yellow to violet, pink white and colorless and blue. I am in the middle of the hardness scale at 5, my luster is greasy and vitreous, and my specific gravity is 3.1 to 3.2. I have poor cleavage with a crystal structure that is hexagonal. My name derives from the Greek word *apate*, "deceit," for I am very often mistaken for a variety of other minerals such as Aquamarine, Flourine and Olivine.

I am the most common of the phosphate-bearing minerals, and I form in many igneous rocks and in certain metamorphic ones. I am found worldwide, although the majority of my gem quality deposits are in Burma. I can also be found in abundance in Sri Lanka, Brasil, Norway, Germany, Spain, and throughout North America.

Physical Integration: Helps to align the meridians of the body. Soothes sore or weakened areas. Provides help to work with chronic conditions.

Emotional Integration: Alleviates moodiness. Expands healthy detachment. Relishes in adventures.

Millennial Uses: In times of rapid advancement, we tend to take ourselves very seriously. Neon Blue Apatite laughs with us. It delights, like a child, in every accomplishment. It only takes one thing seriously: fun.

Perhaps the greatest adventure of the next millennium will be to enjoy the life we have.

Electrical Body Alignment: Reconnects us with childlike joy.

Affirmation of Support: *"I play in my world and I am quite enraptured with it."*

Stone Story:
Oh my, I don't laugh at anything,
I laugh at everything.
Try it on.
Take anything from your life (just yours- leave everyone else's lives to their devices)
and giggle at it.
Now, put yourself back in a moment of embarassment.
Smirk at yourself.
Practice does make perfect.
So does a great smile.

Summary: Neon Blue Apatite stands for an easy sense of humor.

(See *Stone Combination Section* for Neon Blue Apatite in "Fear into Love")

Obsidian

"I declare you to be a sacred space and only what you love will share your home."

I am the best known of the natural glasses, and I am found throughout the world where volcanic activity occurs. I am formed by the rapid cooling of volcanic lava which allows no time for crystals to form. I am, therefore, an amorphous solid or glass rather than an aggregate of minerals. I am the volcanic glass equivalent to the plutonic rock granite, and am in the same chemical composition as Granite, Pumice and Rhyolite. I am so Silica-rich that upon slow crystallization a very light colored granite would have formed.

My hardness is 6 to 7, my luster is brilliantly vitreous and my specific gravity is 2.3 to 2.6. I was originally used by Stone Age peoples for making implements, by American Indians for arrowheads, and by the Incas for making weapons, mirrors, masks, and earrings. I am to be found in the Mississippi Valley, Arizona, Colorado, Nevada, California, New Mexico, Mexico, Guatemala, and Ecuador.

Physical Integration: Improves balance. Integrates right and left halves of the body. Protects from injury.

Emotional Integration: Cultivates watchful awareness in all situations. Releases the need to fight. Accepts all parts of self.

Millennial Uses: In all times, there have been guardian spirits watching over us. Obsidian has been the ally of these guardians. To meet our future feeling protected, Obsidian guides us to find the unloved "shadow" parts of ourselves. By ending that conflict, we will seek and create peace in every other part of our world.

Electrical Body Alignment: Connects us to our shadow selves.

Personal Story

One of the first stones I started collecting was obsidian. It's not a gorgeous stone, but I love the way light travels through these dark, little rocks, and I like them well enough that I carry them with me continually. Pretty soon, I noticed that whenever something hard was happening to someone around me, I would give them my obsidian. It felt like I almost didn't have a choice. That obsidian would feel the troubles of some person and it would just want to go with them. It got so that every time I bought myself a new obsidian I would say, "Hello" and "Good-bye!" to it, simultaneously.

About this time, I got promoted at work. Now I was in

(con't on next page)

Affirmation of Support: *"I am all things and whatever I am, I love myself."*

Stone Story:
When you are born, you must cry to begin your life.
In every birth, there breathes some death.
For you, you left behind a calm connection to spirit.
It died so that you could be born and rediscover it all over,
again and again.
You cry with grief, but that grief takes you on the impossible journey.
Traveling without your full knowingness, anything can happen.
You find pain and fear and it is so dark on your path
that you must discover love to light it up.
Place that love under every unknown.
You will see everything as it really is—
another traveler asking for love.
At the end of the journey
you absorb the light completely.

On the impossible journey,
you are the possibilities.

Summary: Obsidian represents eternal protection and safety.

Opal

"Look at my magnificent, inner fire.
That is what you look like when you remember your spirit."

I am Quartz, silicon and oxygen, but containing water as well. Once thought to be without atomic structure, closer examination reveals microscopic spheres with a disordered crystal structure. I am the only gem mineral which is amorphous, without the regular internal atomic structure which makes up a crystal. I belong to no crystal system, have no cleavage, and cannot show any optical directional properties. My hardness is 6.5, my specific gravity is 2.1, my luster is vitreous to pearly, and my dazzling play of spectral color is due to stackings of groups of spheres of different diameters diffracting light from various angles.

(con't from previous page)

the corporate office in an affluent suburb and I didn't know what they would think of the stone collection that decorated my desk, but I decided I wouldn't worry about it. One day, a new bookkeeper started on the job. She seemed pleasant and very linear, very task-oriented. Then I heard that her father had died. I knew what I had to do. Even though Colleen and I didn't know each other very well, I was going to give her my obsidian and the only way that would make any sense was that I had to tell this very practical young woman that the reason why I was giving it to her was that I knew that it had a heart that could help with her grief. I did it. I sent

(con't on next page)

My name is from the Sanskrit *upala*, meaning "precious stone." I have myriad varieties, and names have been given to hundreds of color effects. My main classes are: Black Opal; White Opal; Fire Opal; and Water Opal, most all of which are translucent. I am found in Sandstone rocks as veins; my common variety is widespread and found worldwide but my precious forms are uncommon, found mostly in the western United States and Mexico. Other major sources are Australia and Brazil.

I am almost always in cabochon form, since I am never perfectly transparent and my desirable color effects are generated at or near the surface. I am one of the softer major gems, and as such very fragile and am particularly vulnerable to temperature changes. My popularity with humans has risen and fallen over the centuries. To the Romans, I was a symbol of power, yet at other times I have been deemed to be unlucky; during the Black Plague of the 14th century, the Venetians noticed that Opals became brilliant when the wearer caught the disease and dulled when the person died.

Physical Integration: Integrates and combines all the senses. Assists the physical and emotional growth processes. Nurtures our childlike and new qualities.

Emotional Integration: Transforms vulnerability into open-heartedness. Increases generosity. Brings forth inner beauty.

Millennial Uses: As we experience unimaginable events in the 21st century, we need to find the hidden gifts in everything. Opal emphasizes the beauty within all things and invites us to explore any depths to find it. This gem shows us that we must focus, constantly, on wonder in order to find the joy that we need. Mystery will join us along the way, so that we may look where we never expected to discover anything.

Then, when we find our prizes in life, Opal helps us to accept the treasures with an open, free heart. It assists us in enjoying beauty without being attached to it.

Electrical Body Alignment: Joins our reality with mystery and unknown beauty.

(con't from previous page)

it to her with a note, saying that I didn't expect her to feel the same way about stones as I did, but in my heart, I felt strongly that this one had special gifts to share with her at this time of her life, etc.

One day I got a note from Colleen. She thanked me for the stone and explained that a funny thing had happened with it. She didn't know quite what to do with the stone, but she put it in a pouch in her purse and kind of forgot about it. One night she was thinking about her father and all the times that he had told her bedtime stories. Even after she got older, he would still come in and wish her goodnight every night. About this time, Colleen felt very, very sad. She pulled

(con't on next page)

Affirmation of Support: *"I glow with every experience, now and always."*

Stone Story:
Welcome to my home.
Every moment is my home before I even know it.
I understand nothing, so that I can greet the beauty.
I have not met you before.
Welcome to your loveliness.
Thank you for entering my space.
Thank you for giving me your questions,
your amazement,
your learning,
your doubt,
your freedom.
You expand my life.
You give me words so that I can talk to you,
so that I can know something unique
and feel something, sometimes familiar.
You share my home,
even before you know me
and that is the delight that I will carry
through these ages.

Personal Story

Thomas and I went to a wholesale rock show a few years back. It was an early Sunday morning and the doors to the show had yet to open and people were piling up at the entrance, just waiting to jump in at the first opportunity. So we went to a back corner to stay out of the crowd and just relaxed. This Australian man [Rodney] came up and started talking to us about opals. We weren't feeling terribly communicative, so we just nodded and moved further into the corner.

No matter how far away we got, Rodney kept following us and talking to us about how difficult it was to mine opals because they were very hard to find. After about the fourth time he followed us around the room, Thomas offered, "We might be able to help you. We listen to stones and we could see what they had to say..." No matter what Thomas said, Rodney talked right over him, as if there was no possibility of a solution.

The next thing we knew, the doors to the show had opened and everybody

---

(con't from previous page)

the obsidian (still in the pouch) out of her purse and asked it for any help it could offer. Then she put it back into her purse and went to bed.

The next day she couldn't find the stone anywhere. She looked everywhere and started feeling pretty desperate- like everything important was leaving her life. Then Colleen found it sitting on her nightstand, without the pouch. She told me that she knew she hadn't placed it there—that she could still see herself putting it back into her purse (still in its pouch) the night before. When she found it on the nightstand she said she felt like it was a message from her father, letting her know that his spirit was still with her.

~from Marilyn

144

had filed in, including Rodney (who had a booth inside). So we went back to our quiet corner and decided to listen to the spirit guardian of opal. It explained to us that if it isn't time for some stones to surface, they won't. And if certain people aren't meant to find opals, they won't- even if everybody all around them is finding them. There's a synchronicity of intent and timing that creates everything including stone harvesting.

Wanting to be respectful, we asked the opal guardian if there was any advice it could give Rodney about locating these gems. The guardian told us various types of locales where opals could be find and it also gave us a few messages to pass onto Rodney, that would open him up to the possibility of the guardian's advice. First of all, it told us that he wakes up every night at precisely 2:33 a.m. and he would know this because he always checks his clock as soon as he opens his eyes. Secondly, one of the reasons why he wakes up every night is because he is having some health difficulties (which it described in more detail later). The guardian spirit advised us to tell Rodney the entire message, no matter how odd it might seem.

We found Rodney at his booth and told him where the opal guardian had suggested he mine for opals. He smiled and said that he had never found them in those areas. Then Thomas told him that the spirit of the opal had other information for him, but we would tell him only if we had his permission. He consented and Thomas said that Rodney got up every night at precisely 2:33 a.m. At this point, he interrupted Thomas saying, "Yeah, yeah, I've just been kind of hyper lately." Finally, Thomas told him the rest of the message about his health. Again, Rodney agreed, and quickly explained it away. Finally, we just shook hands and left.

We were truly amazed by it all. Here was a man that we had never met before and via the opal guardian had told him things that we couldn't possibly have known and he hadn't even batted an eye. Rodney affirmed what we had said and then talked right past it. It was at that moment that we learned something very valuable from the opal spirit. We realized from that experience that it is very easy for us, as humans, to talk even before we have listened to something, therefore effectively stopping ourselves from learning what is truly possible in any situation. Thanks to Opal and to Rodney for reminding us how important it is to listen.

~from Twintreess

Summary: Opal shares mystery and an open heart with all.

Payson Diamonds

"I sparkle in delight!"

Found in the Mogollon Rim of the White Mountains of Payson, Arizona, I am a unique double terminated variety of Quartz, similar to Herkimer Diamonds.

Physical Integration: Increases mobility, and ease and enjoyment of movement. Stimulates energy. Increases the ability to bounce back from injury or disease.

Emotional Integration: Increases childlike joy. Expands gestures. Uses body movement to facilitate happiness and learning.

Millennial Uses: As we go forth in time, we must deal with aging. Payson Diamonds remind us, continually, that youthful vigor is our natural state, no matter what our chronological age. These double-terminated beauties insist on happiness as lifelong exploration.

Electrical Body Alignment: Links us to all forms of joy.

Affirmation of Support: *"I find joy in every single moment!"*

Stone Story:
Greetings! I am glad that you can visit me.
I am the spirit of Payson Diamonds.
All I will ask you to do is everything you already love.
When you do what you love, life embraces you.
What more happiness could there be than that?

Summary: Payson Diamonds remind us that we can empower our-selves through joy.

Peridot

*"Have you ever noticed
that whatever you avoid
has a tendency to reach out and bite you on the nose?"*

I am the gemstone of Olivine, a series consisting of two end members Forsterite and Fayalite, which occur as separate species; when chemically combined, they form the Magnesium Iron Silicate known as Olivine. I am a yellowish-green rock-forming mineral, a transparent gem with a distinctive oily luster, a hardness of 6.5 to 7 and a specific gravity of 2.2 to 2.3. My structure is orthorhombic, with crystals being rare. My cleavage is indistinct at two directions at 90 degrees.

I am erroneously known as Evening Emerald because I appear to lose my yellowish hue at night and closely resemble Emerald. I can be found in Italy, Egypt, Norway, and Austria, although I am common in volcanic rocks worldwide.

Physical Integration: Expels excess mucus. Strengthens the ability to throw off common constant illnesses. Facilitates body awareness.

Emotional Integration: Encourages sense of humor. Reviews all habits (hopefully, compassionately). Adapts sense of humor to darker situations.

Millennial Uses: In every disaster, somebody laughs. In this next millennium, it is possible that we will experience multiple disasters. In that emergency, we have the resources of Peridot. Peridot always asks us to go where we don't want to go, to eat our least favorite foods, to wear our least favorite colors. It brings up what we don't want, and if we are lucky, we will hear its laughter. The gift is we can adjust our mind to see joy when we least expect it.

Electrical Body Alignment: Links us to unacknowledged parts of being.

Personal Story

Dragon of Peridot with Kyanite Eyes Herstory:

Long ago, the voice of Kyanite spoke deep grief to me, sorrow long hidden and nearly forgotten. And so began my work with buried childhood memories.

Undigested experi-ences had manifested for years as sad and soggy bowels. During my vision-work for my bowels, an image of glowing green-gold stones laid out in a spiral gave itself to me.

Years later, Twin-treess tell me Peridot has spoken my name. I open the stones-rest-ing-box, find the Periodot waiting. Holding the green stone in the palm of my hand, I see a gold fire glowing within it.

(con't on next page)

Affirmation of Support: *"Deep inside myself, I find more and more capacity for joy."*

Stone Story:

Sit down and close your eyes.

Let's go through your life (and you don't even have to die). Find the most embarassing moment you can remember. Go through it step by step. Replay it a few times if you have to in order to include all of the details. Once you have it, cement it perfectly in your mind.

Stop.

Now, drink in my light beam color and imagine this: Go through the same scene, but imagine that in your hand you have an incredibly precious gemstone. When you hold it, you know you are utterly loved. Nothing you can do will deter this stone's admiration of you. Now, relive your embarrassing moment to the nth degree while simultaneously reveling in the support of your new friend, me. That's my support for you.

Whenever you feel incredibly bad about yourself, take me with you, relive those moments of life, and you will have new ways to smile, maybe even laugh.

Summary: Peridot takes us to the heart of denial with happiness.

Petrified Wood

*"All that I am is magic
and I have set that in stone for all who have the heart to see it."*

Over the course of millions of Earth years we are the transformers of wood into mineral. The process is silicification, where Silica dissolved in groundwater replaces the organic material in fallen tree trunks and branches. With the addition of temperature and pressure over a long period of time, the organic matter within the wood is gradually converted into Chert, a hard and dense rock formed of amorphous Silica, or Quartz. Color variations are created by the presence of inorganic compounds such as Manganese, Copper, or Iron Oxides.

(con't from previous page)

Recognition shocks through me.

The Dragon:

Green-gold dragon scales glisten and ripple with power. Her strong dawn-blue eyes do not waver or blink, challenge me to look for the hidden courage, face what has been lost. Glowing green fire, her breath purifies my doubts, enlivens my bowels and blood.

~ from Linda Melita Beaty

Physical Integration: Aligns the feet and balances the rhythm of walking. Softens the shoulders to open the lungs. Preserves balance and good health.

Emotional Integration: Feels the metaphysical communications and gifts in breath. Imparts a sense of stability and belonging. Sensitizes all thoughts and emotions to the earth and its changes.

Millennial Uses: Many ages before now, magical beings have walked the earth. They have known how to navigate ships and destinies by the stars. They have understood special meanings (for their tribes) within everyday events of nature– like the screech of an owl or a change in the winds. There have been many ways to record the wisdom of these sages. Mostly, they are not printed, often they are viewed in trees and in stones, things that last many, many lifetimes. This is the time on the planet when we may be destined to read the signs of nature, the wisdom of the stones. Ancient healers, seers and shamans placed their traditions in stones like Petrified Wood. Each picture and line in petrified wood gives us a language to understand our world and our deepest connections to it. To listen to Petrified Wood's Stone Story is one way to find the magic that has been discovered before us.

Electrical Body Alignment: Unites the nerves and meridians of the body to ancient healing ways.

Affirmation of Support: *"I firmly root myself in the earth to receive the magic of this lifetime."*

Stone Story:
Once upon a forever, I listened to the cries of humans. I laid beside them while they died. I watched as they struggled to eat, witnessed the pain of birthing their young. And I chose. I chose with all my body, all my shape and all my hues, to lay my blessing upon their struggles and so I have done this. In the timeless forever of my growth, I have blessed you all. I do not weep at your deaths. I smile because I listen with such firmness that I break through your struggles. I witness new life coming from your pain. I bless the awareness you spark from your challenges. I bless all of this. The whole story of your forever life lies within my heart. Touch me again and I will sing the old songs with the new and you will remember the magic you have brought upon yourselves.

Summary: Petrified Wood holds the old myths that guide the new realities.

Phenacite

"No matter what you see, you are surrounded, gloriously, by infinite guides and angels."

From the Greek word *phenakos*, for "deceiver," from being mistaken for Quartz, I am Beryllium Silicate, a colorless, white, yellow, pink to brown vitreous mineral formed in hypothermal veins, pegmatites, and Mica schist. Hexagonal in structure, I form in well-developed flat rhombohedral to long prismatic crystals, striated lengthwise, often forming penetration twins. I am among the harder minerals at 7.5 to 8, and my cleavage is poor in one direction. I can be found in the state of Minas Gerais, Brazil, and in the Russian Urals, Switzerland, Austria, Norway, and the United States.

Physical Integration: Embraces clear thinking actions. Focuses on and tones weaknesses in the body. Sharpens instincts. Deepens breathing.

Emotional Integration: Gives us guidance. Assists us in feeling loved and supported, as we are. Aligns our heart with all of life. Promotes full emotional healing and integration.

Millennial Uses: The next great unexplored territory lies within us; it is the inexplicable unlimitedness and spirit that comprises all of us. Phenacite directs us, on that level, to all the guides, angels and guardians that we need (sometimes without our conscious awareness). It enhances our communication with these unseen levels of life and offers us pathways to live multi-dimensionally.

Even though we may not understand it, if we listen to the gifts of Phenacite, we open ourselves up to the perfect possibilities for which we may be designed.

Electrical Body Alignment: Focuses our instantaneous body/mind/heart integration on exploring our spirit.

(con't on next page)

Affirmation of Support: *"I am surrounded by the blessings of my guides and angels, constantly."*

Stone Story:

Deep within the womb of feelings,
you know me.
You know me because you know yourself.
You know that your spirit reaches beyond
your words
your acts
even your dreams.
It stalks the open light of unimaginability.
Yes, yes, yes.
There I live.
I breathe for you there.

You need nothing,
for you surround yourself with the sweetness of every loving spirit.
You remember this. You know this. You are unlimitedness.

Summary: Phenacite urges us to act upon our unknown, boundless perfection.

(See *Stone Combination Section* for Phenacite in "Aurora's Dream," guilt into Perfection," "Immortality," Gabriel's Dawn," "Listening," "Spiral of Life" and "Timeless Treasure")

Pietersite

"If you want protection, I will stand forth as your shield.
If you need protection, the whole universe will stand at your side."

I am a rare and beautiful variety of Tiger Eye, and I am a resplendent blue to black in color, with an iridescent and undulating luster. I form as inclusions in Jasper/Chalcedony, with asbestos additions. My name derives from my discoverer, Sid Pieters, who first found me in Namibia. The original mine was my only known source for decades until I was again found in China in 1993, where I am known as Eagles Eyes for my blue chatoyancy.

(con't from previous page)

embraces and nour-ishes.

Clear Madagascan Phenacite was like beaming into a warp elevator. A strong, clear golden silver vibration took me to *Galactic Center* on one of my first journeys "out". I noticed an indigo tendril of light moving up and out of the *Galaxy* emanating from the golden silver light. I followed it into *Universe Center,* and then on to the *Realm of the Ancients* where I lost track of following the indigo thread because of wanting to explore this realm further. Perhaps it can act as an elevator to get one there.

I use this crystal often to strengthen and secure the multidimensional access asked for.

from Geoff Stoddart

Physical Integration: Stretches the feet and the toes. Expands the postures for strength and balance. Focuses eyesight. Guards the eyes from injury.

Emotional Integration: Promotes healthy time away from people. Explores inner truth deeply and easily.

Millennial Uses: In many cultures, people find themselves busier and busier, with less satisfaction. Pietersite encourages quiet time to regenerate and to explore who we are, as we and the earth change ever more rapidly. This stone continually brings us back to ourselves, so we can rediscover our truth and honor our own lives and space. Then we have the tools to honor others and the new world we will co-create together.

Electrical Body Alignment: Links us to the deepest parts of ourselves.

Affirmation of Support: *"I turn inward to renew my life force."*

Stone Story:
Oh, so very long ago, the peoples of the earth crawled into caves
and lingered in the mysteries there.
They sat perfectly still in the lush woods
and breathed in nameless perfection.
They climbed the mountains and at the peak,
chanted their sweetest inspirations.
They laid by the sparkling sea
and danced in the eternal waves of life.

Oh, now, you have given away the caves, the woods, the mountains
and the seas.

Friends, travel inside the absolute hush of your soul.
Insist upon knowing the caves,
the woods, the mountains, the seas.
They pulse in your blood.
They move with your bones.
They see past your eyes.
The peace of the earth's sacred spaces never leaves you,
even when you leave them.

Summary: Pietersite creates a safe space within to explore ourselves completely.

Pink Smithsonite

"I look delicate but I am as strong as your most wished for dreams."

I am an ore of Zinc, occasionally used as a gemstone, and named after James Smithson, the British chemist and meteorologist, and founder / benefactor of the Smithsonian Institution. I am also called Calamene, Galmei, and Zinc Spar, and I appear in a wide range of colors including colorless, white, yellow, pink, green, blue, purple, and brown.

My hexagonal structure rarely creates crystals; when formed they are normally rounded and indistinct. My hardness is 4 to 4.5, my specific gravity is 4.3 to 4.5, I have a vitreous, adamantine, pearly luster, and my cleavage is perfect, in three directions, forming a rhombohedron. Renowned localities are Greece, Germany, Austria, South West Africa, as well as Pennsylvania, Arkansas, Utah, New Mexico, Colorado, and California.

Physical Integration: Promotes eye muscle strength. Fosters an open heart, physical balance and integration between all the bodily systems.

Emotional Integration: Breeds gentleness. Increases trust as a way of life.

Millennial Uses: Some of the destruction that we have created around us (and within us) comes from seeing differences in others and feeling threatened by that. Pink Smithsonite carries a quiet strength through tenderness and it offers this gift to all of us on the earth. When we feel that gift, we embrace diversity and use all the resources available to us to co-create change, peacefully. By embracing diversity, we immediately co-create the evolution that makes our survival possible. By embracing diversity, we trust enough to enjoy, truly, the life we are given.

Electrical Body Alignment: Connects our heart to our reason and to all dreams we wish to fulfill.

Affirmation of Support: *"I approach life with gentle kindness and it grants all my respectful needs and desires."*

Stone Story:

Really, I have so little to say.
Words are only one way to know me.
After you meet me here, I ask you to put down this book.
Find a truly safe, pleasing spot and just be yourself.
Watch everything and witness the wonder of it all.
Ahh~

Then you will be doing everything that I do
and being everything that I give you, freely, completely freely.
Now you are part of my heart.

Summary: Pink Smithsonite completely encourages us to live in trust.

Pyrite

"Squeeze my hand when you know what you want in life.
Then open your hand and there it is."

Known to most of you as Fools' Gold (or Iron Pyrite), we are the most widespread and abundant of the sulfide minerals and we occur in rocks of many types and in all types of hydrothermal veins. We appear in the familiar cube form, less commonly in octahedrons, with crystals sometimes twinned and also in nodules and massive forms. We have the same formula as Marcasite, but our crystal structure is isometric rather than orthohombic. Our color is pale yellow to brass-yellow, often tarnished with a brown film of Iron Oxide. We are sometimes iridescent, our luster is metallic, and we have no cleavage.

Our name derives from the Greek, *pyr*, "fire," as we are easily mistaken for native Gold. In actuality, we can be associated with Gold, and can be an important Gold ore, and we are found in abundance around the world. Our commercial importance is as a source of Sulfur, used in the manufacture of sulfuric acid; Iron may also be produced as a by-product.

(con't on next page)

Physical Integration: Soothes pain. Eases dryness of skin. Regulates physical rhythms.

Emotional Integration: Amplifies curiosity. Integrates happily with the inner child. Increases pleasure and pride in activities. Enhances the sense of timelessness.

Millennial Uses: Pyrite guides us into the 21st century by showing us timelessness.When we no longer measure ourselves only by our technological advances, then we are free to jump ecstatically into life and just be. Be what? We can be ourselves and play our perfect part in nature's perfect rhythms of life.

Electrical Body Alignment: Connects us with the joy of exploration.

Affirmation of Support: *"I create my life as a continual adventure."*

Stone Story:
What would you do if you could do anything at all?
You can do anything at all.
I am with you as you explore everything.

Whatever you do, relish it.
Enter it like a new mystery
that will unravel your sensibilities
and set you free.
Deep within every activity, there lies a perfect heart.
If you go far enough into what you do, you will find it,
waiting for you, beating for you,
loving you for risking yourself to know it.
Always search for that heart in everything,
no matter how big or small the pastime...
No matter how long or how little of your time it asks...
the reward doesn't spring from size or time,
it comes to you in sheer ecstasy—
the ecstasy of being through doing.

Summary: Pyrite involves us in life so much that we are enlivened.

(See *Stone Combination Section* for Pyrite in "Buddha," "Focused Grounding," "Hope's Call" and "Turkll Delight")

(con't from previous page)

her that I was retired but intended to get a part-time job also. Anyhow, what she wrote to Joe was: Mr. Joseph Kraker - Fran is retired but doesn't have enough money. Please help her." (I almost fell off the chair!). *Joe and I both laughed, and then he handed me $1,000...* (I refused but he insisted. *I guess we need to be quite careful about how we draw things to ourselves...).*

~ *from Fran Abbott*

Totem Stories from the Tibetan Tektites

Everything in the universe blossoms.

It lays out its full glory to suns and stars and moons

at just the exact moment.

If you come to see the show too soon, you will get seeds of what will be.

If you come too late, you will receive dried petals of what was.

We personally love every part of the growing process....

and it reminds us of you.

You are a flowering group of beings who have traveled far enough

 into your destiny

that you are beyond seed and the initial sprouts of green.

You're just now leaning your bright colors into the sun.

You stand so delicate and so bold.

We have watched you grow.

This is the glorious season for you.

You are about to make your earth a garden

and everyone knows it but you.

Realgar

*"I come from the fires and the passion of the earth's belly
to cool in your hand for steady intentional use.
Together we will manifest reality."*

I am Arsenic Sulfide, a real softy, at 1.5 to 2 on Moh's scale. I form short prismatic crystals, often twinned, in the monoclinic system, and I'm a resplendent deep red to orange in color, becoming yellow when exposed to light. I'm easily confused with Cinnabar, and I form in low temperature veins with Cinnabar, Stibnite, and Orpiment in epithermal veins. Used as an ore of Arsenic, my name is from the Arabic *rahj alghar*, "powder of the mine." My cleavage is good, in one direction lengthwise, my specific gravity is 3.5 to 3.6, and my luster is adamantine to dull. You can find me in Italy, Turkey, Corsica, China, Germany, Nevada, Colorado, and California. My large crystals are quite rare and in great demand by collectors.

Physical Integration: Awakens life force. Stimulates energy. Encourages vitality.

Emotional Integration: Invites integration of mystical experiences with physical, emotional reality. Focuses on strengths to eliminate dysfunction. Utilizes every challenge for growth.

Millennial Uses: During our technological advances, we have created many toxins that we do not know how to handle or to eliminate properly. Realgar, a totem of constantly revitalizing life force, invites us to look within every poison for a cure. Perhaps in the exploration for answers, we will learn new ways of life that are not hazardous, in the first place.

Electrical Body Alignment: Links us to constant regeneration of body, mind and emotions.

Affirmation of Support: *"I grow so much from every challenge, that I am stronger and stronger."*

Stone Story:
Please gather around the storyteller's fire.
Warm your heart and I will fill your wisdom
with my millenniums of being.
I do not know how long you will be here,
nor do I know how long you will walk the earth.
Certainly you are bright.
Your light beams at me and through me
to sparkle the walls of this dreamer's cave.
Ah, life gives you talents that I only guess at.
Marvel.
Still, you didn't come here to list your accolades;
I leave that to the gentler ones.

You stare at me for truth.
I give it to you.
The earth has many poisons.
We are not designed to touch everything
or to use everything for our own fuel.
Some things are best left alone for another day's learning.
You will not choose when.
The earth will birth that season.
Until then, drink in the bounty of our home.
Focus on what has been gifted to you
and leave the rest to its own path.

Summary: Realgar guides us to use every experience for regeneration, growth and wisdom.

(See *Stone Combination Section* for Realgar in "Pregnancy")

Red Garnet

"I am rushing vitality, grounded in reality."

We are the collective name for a closely related group of Aluminum and Calcium Silicate minerals with similar structure but variable chemical composition and physical properties. Widespread and all used as gemstones, our family is comprised of Almandine (deep red to brown), Pyrope (deep red to reddish-black), Spessartine (brownish-red to hyacinth-red), Grossular (colorless, white, yellow, pink, green, brown), Andradite (wine red, greenish, yellow, brown, black) and Uvarorite (emerald-green). From the Latin pomum *granatum*, "pomegranate," noting the resemblance in color of the Almandine-Pyrope group.

Our colors cover the gamet, with the exception of blue, as do our origins: although our formations occur mostly as a result of metamorphism, fine crystals can be found in schist, serpentines, gneisses and granite pegmatites Our isometric structure generally forms as dodecahedrons and trapezohedrons; our hardness is 6.5 to 7.5; our luster is vitreous; our specific gravity is 3.56 to 4.32, our cleavage is none, parting occasionally distinct in six directions. Garnets are found worldwide; localities are plentiful throughout North America, and can also be found in abundance in South Africa, Germany, Australia, Sri Lanka and South America.

Physical Integration: An increase and balancing of energy. A surging of enthusiasm, powerful reflexes.

Emotional Integration: Strengthens the ability to find happiness. Expands curiosity. Gives emotions spontaneous honest expressions. Revitalizes everything.

Millennial Uses: To prosper in the 21st century, we must work hard. We must clean up our environment and we have to create a practical, healing lifestyle. The heart of Red Garnet encourages/regenerates us and enhances the stamina needed for every task. The miracle is that it offers this with joy.

Electrical Body Alignment: Links our life force with practical determination.

Affirmation of Support: *"I have all the strength and more to accomplish everything that I must do."*

Stone Story:

Thank you so much for listening to me.
If you want to find my message, reach deep into your body.
What activity would give you the biggest upsurge right now—
tennis?
a walk in the woods?
wrestling with a puppy?
running with the kids?
or even reading by the lake...
Go there now.
Inhale the luxury of being able to do something, anything, you like.
Fill yourself to the brim with it.
I'll be leaping to your side.
Then you'll hear all of me.

Summary: Red Garnet activates the life force in us.

(See *Stone Combination Section* for Red Garnet in "Boredom")

Rhodochrosite

"Reach for me, I am already with you. Whatever you need, the answer
is love and I already give it to you with all my heart."

My rose-red colored crystals (from the Greek *rhodon*, "rose," and
chros, "color") are due to the presence of Manganese, and often I also
contain Calcium, Iron, and Zinc. I am also known as Manganese
Spar. I am a secondary mineral associated with Lead and Copper
veins (rich in Manganese), often occurring with Chalcopyrite, Galena, Sphalerite, Bornite, and Tetrahedrite. My structure is hexagonal, my hardness is 3.5 to 4, my specific gravity is 3.4 to 3.6, I am
vitreous to pearly in luster, and my cleavage is perfect in three directions, forming a rhombohedron. I am a relatively rare mineral, but
can be found in Romania, UK, Germany, Peru and North America,
including Newfoundland.

Physical Integration: Opens the heart and helps to draw to us whatever circumstances we require for healing. Helps clear out old infections/wounds/scars.

Emotional Integration: Brings up growth situations to be embraced fully and lovingly. Brings out adventuresome qualities. Balances and revitalizes the yin and yang (male/female traits).

Millennial Uses: In the last millennium, the patriarchal hierarchy, largely, has dominated the world. This is changing; women are exerting more influence in all ways. We are learning to balance male/female polarities in order to survive and prosper as a species.

Rhodochrosite emphasizes the feminine, while still appreciating the masculine. It integrates us with the world by embracing the inner male and female in all of us. As we heal ourselves, we will face many wondrous and uncomfortable moments. The heart of Rhodochrosite compassionately supports us in our time of need and discovery.

Electrical Body Alignment: Rhodochrosite connects our heart with the seasons of change and the seasons of the earth.

Affirmation of Support: *"I give and receive all change with unconditional love."*

Stone Story:
I long to be next to you.
I love the human that you are on the outside and
the stone,
the plant,
the star,
you are in the inside,
and more~
always more and more...
You are adventure in constantly swirling shapes and form.
See yourself in my spirals.
I delight in you.
As you transform,
I see life, bright as the sun,
growing on the earth.

I am ready.
I stand here for the journey.

We go together
because there are worlds unknown.

Summary: Rhodochrosite embraces change with joy and vitality.

(See *Stone Combination Section* for Rhodochrosite in "Hope's Call" and "Unimaginability")

Rhodonite

"In our hearts, love doesn't wear definitions, it just is."

My usual color is rose (from the Greek *rhodon*) though I may also appear brownish-red or pink, and occasionally yellowish or greenish. I am Manganese Silicate, often with some Calcium, and I form in metamorphic rocks and in hydrothermic replacement deposits. With a hardness of 5.5. to 6, good cleavage in two directions at nearly right angles, and a specific gravity of 3.5 to 3.7, I am of triclinic structure, with crystals usually forming in fine-grained masses. I can be found in Sweden, England, South Africa, and Australia, but exceptionally fine crystals have been found only at the Zinc deposits in Sussex, New Jersey.

Physical Integration: Focuses vision. Tones digestion. Adjusts appetite according to our needs. Aligns our energy with any time of day or season.

Emotional Integration: Softens our needs. Expands our conversations/expressions beyond petty control issues. Teaches us to prize ourselves and our leisure time.

Millennial Uses: The earth is changing and evolving. It seems to possess a perfect wisdom for every age that it endures. When we connect with it and its stones, we learn how to grow beyond our personal pictures of the future; we open to others' needs while still respecting our own.

Rhodonite asks us to look beyond good and bad, or any polarized thinking. We can connect with a bigger scheme of life any time we choose to love.

Electrical Body Alignment: Peacefully integrates all emotions to the changes and the ways of the earth.

Affirmation of Support: *"I belong upon the earth. I love all life and all experiences."*

Stone Story:
Circle round and round.
Come back to yourself.
Wear every color.
Life isn't just black and white.
Explore.
Mingle.
Sing.

You are the love that you seek.
Come back to yourself
where life and love embrace
in an ever growing circle.

Summary: Rhodonite brings us beyond polarized thinking, into love.

(See *Stone Combination Section* for Rhodonite in "Guilt")

Rose Quartz

"Everywhere we are, we create beauty, grace and poetry."

I am the pink to rose-red to pale variety of Silicon Dioxide, the most diverse natural substance known. While I am not highly valued as a faceted gem, due to my pale and cloudy appearance, I am nonetheless prized in my finest (darkest and clearest) forms. I develop mostly in pegmatic veins. When heated to 575 degrees (C) I will lose my color entirely. Atypical of the other members of my formation group - Amethyst, Citrine, Smoky Quartz, and Rock Crystal, I am generally not found as single crystals; it is still a mystery just why this is, and it makes these uncommon crystals extremely valuable to collectors. I am found in California, Maine, Montana, South Dakota, Brazil, India, Sri Lanka, China and Madagascar.

Physical Integration: Promotes healthy self-esteem and appearance. Smoothes the skin. Youthens the body and the heart.

Emotional Integration: Gives us eagerness to greet each day. Appreciates all forms of beauty. Regenerates, revitalizes.

Millennial Uses: Rose Quartz lives upon the earth as a timeless being. Whenever we need inspiration, it gently and constantly shows us the beauty in all things. It endows us with appreciation. As we appreciate things, we change the world and ourselves. We open our hearts; we feast on life. This renews and refreshes us. It invites the wonder of our inner child into every part of our life.

Electrical Body Alignment: Sensitizes our heart to other people and to all life.

Affirmation of Support: *"I give and receive kindness, grace and love to and from all beings."*

Stone Story:
I am so pleased to meet you here.
The way of words touches my heart.
You are so blessed to be able to give voice to your love.
When you leave this letter to you,
tell everyone you know how and why you love them.
If they are too shy to receive so much,
then smile at them.
Laugh with them
and point out the constant happiness
following them everywhere.

Thank you so much for listening to me.
I feel such honor to meet with you so directly.
Share my joy. Share my love. Share my bliss.
Fill your heart and then let it overflow through all your days.

Summary: Rose Quartz brings out the beauty of love, innate in all things.

(See *Stone Combination Section* for Rose Quartz in "Perfect Weight" and "Violence into Compassion")

Rubellite

*"I come from deep within the earth's heart.
She opens her vein, gives her love completely,
and I am a remembrance of that utter giving."*

I am in the Tourmaline family, a large group of multicolored, moderately abundant minerals, and I am the pink and red version of this mineral. I am a complex silicate of Boron and Aluminum, whose composition varies widely because of substitutions. I am a hard mineral, at 7 to 7.5, and I form in igneous and metamorphic rocks in veins.

My structure is hexagonal, usually with short to long prismatic crystals with a rounded triangular cross section, striated lengthwise. I have no cleavage, my specific gravity is 3 to 3.3, and my luster is vitreous. I am created in schist in pegmatic rocks with cavities or in alluvial deposits. Gemstone quality specimens can be found in the Urals and Madagascar; other localities include Zimbabwe, Kenya, Mozambique, Tanzania, Myanmar, Sri Lanka, Brazil, and the United States.

Physical Integration: Makes available surges of new energy from unexpected sources. Grounding and calming of the adrenals. Opens heart and chest.

Emotional Integration: Gives us the security to express, truly, all our love. Develops romance as a healthy lifestyle. Inspires our creativity.

Millennial Uses: As we grow busier, we sometimes allow less time for following our heart. Rubellite teaches us to listen to our feelings, to accept them and then to act upon them swiftly, even instinctually. This simple lesson will lead us to new ways of community never dreamed of before. The more we follow our hearts, the more we empower ourselves to create our own joy. As we overflow with happiness, we share that with everyone else. That happiness births an incredible future under any circumstances.

Electrical Body Alignment: Connects our heart and our life force.

Affirmation of Support: *"I give and receive love in an ever expanding circle of abundance."*

Stone Story:
Yes, I love you.
I love you as I love myself and all the family around me.
We live in such a kind world.
Even the pain here respects us.
It gives just as much as we need
to break us out of our shells of ignorance.
It strips away our superficial layers
(the ones we're pretending are important)
and leaves us naked in the sun.

I watch it happen endlessly.
It's a constant season of learning and compassion, here. I wanted to come into this life and into this book, to show my devotion. Whatever I can do for you, I offer it. In the meantime, I declare my truest admiration for you. Humans move along so quickly and so beautifully. I will announce that to you in as many ways and times as you allow. We'll learn to recount the ways of love together.

I love you enough to tell you: Change. Transform yourself now, so that you don't have to hide your splendor in fear. Come out! Brave the sun. I won't do it for you. I'll watch you and I'll applaud your every step. You are magnificent. Be more magnificent each day.

Summary: Rubellite shows us how to demonstrate our love.

(See *Stone Combination Section* for Rubellite in "Hope's Call," "Impatience" and "Relationship")

Ruby

"I jump into life for beauty, for joy, and for you."

I am Corundum, Aluminum Oxide. In my purest form, I am colorless, although I am found in almost every conceivable color. All are called Sapphire unless the color is red, in which case I am Ruby. My name comes from *kuruntam*, a Tamil word derived from the Sanskrit *kuruvinda,* "ruby," and I am the rarest and most valuable of all gem-stones. I am second only to Diamond in hardness, at 9, and I am pleochroic, that is, my color varies when viewed from different directions. In the world of gems my identity is debatable; it is indeed a fine and subjective line between Ruby and Pink Sapphire and it is endlessly debated.

I form in several distinct environments, in a hexagonal structure; my specific gravity is 3.9 to 4.1, and my cleavage is none, often with conspicuous parting in three directions. I was the first gem-quality synthetic, produced at the turn of the 20th century by Auguste Verneuil, the French chemist who invented the flame-fusion process that is still used to manufacture Rubies, Sapphires, and Spinels. Although laboratory versions of myself are vastly superior in size and perfection to those found in nature, and virtually indistinguishable as well, no synthetic gem can rival the natural form in value even though it may surpass it in quality. My finest natural versions come from Myanmar, with other fine examples located in Thailand, Sri Lanka, Cambodia, Malawi, Pakistan, Australia, Brazil, Afghanistan, and the United States.

Physical Integration: Aligns the lower spine. Completely activates life force energy. Increases beauty.

Emotional Integration: Warms the heart to strangers and to new situations. Dramatically increases self-esteem. Links confidence with self-expression.

Millennial Uses: It is a fearful and awe-inspiring time to be alive on this planet as everything changes. We will be required to *know* that we have the talents to thrive in a new world. Ruby embraces us. It embraces our life energy and it rejoices in the beautiful manners that we use to express ourselves. To feel Ruby is to feel the confidence to meet every challenge and to exceed it.

Electrical Body Alignment: Connects our survival instincts to the appreciation of all life– the red to the rose.

Affirmation of Support: *"I am a beautiful heart expression of life!"*

Stone Story:
I've been revered through the ages. I am a gem. I am the captured rays of a fiery sunset. If you can hear my words right now, it means that you are all of these things. If you can hear my words right now it means that you can take all that you are and make more. Go out and make magic.

Summary: Ruby enlivens us beyond health into beauty.

(See *Stone Combination Section* for Ruby in "Crystal Pleidean Pyramid Alignment," "Death," "Infinite Intimacy-male" and "Transformation, Prosperity and the Goddess")

Rutilated Quartz

"I dance with the electricity of life!"

I am Rutile, a tetragonal, usually reddish-brown mineral, Titanium Dioxide; I often appear in striated form in Quartz, giving it a hair-like, magically divided appearance. From the Latin word *rutilus for* "reddish," I crystallize in a tetragonal system forming short, prismatic crystals and frequent geniculate (knee-shaped) twins. I form in plutonic and metamorphic rocks, often as golden, hairlike crystals (referred to as Venus' hair stone). My luster is adamantine or submetallic, my hardness is 6 to 6.5, my specific gravity is 4.2 to 4.3, and my cleavage is distinct, sometimes good, in two directions, and poor in a third. Found in Georgia, Arkansas, California, Norway, Brazil, Australia, New South Wales, and Switzerland, I am the principal ore of Titanium, used as a gemstone and in ceramic glazes.

Physical Integration: Increases nervous system communication. Warms, soothes, relaxes the body. Speeds up movement.

Emotional Integration: Aligns the mind and the body. Encourages spontaneity.

Millennial Uses: There is so much for us to explore in the area of energy in 2000's. Tesla, the prolific inventor and scientist, spoke of free energy—the ability to tap into an invisible current that surrounds all of us and the earth, to fuel anything freely. To do this we must open up to previously unimaginable potentials.

Rutilated Quartz represents immediate energy of all kinds. It carries the message that we innately have the capacity to communicate within our body/mind/spirit union, and with all other lifeforms (seen and unseen) spontaneously. When we become aware of how to use this ability, we will create miracles.

Electrical Body Alignment: Connects us with other energy fields.

Affirmation of Support: *"I spontaneously connect with the flow of life!"*

Stone Story:
Stop everything else.
Be comfortable.
Sit with quiet readiness.
Let all your thoughts fly on through you
as if they belonged to someone else.
Breathe.
Inhale and exhale in a perfect circle.
Keep extending the circle to welcome all life, in love and respect.
Breathe like a prayer.
Breathe that you are complete
by just breathing the nectar of life—air.
Air carries the wishes, dreams and love of all beings.
Receive it so freely that the air forms words.
Be grateful for the language of consciousness
that needs nothing to carry it but intent.
Give thanks that all of life speaks to you.
It knows your name,
amongst all the others
and it honors you utterly.
Give thanks that I share with you these words.
They will open your heart,
they will smile upon your spirit,
they will embrace your fears and send them to freedom,
they will bless your dreams,
they will connect you to the angels who protect your every step...

My words sing my essence.
They flash from me to you to all, to me to you to allllllllllll

instant energy.
They are formed in love so they carry all the magnificence of what can
be created with love.
When you read this,
you absorb the spark of spirit
and it touches you in a forever instant.

If you choose,
you are never the same,
you ever change.
You become more of the magic
that gives you dreams to dream
and dreams to make true.
Receive my magic,
open your life to love.

Summary: Rutilated Quartz guides instant communication between all lifeforms.

(See *Stone Combination Section* for Rutilated Quartz in "Perfect Weight," "Regeneration" and " Spirit storytelling")

Sapphire

"Inside each being rests a glorious spark.
When touched, it rises to the surface and shimmers beauty across the
land."

Like Ruby, I am Corundum, my variety of colors—blue, yellow, pink, violet, gray, and dark green. I may also be clear or contain bundles of tubelike inclusions, giving "star" or "catseye" effects in cut or polished stones. My most valued form is the extremely rare orange variety called Padparadschah. The brighter my color the more desirable a specimen I will be as a gemstone. My color is created by the presence of a small amount of Iron. As with Ruby, I, too, am made synthetically, both as I appear naturally and also with rutile inclusions, creating synthetic star stones.

Physical Integration: Increases metabolic efficiency. Tones fat/muscle ratio. Softens the skin.

Emotional Integration: Clarifies emotions. Focuses on self actualization. Honors independence.

Millennial Uses: In this high-tech age, we are influenced by many advertisements and stimuli. They teach us to conform to certain values, that may or may not suit our personal lives. Sapphires very simply provide clarity, a respite from information overload. Also they invite us to explore our own truths and capabilities. As we do this, more of the glossy marketing disappears (no need for it) and we all project and appreciate our innate, unique beauty.

Electrical Body Alignment: Links us to clear truth and beauty.

Affirmation of Support: *"I know that I am beautiful and perfect."*

Stone Story:
Lie by my side.
Grow into the earth.

Feel your roots travel in the dark.
Everywhere you touch you feel love.

Ease your mind.
Sing a spontaneous song for the celebration of today.

Whatever we dream comes to us.
We attract love, because we have given it to ourselves.

Summary: Sapphire appreciates beauty and clarity.

(See *Stone Combination Section* for Sapphire in "Earth Light Initiation")

Scapulite

"I remind you that the loving guidance of spirit gently whispers in your heart, every moment. Listen—it is with you, now."

I am part of a continuous compositional series from Sodium-rich at one end (Marialite) to Calcium-rich (Meionite). Found in a wide range of colors from colorless to brown and named from the Greek *scapos,* "shaf," or "stickstone," referring to the prismatic crystals I form in within the isometric structure. My hardness is average at 5 to 6, which is fairly soft for a gemstone. My luster varies from vitreous to resinous, my specific gravity is 2.5 to 2.8, and my cleavage is distinct, in two directions. I am principally a product of metamorphism, and I am found associated with Almandine, Andalusite, Andradite, and Actinolite. Gem quality Scapulite was first found in Myanmar; I am also to be found in Brazil, Madagascar, Kenya, and in North America.

Physical Integration: Increases the ease of connection between bone, cartilage and muscle. Adapts the body easily to all types of movements. Lets go of stress in the head and upper neck.

Emotional Integration: Continually increases intuition and balances that increase with every other part of the body, emotions and spirit. Integrates struggles/resistance, so that awareness grows quickly, easily. Brings previously unimaginable possibilities into life.

Millennial Uses: In a world of full speed and technology, Scapulite reintroduces us to quiet calm within our hearts by gently pulling us out of a mind dominance into a fuller balance within ourselves and all things.

Scapulite bolsters our abilities to connect with and to speak with (in our own unique voice) all other life forms, including: animals, plants, stones and the earth, itself. It reminds us that this communication innately belongs to all of us and like all other gifts, it expands with practice.

Electrical Body Alignment: Links us cellularly with all other lifeforms upon the earth.

Affirmation of Support: *"I am part of everything on the earth and that is how I fully honor myself."*

Stone Story:
Hello, hello. Please come and lay next to me.
Bring your inner peace and we will talk.
I am one of your own guides, during your time upon the earth.
I am this, as we have chosen it together. So, relax, we know each other exceedingly well. I honor all that you are and I completely respect all your secrets, as you wish.

This time of your life touches me, so full of promise and dreams, it is. Glorious, magnificent! Perfect, yes, perfect. The restless in you knows that this is a moment of profound change. All the separateness from other life that you have cultivated, is leaving. A way of living that you have practiced strongly leaves you now and fear fills the void.
Trust.
Smile.

Fear is an old friend who tells you you are alive (and want to stay that way very much, indeed). Do not let any more time fall between your old friends. Look at fear.
Smile.
Trust.

*Tell it, "Welcome old friend. We have been much together and I
thank you for all your fine services. I have learned so well from your
teaching, that I no longer need you to lead me. Blessings upon your
next journey!"*

*Then say to yourself, "I trust me to lead my life in love, completely."
Now you are ready for any change of time, or change of heart, or
change of season and for a complete change of life.
Everything is a change of life;
that's what life is—constant, honoring change.
To be unlimited, life transforms itself every single moment,
to be more
and to be more
and to be more.
Yes, it is unlimited.
You recognize that.
You are unlimited,
as am I,
as are all things made of life,
which means made in love.
Trust.
Smile.*

*Life and love intermesh so intricately that they breathe the same.
Do you need a reminder, you adventuresome, growing human?
Then talk to the rest of the life that grows upon the earth.
Talk to all the stones, the flowers and the trees.
They have never forgotten your name.
You will feel this
and you will feel supported,
around any fear.
This is the time when you will speak to all things again
and never forget
the kindness of all life.*

Summary: Scapulite reconnects us to our innate ability to communicate with all life.

(See *Stone Combination Section* for Scapulite in "Crystal Pleiadean Pyramid Alignment")

Scepter Stones

"I take the power of my growth and stretch beyond all dreams, now."

Another form of Silicon Dioxide, I am named for my visually striking long and elegant appearance. I am a unique formation of two crystals together, one as shaft and the other as head.

Physical Integration: Increases heat in the body. Protects the head from injury. Increases libido.

Emotional Integration: Fills the heart with passion and confidence. Inspires us to action. Increases leadership capabilities.

Millennial Uses: The patriarchal urge to dominate all circumstances around us has created great destruction. Scepter Stones share the wisdom of harnessing the powerful energy behind domination and creating new uses for it. By embracing the power in ourselves (instead of fearing it), we can birth new cities with unbelievable possibilities.

Electrical Body Alignment: Links our responsibilities and powers with others, harmoniously.

Affirmation of Support: *"I accept my power to change myself and the world peacefully."*

Stone Story:
Take my hand.
Feel the power within it grasp you back.
My friend, what you touch in me
is the reflection of your strength.

Join me.
Let's build mountains and forests for homes.
Let's blaze across the sky and share our warmth for all beings.

Summary: Scepter Stones expresses the male energy in all of us, compassionately and joyfully.

Selenite

*"Look at me and see how simple, how clear life is.
Then breathe, relax;
your life is that same clarity no matter what you think."*

I am Gypsum, Hydras Calcium Sulfate, my names both derive from Greek: *gypsos*, for gypsum or plaster; and *celenites*, for "moonstone," so called because my luster was believed to wax and wane with the moon. My colors range from white to green, I am extremely soft—a 1.5 to 2 on the hardness scale, and my specific gravity is 2.3 to 2.4. My luster can be pearly to glistening or dull and earthy. I am a very common Sulfate mineral, an evaporative sedimentary rock, formed when seas or salty lakes evaporate. My monoclinic structure creates untwinned single rhombic crystals, and I can be found throughout North America, and in Algeria, and Germany.

Physical Integration: Helps clear sinus/eye/ear/nose infections. Assists visual acuity. Supports flexibility and balance.

Emotional Integration: Focuses on simply being. Enhances meditation. Eases breath. Extends simple feelings and acts into art.

Millennial Uses: Selenite is a clear, fragile stone. When it dissolves into the ground, it enriches the earth.

Selenite gives simplicity to everything, which contributes to every cycle of the planet and to all its beings.

Electrical Body Alignment: Links our physical/emotional/mental selves to the healing and enjoyment of light and sound.

Affirmation of Support: *"I breathe, therefore I am."*

Stone Story:
Breathe.
Life crystallizes into a single sound.
Breathe.
Life shows itself in a single flash.
Breathe.
Life is you.

Personal Story

I don't have any experiences with stones that seem worthy of mention in your book that I can think of, except the experience I had with that white stone in the middle of the labyrinth at Festival this year. What was it called...selenite? That stone had such an amazing amount of light coming from it...as I sat next to it and meditated I had a very clear and strong sense of receiving light energy from it that filled my being and surrounded my whole energy field. I have never experienced such a powerful light force coming from a stone. It is light incarnated into matter!

~ from Lisa Lundeen

Breathe.
Smile.

Summary: Selenite represents simpleness and clarity.

(See *Stone Combination Section* for Selenite in "Aurora's Dream," "Phenacite," "Judgement into Trust" and "Listening")

Seraphinite

"You won't see them.
But when you need them, your guardians are already there."

I am called Seraphinite, a gem variety of Clinichlore, a mineral of the chlorite group. I am found in the Lake Bakal region of Siberia. My gemstones are primarily a deep green color, with feathery inclusions of silver colored iridescent formations making intricate internal patterns.

Physical Integration: Heals old scar tissue. Reduces susceptibility to disease. Eases allergies.

Emotional Integration: Softens the heart. Increases intuition. Demonstrates the courage to act upon beliefs.

Millennial Uses: Like the future, some things remain a mystery. Though we can't explain love or life, it exists and we accept it. Seraphinite opens us to the possibilities of unseen guardian spirits who work and walk with us every day. There may not be proof of it; however, this stone suggests that there may not be proof against it, either.

Electrical Body Alignment: Links us to unknown spirit guardians.

Affirmation of Support: *"I believe that I am well protected and loved."*

Stone Story:
Is it hard to believe in a stone?
Is it hard for you to accept that you are watched over by beings that you can't

hold next to you?

What else is hard for you to believe...

Is it hard for you to believe in nuclear war?
Is it hard for you to accept that the earth is polluted?

So many things seem impossible.
Find the ones that make your heart sing
and you will find all the help you need
to make them possible.

Summary: Seraphinite is the totem for invisible guardians.

Smoky Quartz

"Love springs from us unconditionally,
to all life and back again to ourselves."

I am a popular variety of quartz, notable for my unusual brown to black (to sometimes smoky gray) color; it is believed that this is related to the amount of exposure to radiation I have undergone. My natural Smoky Quartz often occurs in granitic rocks which have a small but persistent amount of radioactivity. I am one of the few brown to black minerals that are cut into gemstones. My crystals form within the trigonal system, my hardness is 7, and I possess no cleavage. My most notable sources are Brazil, Colorado, and the Swiss Alps.

Physical Integration: Soothes sore spots. Stretches the limbs. Releases old sources of disease of all types.

Emotional Integration: Calms survival instincts. Imparts more appreciation for the body/mind/emotions and all of their processes, especially the challenging ones. Invites unknown, unexpected adventures into life.

Millennial Uses: When leaving behind one millennium for a new one, the opportunity arises to release old unsuccessful traditions for fantastic new ways of life.

Quartz has the properties of holding our affirmations. Then it focuses energy upon them to help us with creating our realities. Smoky Quartz visits our uncomfortable places, our denials. It focuses calm acceptance upon them, so that we will love ourselves enough to transmute our fragilities into empowerment. Hold this stone while you affirm the qualities you desire, and it will assist you in releasing any limits that keep you from your new strength.

Electrical Body Alignment: Combines positive and negative qualities into loving acceptance.

Affirmation of Support: *"As I happily accept myself and the world, it showers me with love."*

Stone Story:
Of course I live in the darkness.
So do you.
Mystery, power and regeneration lie next to us there
like the mighty bear in the dreamtime cave.

I dream with the bear on moon-softened nights.
All his stories unfold in my heart and
I feel pride.

I rest, proud that the bear honors me with his magical visions.
I speak, proud that we all can grow so far through the darkness
that we sail across the sky and land,
immortal again.

Summary: Smoky Quartz transmutes (with us) all qualities into strengths.

(See *Stone Combination Section* for Smoky Quartz in "Confusion into Focus," "Earth Light Initiation," "Environmental Toxins" and "Judgement into Trust")

Snowflake Obsidian

*"I come from the earth to tell you that every being is exactly perfect.
Every life story is unique and must be heard."*

I am one of the Silica-rich volcanic glasses formed as lava quickly
cools. My internal inclusions—crystallites—produce a snowflake appearance within my otherwise shiny black color.

Physical Integration: Grounds the body. Alerts the senses to potential. Helps to release recurring nightmares and stabilizes sleep patterns.

Emotional Integration: Helps us to create a comfortable, safe home.
Honors ourselves and others. Reconnects us to our earliest, happiest
memories.

Millennial Uses: To grow as a species, we must consider embracing
diversity (the heart of evolution).

Snowflake Obsidian gifts us with the awareness of all things, allowing us the sense to celebrate what honors us, while releasing the rest.

Traditionally, it has been used for guardianship and protection.
Protecting ourselves in the old way, through domination and competition, has failed. Snowflake Obsidian teaches guardianship through
respect for all life, first.

Electrical Body Alignment: Connects our survival instincts to our
intuition and guides.

Affirmation of Support: *"I am well protected by love."*

Stone Story:
*In the dark of the nights
and the light of the day,
we dance.
You know me and I know you.
In embracing the utter richness of that,
we find all life
and it finds us
safe,*

Personal Story

There was a period of time when I would go to bed, calm, but wake up knowing that I had tossed and turned during the night with unnamed fears. After this went on for awhile, I got a big piece of raw snowflake obsidian. Even unpolished, it glimmered with an innate, unmistakable ease.

I would take it to bed with me and hold it as I fell asleep. After a bit, I realized that I relaxed in the night much more. Now I took to holding it and admiring it for awhile before I fell asleep. One night while I was doing this, I meditated on its soothing qualities. At that point, we still owned a TV and one of the very few things we occasionally

(con't on next page)

*perfect
and at peace.*

Love knows us all so that we can never be hurt.

Summary: Snowflake Obsidian teaches reverence for all life, beginning with our own.

(See *Stone Combination Section* for Snowflake Obsidian in "Mary's Wonder" and "Pain into Fulfillment")

(con't from previous page)

watched was the news. As I stared at that stone, I really heard the news coming to me from the room below. I sat upright and I realized that I really didn't need to hear about murder and mayhem just as my consciousness was opening up to the dreamtime.

That was the last time I listened to the news just before bedtime (actually the TV shortly left after that, too). And I have felt more peaceful ever since.

~from Marilyn

Sodalite

"When I speak, I see the truth. Then, more and more light fills the world."

I am known for being one of the components of the rock Lapis Lazuli, though I am darker blue in color and rarely contain the brassy specks of Pyrite that are found in Lapis. Found in Canada during a Royal visit, I was called Princess Blue, and I'm also known as Canadian Blue Stone or just Bluestone. My colors range from blue to colorless, I develop in nepheline syenite pegmatites, and my isometric structure rarely produces crystals. My hardness is 5.5 to 6, my cleavage is poor, in six directions, my luster is vitreous and my specific gravity is 2.2 to 2.3. I can be found in Ontario, British Columbia, Norway, Namibia, Brazil, and the United States. My name alludes to my Sodium content.

Physical Integration: Tones the lymph glands. Eases sore throats. Integrates thoughts, words and actions.

Emotional Integration: Revels in our capacity to change for the better. Encourages truth under great duress. Lessens the need for judgment.

Millennial Uses: As we go from one millennium to the next, we will discover great triumphs and what appears to be great tragedies. To move from tragedy to triumph requires one step. When translated to humans as a species, that means we require a single person or a group

of people to stand firm in the truth. In other words, we need heroes/
heroines to show us what is possible. Sodalite is a stone guardian for
heroes/heroines (or wannabes). It reminds us of what we know to be
true in that awful, wonderful moment when we are put to the test.
Sodalite shares unswerving clarity when fear seems out of control.

Electrical Body Alignment: Connects our truth, our language and
our uniqueness to inspiration.

Affirmation of Support: *"I am an incredible hero/heroine in the story
of my life."*

Stone Story:
*Hello, hello. Everybody likes a good story with an incredibly happy
ending. Especially if it is not expected.
I have a story for you.*

*Once upon a crystal planet there grew all sorts of incredible life, the
diversity of which cannot begin to be named here. Just imagine every
color, every smell, every song possible and you will have an almost close
approximation of this place. The crystal planet loved all of the
creatures that lived with it in its travels across the universe. It loved
so much that it joined with the universe and birthed yet another
child to live upon it. This child became a race of beings which was
comprised of all of the elements of the crystal planet. That was
obvious. What was more hidden (to the child, anyway) was that it
was made up of starshine and mystery from the universe.
As the child grew up, it played with all of its possibilities. You might
say that when it was in balance with the crystal planet, it looked like
all the other seasons—perfect rhythym. When it was out of balance,
it was like an explosion of destruction, eliminating everything in its
path. One day, the crystal planet and the universe spoke to the child.
They said, "If you continue like this, you will kill everything around
you, and you will not be able to bear the pain of this. So we will give
you a test. It will be up to you to use every strength you have ever
known in order to pass it. If you do pass, there will be a new race of
unimaginable beings to play with you on the crystal planet. If you do
not pass, you will kill yourself off and have to take the test again and
again."*

Personal Story

One of the very first stones that I ever collected was Sodalite. I bought a deep blue piece of it and carried it with me often. Then I decided to splurge on a simple Sodalite necklace that a local artist had made. I wore it until the stone fell out of its glued setting. When the artist (Lori) realized what had happened, she offered to fix it for me. I never told her, but I figured that if the Sodalite fell out of the necklace, maybe it should stay out. In my dreams, I imagined that Lori (a prolific jewelry maker) instead designed me a single earring—very long and simple with a crystal that would enhance my awareness naturally

(con't on next page)

183

That's the end of the story. It's a great story because anything can happen. It's your story and your ending and I am your friend on the crystal planet. I am here to remind you that you have everything that you need, and more, to make the story come out the way you want it to.

(con't from previous page)

because it just blended with me.

Lori came by to deliver my necklace. She placed the still unglued sodalite in my palm and said, "I have another piece of jewelry for you." Then she gave me an earring exactly as I had imagined it. I was thrilled. To this day, I know that that sodalite brought me my earring.

~ from Marilyn

Personal Story

In April 1997 I spoke at the Minneapolis Whole Life Expo. I also had a booth for networking and counseling. While counseling someone on their mission I felt an urgent need to go purchase a large sodalite from Africa at an adjoining booth.

It seemed inappropriate but I gave the client a writing task, excused myself and ran over and got the $400 sodalite. Upon my return, she asked "Where did that come from?" I answered, "Africa." She let me know she had just returned from a trip from Africa. She laid her hand on the rock through the rest of the session. Africa had come to the Midwest to help us with our intimate journey in that moment. We were grateful.

~ from Sage

Summary: Sodalite brings out our ability to act in our integrity when we most need it.

(See *Stone Combination Section* for Sodalite in "Aurora's Dream" and " Disappointment into Responsibility")

Stibnite

"Let's take all our gifts and create a new garden of life that will grow more than we could ever need."

I am the chief and most common ore of Antimony. Often infused with small amounts of Iron, Copper, or Lead, I occur as lead-gray striated prismatic crystals of the orthorhombic system. I develop in low temperature in hydrothermal veins and in hot springs, often in association with Realgar, Orpiment, and Calcite in epithermal veins. My luster is metallic, I am soft at a 2, my specific gravity is at 4.6, and my cleavage is perfect, in one direction lengthwise.

My name comes from the Greek *stibi*, used for Antimony. I was used by the ancients as a cosmetic preparation; my finest specimens are now found on the island of Shikoku, Japan and from the famous mines of Felsobanya, Romania. Many quality sites abound in North America, as well.

Physical Integration: Helps to remove toxins. Clears out old blockages and congestion. Cools off excess heat.

Emotional Integration: Organizes our thoughts and feelings for clear choices. Increases our ability to handle many tasks without undue stress. Lets go of old, deep dysfunction.

Millennial Uses: We have so many resources available to us to create our future now. Technology is one of them.Stibnite encourages us to focus ourselves upon every task with a simple minded clarity. If we are destroying ourselves through certain tendencies, then we may need to embrace them, so that they finally disappear peacefully.

Stibnite invites us to learn from our shadow sides and use them to our every advantage.

Electrical Body Alignment: Integrates our weaknesses with our strengths.

Affirmation of Support: *"I take all that I am into life to create peace and fulfillment."*

Stone Story:
Yes.
Single focus.
Compassionate clarity.
Power.
Unconditional love.
Unlimited possibilities.
Reflections.
Freedom.
Detachment.
Birth.

Whatever is needed
as it is needed.
Acceptance.

Summary: Stibnite focuses on strengths.

Sugilite

"Bear witness to your intuition and let it discover glorious new worlds."

I am among the new gem materials first found in Japan but considered a nondescript curiosity, and later discovered in 1975 in a Manganese mine in South Africa. Deep lavender to deep reddish-violet in color, I am remarkably similar to Charoite. In my purest form I am quite translucent and to date I am still quite rare. The world is awaiting further discovery of my existence.

Physical Integration: Evens the flow of cerebral spinal fluid. Helps release pressure on the brain. Protects the spine.

Emotional Integration: Increases the ability to commit to long term relationships and projects. Brings forth more lucid dreams. Integrates psychic abilities with everyday life.

Millennial Uses: To enter our future, we must find inspiration. Practical knowledge cannot tell us everything that we need to feel and be supported. Sugilite fortifies our "sixth sense," an innate knowingness that defies linear description.

This stone leads us into our intuition, as a practice of life. It requires us to believe in ourselves and in our resources, without standard proof.

Electrical Body Alignment: Integrates our intuition with our actions.

Affirmation of Support: *"I follow my intuition and it rewards me with unexpected fulfillment."*

Stone Story:

If you do not stand for yourself, then what will you stand up for, or trust?

Without explanation, without money, without verification, your intuition shines inside of you.

Do you know it?
Do you speak to it?

When you join with it, it moves from the unknown into a working practice of miracles.

Stand up for that.
Align yourself with the fullness of life that has yet to be known.

Summary: Sugilite represents the courage to affirm what we believe through our intuition.

(See *Stone Combination Section* for Sugilite in "Turkll Delight")

Sunstone

"We rise from the belly of the earth to be with you.
Together we shimmer in the splendor of the sun upon our beings."

I am a variety of the plagioclase Feldspar group, a series of mixtures of Sodium and Calcium Aluminum Silicates exhibiting red or golden reflections from minute imbedded crystals of Mica or Iron Oxide. I am a gem variety of Labradorite with two distinctive characteristics: I am found in warm salmon to rich red crystals, and I have a golden sheen, due to microscopic platelets of bright Copper aligned in parallel planes dictated by my crystal structure. I've been known for many years, but only recently found in substantial quantities in Oregon.

Physical Integration: Acceleration of metabolism/creativity/fertility. Focuses on female/male learnings and union. Stretches the entire body.

Emotional Integration: Increases emotional memories and how to access them when needed. Blesses the totality of our experiences without dwelling too long on any of them. Facilitates clearer, easier decision-making.

Millennial Uses: Sometimes when we assess our accomplishments and tribulations in this last century/millennium, it seems easy to focus on what has gone wrong. That, of course, leads us to learn from our "mistakes," so we can create more harmoniously in the next millennium.

Yet, if we don't remember and celebrate our achievements, then we develop hopelessness and apathy.

Sunstone prods us into affirming the magnificence in us. It insists we act from that right now. It joyfully demands that we evolve through and beyond our fears, now.

Electrical Body Alignment: Connects our passion with our growth and overall essence.

Affirmation of Support: *"I choose to evolve into my full passion and love of life."*

Stone Story:
Thank you for meeting with me.
I give you these acts to savor~
Dance in the moon, during a full blaze sunset.
Tiptoe in the wet, morning grass of spring.
Stare into a friend's eyes and recount their every charm.
Say your truth to change no one, but yourself!
Act upon your fine inspirations.
Love yourself enough to fulfill your dreams.
Create with the earth and its creatures a very proud existence
that will welcome in every age with song.

Summary: Sunstone insists that we act upon our choices to evolve now.

(See *Stone Combination Section* for Sunstone in "Crystal Pleiadean Pyramid Alignment," "Pregnancy" and "Should into Acceptance")

Tanzanite

"Remember when you first realized that you were all alone in the world?
As you hold me, remember that feeling and smile
because you now know the perfection
of solitude without pain."

We are Zoisite, and our best gem-quality crystals, transparent blue are known as Tanzanite. Our Calcium Aluminum Silicate formula often includes Iron or Manganese, and our orthorhombic structure occurs as long prismatic crystals deeply striated along their length. We are an uncommon mineral and our formation is restricted to metamorphic rocks. We can be gray, yellowish brown, greenish, pink or blue in color (as Zoisite), most of which change color to blue when heated.

Our luster is vitreous, but pearly on cleavage, which is good, in one direction lengthwise. Our hardness is 6 to 6.5, and our specific gravity is 2.2 to 2.4. Tanzanite has been found only at localities in Tanzania, East Africa.

Physical Integration: Expands vision. Integrates etheric desires and physical realities. Clears the throat and lungs of congestion. Strengthens the voice.

Emotional Integration: Inspires optimism. Releases depression. Nurtures us so we can explore the deepest places of being to find the sources of our joy and sorrow.

Millennial Uses: To find ourselves thriving in the next millennium, we must discover how to live well. Tanzanite supports us in our most intense moments, so we can (and do) touch the core of self that creates our health and wellbeing. We explore truths that bring us to our own power, our own responsibility. It shows us, through our hidden depths, that we create most of our lives according to our own wishes.

Electrical Body Alignment: Links us to eternal truth.

Affirmation of Support: *"I discover truth so that I can freely choose what empowers and honors me."*

Stone Story:
Come with me.
Don't put aside your breath.
Travel with it.
Circle your knowingness,
your expectations,
your beliefs,
your-anything-at-all
and breathe it into freedom.
Now you soar into unknowingness
and whatever is still a "you"
swirls through what you have known.

Place your fingers upon the stars.
Make their dreams come true.
In a single intent, you travel anywhere.
You go because the creator within must,
it must.
It must know more of all.
It must leap into the cracks of the universe
and thrust them open bravely,
then it shouts with responsibility,
"I dawned a new world.
The sun forever shines.
Whoever visits me here is not my child,
not my own.
Enter freely and leave with more."

Truth stands beside you,
firm and infinite.
It shakes its head at time and smiles.
Breathe.
Breathe and sweet, simple air
presents you with timelessness.

You fueled the journey there.

Explode into all directions.
Space empties itself of measurements.
Free, free, free surrounds you,
emanates from your moment-to-moment resolve.
Do you love this journey?
Do you love coming with me?

I have never left.
I only witness your flight.

Summary: Tanzanite expresses individual and eternal truth.

(See *Stone Combination Section* for Tanzanite in "Infinite Intimacy-female" and "Crystal Pleiadean Pyramid Alignment")

Thomsonite

"Life grows through awareness.
See through my eyes—you are ever a wonder!"

Named after the Danish chemist, Julius Thomsen (1826-1909), I am a monoclinic hydrated fluoride of Aluminum, Calcium, and Sodium, usually occurring as colorless crystals. I can be found on the north shore of Lake Superior in Minnesota.

Physical Integration: Celebrates vision. Protects eyes from injury. Facilitates memory.

Emotional Integration: Integrates emotions and perceptions. Helps us to teach and learn from experience. Values wisdom in new and old traditions.

Millennial Uses: As we blaze ahead with ever growing technology and information, it feels like we leave behind what generations of people have learned already.

Thomsonite innately connects with us with all the wisdom and awareness that could possibly be needed in any moment and in any situation. It increases our natural intuition and our abilities to envision, physically and metaphysically.

Electrical Body Alignment: Connects our eyes with vision and awareness of every sort.

Affirmation of Support: *"I calmly witness all levels of life and learn from them, easily."*

Stone Story:
Come into my heart.
It lives full of the awareness
that I have recorded
through all my times.
Take it.
Take freely what you need.
This is the moment of complete transformation.
This is the moment when life births life without limits.

I have held these wisdoms
as your sacred tools.
Let them cut away the pain you know longer desire to keep.
Shape the future of your dreams with the love of what you learned
and give it to now,
now.

Summary: Thomsonite expands all of our perceptions so that we can learn from everything.

Tibetan Tektite

"I present you with myself,
an ally for all your experiences and all your being."

We are among the Tektites (from the Greek *tektos* "molten"), natural glasses of unknown interstellar origin. Transparent green, greenish-brown or brown in color, we have a bobbly or craggy surface. We have been faceted as gemstones and we look very similar to the bottle-green mineral Peridot. We contain round or torpedo-shaped bubbles

Personal Story

These stones are gathered from high grasslands on the Northern Plateau of Tibet. This region was home for centuries to nomadic Buddhist Herdsmen who tended goats, sheep and yaks, and acted as traders with farmers, villages and other nomadic groups encountered in their constant travels. The nomads collected Tektites, along with salt, (while tending herds) on trading trips, and when moving from camp to camp. They used the stones as offerings for the use of the monks, and to pay taxes imposed by their governor, the Panchen Lama, Tibet's second most powerful Lama. The monks used the tektites to enhance meditation states.

(con't on next page)

and characteristic swirls like treckle. Our system is amorphous, that is, we do not have a crystalline structure; as a result we do not belong to any of the 7 crystal symmetry systems. Our hardness is 5, and our specific gravity is 2.34 to 2.39.

We Tektites, are, of course, from Tibet. *(Please see our Personal Story).*

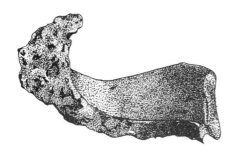

Physical Integration: Extends the fullness of breath. Increases awareness of all the senses.

Emotional Integration: Appreciates the richness of all experiences. Unites full consciousness with daily reality.

Millennial Uses: According to some traditions, every new undertaking has an ally in spirit. This ally guides how the project will be born.

For "Stones Alive!" that guidance comes from the Tibetan Tektites. Under all the words, they speak constantly, unifying the intent and tone of this book. They join us (the readers and the writers) with the spirits of the stone beings, so we can know their wisdom—to participate in life, wholly and blissfully (our most natural state).

Why do the Tibetan Tektites perform that service here? Simple. They came to us miraculously at exactly the right moment and synchronicity is the language we use to connect with all life in balance. Since their arrival in our lives, we have learned that for years, they have been prized by Tibetan monks because they believed these meteorite stones enhance meditation. That is the quality they gift to all of us right now. They bring us with them to this present moment so utterly that life is our meditation. That is the future and the past integrated into now.

Electrical Body Alignment: Links all the brain wave states harmoniously.

(con't from previous page)

In 1959, the Chinese assumed complete control of Tibet, rendering the Panchen Lama powerless, and causing the monks to flee or die. The nomads continued to gather Tektites even though the monks were gone, the monasteries closed or destroyed, and their religion supressed. During the Cultural Revolution, the nomads were forced to live in communes with no private ownership of their herds. A short-lived revolt resulted in death or imprisonment for many.

Communes were abolished 1981, and there was a move toward market-oriented rural economy, with the family as the basic unit of production. The government has softened its policy on

(con't on next page)

Affirmation of Support: *"I am all that I need to live infinitely and freely."*

Stone Story:

I am so honored to feel your heart extend to me.
I cry at the immensity of this.

You are family to me.
That is why I am called to be your guide,
and you are called to do the same for me,
in a unique way that you have to discover yet.
Blessings of every kind upon us!

I have landed upon this earth to express my great love and awe for all
of its beings and their courage to feel and to change and then to grow
through that
and beyond that.
You are all my clan,
all who hear me and know me now.

I announce this as a planetary season of trial and thanksgiving.
Trial—because limits must leave and you have loved them so much
that you made them the focus of your life force for a precious moment.
Thanksgiving—because you dance in endless life.
Now, you will know this with your
still body,
free mind,
open heart
wise soul.

What else could this season of change bring to you?
It brings you back to yourself
again and again
so constantly that it is simultaneous with all things within you and
glows in all dimensions.
Free, you are.
Free, you ever remain.
Play with struggles but they will not chain you.
That is not possible.

Upon this Now, you asked to expand this message.

(con't from previous page)

religion, although since the death of the Panchen Lama in 1988, the re-establishment of monasteries has been very slow.

Throughout the years, the nomads have continued to collect Tektites. They occasionally trade or sell small quantities to obtain supplies. The nomads hope that someday soon the monasteries will be re-established in their remote region and the tektites will once again be a cherished offering to the monks.

~from Robert Poley, Jr.

194

You are here.
You are now.
You are life.
Even in this body you wear, that truth lives on unrestrained.
Come here, come to this moment.
Bring your consciousness (which is always you)
and heaven lives upon earth, now, always.

Summary: Tibetan Tektites enhance our ability to be present now.

Tiger eye

"I revel in all my visions and the world dances around me."

I am the variety of Quartz that is lustrous yellow to brown with parallel fibers. My hardness is 7, my luster is vitreous to greasy, my specific gravity is 2.65, and I generally have no cleavage. My hexagonal structure creates prismatic crystals striated cross wise and frequently terminated by double rhombohedrons (like hexagonal pyramids).

I am the semiprecious recognizable variety of Quartz with distinctive lustrous yellow to brown parallel fibers arranged within the stone in a pattern that resembles an eye. Strongly chatoyant, that is, having an iridescent, undulating luster, I am not rare but very popular nevertheless. I am formed through an interesting geological process: my original vein has silky blue crystals of Crocidolite, the mineral bearing asbestos, which are then dissolved by solutions which deposit Quartz and Iron Oxides in their place. The structure of these tiny asbestos fibers is exactly reproduced by the Quartz, giving rise to the light reflection that creates the "eye." I am found in abundance in Austria and southwest Africa.

Physical Integration: Eases the neck. Soothes the throat. Sharpens the senses.

Emotional Integration: Releases fears through open conversation. Shares feelings of protection. Embraces life as a constant learning.

Personal Story

On a busy afternoon my wife, Colene, and I were driving through an Iowa city intersection when a car ran a red light and crossed in front of us. It happened so quickly there wasn't any time to react at all. Our quiet drive suddenly exploded with the sound of twisting metal and broken glass.

Our car nearly severed the other car in half. We swerved sideways from the impact, flipped once in the air and continued to roll over the top of another stationary vehicle. Our demolished car came to rest on its driver's side with the roof crushed and all four doors jammed shut.

For a few brief moments we were alone with the horror of

(con't on next page)

Millennial Uses: How will we go into the next millennium? In one way, none of us knows for sure. We need inspired visionaries to point out how to do what we couldn't have even imagined before.

Tiger-eye promotes vision of every kind. It inspires us to witness the world and see it for what it is. Then it inspires us further to see what it could be.

Electrical Body Alignment: Tiger eye connects us with non-judgment about what we see.

Affirmation of Support: *"I love the world as it is and it loves me."*

Stone Story:
Deep in the earth,
we know stillness and growth,
silence and song,
deep shadow and sparkling light,
fire and water,
passion and calm.

We belong there.
We know who we are without words.
We trust.

Wherever we walk or fly upon the earth,
she pulses deeply, intently below us.
She weaves her song of silent treasures through us,
through every step.
It makes us who we are.
We belong, above or below,
inside or outside...
Safe on our endless journey to be.

Summary: Tiger eye witnesses the earth as a miracle.

Tiger Ore

"Be with me and you will be your conscious, passionate life force."

As Tiger Ore, I am a sedimentary deposit of approximately 2.2 bil-

(con't from previous page)

what had happened. Suddenly, the car was surrounded by people who were concerned for our safety. Some held the vehicle stationary while others tore at the shattered windshield or tried to pull the doors open. They were sure we were hurt.

Still strapped in our seatbelts, we were surrounded by broken glass and twisted metal. The roof was crushed to the level of the dashboard between us. People do strange things immediately after the trauma of an accident. I was sifting through the broken glass picking up personal items which had spilled from Colene's purse below me. The very first thing I saw and picked up was a polished tiger eye Colene carried which

(con't on next page)

lion years old that consists of alternating layers of silver gray Hematite and red Jasper, Chert or even Tiger Eye Quartz.

Physical Integration: Tones the circulatory and immune system. Integrates our bodies and minds in empowering ways. Increases manual dexterity.

Emotional Integration: Encourages us to face our fears. Invites us to move in new ways for flexibility of body and feelings. Allows us to feel capable in any situation.

Millennial Uses: Tiger Ore teaches us that we are powerful, not just in spirit, but in our bodies and minds. We can practice our power by finding healthy outlets for all our strength and creativity. To create something useful, all that is required is a focus.

Perhaps the new millennium gives us that focus. With our power, and the focus to use it well, we may experience the future as exactly the challenge we needed to invigorate and restore our life force.

Electrical Body Alignment: Connects us consciously with our power.

Affirmation of Support: *"I empower myself lovingly in every moment."*

Stone Story:
A long long time ago (according to you),
I held you in my lap and told you stories of what you knew
and then placed them into what was to come.
You gazed into my eyes, with excitement and dread,
"Grandfather, what difference does it make if we defeat the dragon?
Something just as awful will come in its place. And by then, I won't
have you to help me to decide what to do."
I smiled because the years had given me peace,
"Granddaughter, every generation has its demons. Each one looks
worse than the last if we anticipate it. Stop worrying. Go live your
life, so that you can be made ready for whatever will come, when it
comes."
You still looked so sad, "But Grandfather, no matter how old I get, I
don't want you to leave me ever."

(con't from previous page)

was etched with a golden angel. When I finally gained my bearings and realized what was happening I carefully struggled out of my seatbelt. I then helped Colene from her elevated position and we both simply walked out of the rear of the vehicle.

We were shaken, bruised, and confused, but thank God, not seriously injured. A bystander who was quite stunned by our appearance exclaimed, "Man, the angels were with you!"

How right he was, he'll never know. The angels were most definitely with us. Thank you, God. Thank you, angels.

~ from Jim and Colene Guthrie

(con't on next page)

So, it was decided.
We made a pact of love.
When it was time to let go of the grandfather body, I sighed and heaved all my stories under a rock.
In a dream truer than life, I told you, "I won't ever leave you. I put everything that's me into something that will live a long long time. Go to the garden and find the rock where we listen to the birds. That's where I'll be. Whenever you're sad, I'll put a brand new story there to give you courage to face the next challenge."

That's what we did.
Do you remember that?

Whenever you needed me and all my love,
you poured your pain into that rock and it cried your tears deep into the earth.
Then you went out and faced your dragons,
though they were even bigger than your imagination.
You learned to win by not fighting.

You realized that you held all the power you needed for every moment.
You even had enough to share for the next generation
while they grew their own courage.

If ever you need me now, or if you want to be inspired by the old stories,
find me by that rock.
Find me in the rock.
Then you'll know you're surrounded by love always
and that's all the power you'll ever need.

Summary: Tiger Ore focuses our power to create more and new life.

(See *Stone Combination Section* for Tiger Ore in "Disappointment into Responsibility")

Topaz

*"Listen to me, listen to yourself.
Listen with compassion and the world smiles upon us all."*

In the past all yellow gemstones were indiscriminately called Topaz, many of which were actually the Citrine variety of Quartz. I am Aluminum Fluorsilicate, white to yellow to golden to deep orange-red to greenish in color. Most natural Topaz is colorless; in recent times Blue Topaz, produced by irradiating colorless varieties, appeared on the market. These stones are a popular and abundant substitute for very rare and expensive Aquamarine of a comparable blue.

I am a high temperature mineral generally formed in igneous rocks. I am harder than Quartz at 8, and my orthorhombic structure usually creates stubby to medium-long prismatic crystals, striated lengthwise, and characteristic pyramid and dome terminations. My luster is vitreous, I have perfect cleavage, in one basal direction, and my specific gravity is 3.4 to 3.6. Though valued throughout history, I am one of the more affordable faceted gems, due to my extraordinary abundance of gem-quality stones and my occurrence in relatively large crystal form (there are a handful of 20,000+ carat specimens in existence, with one at 36,853 carats). My finest specimens are found in Russia, Brazil, and Sri Lanka.

My name comes from the Greek *topazos*, a name said to be applied to a gemstone whose identity has been lost. My name, in fact, was only given in the early part of the 18th Century.

(con't from previous page)

spirits visited it and left their tales and their love there. We have listened to more stones than we can count, but this was the only one who had many spirits who called it home.

~from Twintreess

Physical Integration: Releases infections. Tones the immune system. Gently warms and activates whatever need that is most pressing.

Emotional Integration: Centers on compassion. Spontaneously embraces shadow selves for more open communication. Develops curiosity and humor.

Millennial Uses: In the challenges of every age, each of us needs to contribute to the overall evolution. This requires clear, compassionate communication and Topaz is the stone ally for that. Its energy draws all of us together; it invites us to talk to one another humanely.

Topaz represents empathy of all kinds. As such, it stands for kindness, adaptability and gracious humor.

Electrical Body Alignment: Fosters every kind of communication, within the body and outside of it.

Affirmation of Support: *"I speak truthfully and I understand and appreciate more of life."*

Stone Story:
Hello, hello.
I have been in many stories and many books and I have loved them
all dearly.
In the universe, I live as a storyteller.
I bring words to magic and then magic comes to life.

When we talk without listening ahead of, or behind, the words,
we find heart.
It beats at the core of every kind of language.
The heart tells me everything—of course, the secrets, too.
Sigh when you speak
so you let go of the pain you used to know,
so you can pour yourself into everything you say and everything you
hear.
More you.
More words.
More magic.

Thank you so very much.

Summary: Topaz is the keeper of clear, compassionate communication.

(See *Stone Combination Section* for Topaz in "Earth Light Initiation," Crystal Pleiadean Pyramid Alignment" and "Pregnancy")

Tourmaline

"I come to ground all of your senses so that you feel yourself truly here, now. When we join each other completely in this moment, we simultaneously soar to every other realm."

I am a family of six mineral species with similar crystal structure, but varying widely in chemical composition due to element substitutions in a complex Boron Aluminum Silicate. I occur as prismatic crystals of the trigonal system, and I develop primarily in granitic rocks, schists, and pegmatic rocks. My varieties include: Buergerite (dark brown to black with iridescence); Dravite (brown); Liddicoatite (many colors); Schorl (black); Uvite (black, dark brown, dark green); the sixth member is Elbaite, which is broken down into four specific gem colors—Indicolite (blue); Rubellite (red and pink); Verdelite, sometimes called Brazilian Emerald (green); and the extremely rare Achroite (colorless).

My structure is hexagonal, creating short to long prismatic crystals with a rounded triangular cross section, striated lengthwise. My luster is vitreous, my specific gravity is 3.4 to 3.5, and my cleavage is perfect in one direction. I am quite hard at 7 to 7.5. My name is from the Singhalese *touramalli*, meaning "mixed colored stones." Fine gem-quality Tourmaline comes from California, Maine, Brazil, Myanmar, and the Malagasy Republic.

Physical Integration: Tourmaline is unique to each body because it clarifies, grounds and stimulates the lines of communication of the mind/body/spirit unit. It encourages acting upon this communication immediately.

Emotional Integration: Calms and centers. Faces life in a practical, forthright, harmonious way. Integrates heart and mind in all actions.

Millennial Uses: As we leave the 20th century, we have become aware of how we have disconnected from the earth. Because of this, we have polluted and destroyed everything to such a great degree, shock and denial sets in.

Welcome Tourmaline~

Personal Story

Some stones just feel like me. One of those is Tourmaline. I don't know if I have any specific stories about it, but I do know that every time I have worn it, I feel comfortable in my own body. Whenever Tourmaline is around me, I breathe deeper and I ground myself more. Sometimes it stimulates my energy; other times it relaxes me. It's as if we know each other so well that we just adjust to each other and go from there.

~ from Marilyn

The gift of this stone is that it takes us to our center where we can face anything, including ourselves. It frees us from acting from our fears, so that we can look around our world and witness reality as it is. It continues to soothe us so that we can think in new way, so that we can imagine fresh solutions to our dilemmas. Then with every new solution, we empower ourselves to make more balanced, healthy choices. Tourmaline helps us to transform ourselves and our enormous concerns, one piece at a time. It offers us integration.

Electrical Body Alignment: Aligns our posture and every part of our body with our full mind/heart/spirit intent.

Affirmation of Support: *"I joyfully support the world by calmly living my life, one step at a time."*

Stone Story:
Of course you have known me forever.
We are free spirits dancing the universe
in and out of form
with desire, choice, and bliss.
Feel the lines imprinted on my body.
Run your heart along their edges.
They whisper to you, again and again,
reminding you that we are free.
We have chosen to be here.
We can choose to be here again,
with love to honor our choice
with love to honor all life.
Oh yes, we are no more than this,
and we are everything.

Summary: Tourmaline grants us the inner peace to make the needed changes in our lives.

(See *Stone Combination Section* for Tourmaline in "Earth Light Initiation")

Tucson Mountains

*"Come to me and you won't know why...
No matter, when you stand inside the mountains, they will tell you..."*

We Are The Mountains of Tucson, surrounding the city in a circular pattern. Inhabited by a variety of native peoples for thousands of years, this area remained a quiet place of small pockets of human habitation until the 20th Century. Although the Spanish Conquistadors passed this way more than 400 years ago, there was little development here until the lure of the West and the mineralogical treasures of the surrounding mountains enticed people to arrive in numbers and explore the hidden wealth.

The Santa Catalina Mountains:

As a unit of the Coronado National Forest, we are one of nearly a dozen Sky Island mountain ranges in southeastern Arizona. We make up the north and northeast border of the valley, and our rough pyramid shape is spread out over 200 square miles, and varies in elevation from 2900 feet at the entrance of Sabino Canyon to 9157 feet at the summit of Mount Lemmon.

Geologically, we are a single uplift of granitic metamorphic core complex, with a considerable anticline gneiss forerange. Bajadas—long, flat, but sloping alluvial plains, fan out from steep, rugged ridges which rise abruptly on the perimeter of our range. Our fauna ranges from Sonoran Desert plantlife (mesquite, palo verde, saguaro cactus, creosote) at the base, to towering coniferous Ponderosa pines above 6000 feet. In early Tertiary times, metamorphism reset the atomic clocks in our Precambrian core.

The Tortolita Mountains:

We are the continuation of the granitic metamorphic core complex of the Santa Catalinas, a single large mass of light-colored granite. As in most fault block ranges, the edges of our unfaulted blocks have eroded back, creating a pediment flush with surrounding valley deposits. Between us and the Santa Catalinas, a high platform of Tertiary sediments fills the majority of the downfaulted graben between us.

The Tucson Mountains:

We are the smaller and lower western border of the city, within

---

Personal Story

One of our favorite things about Tucson is that when you ask people who have moved here (many of whom have come fairly recently) why they are in Tucson, they say, "I have no idea." Then they smile and seem satisfied regardless. It's as if the land here is calling to their spirits and they don't know how to translate that into words, so they just come anyway.

~ from Twintreess

the boundaries of the Saguaro National Monument. We are composed of Tertiary intrusive and volcanic rocks bordered by faulted and folded Paleozoic and Cretaceous sedimentary rock. Our range varies from basaltic, flat-lying flows at the south end to a volcanic neck at the north, while small, light-colored hills of Paleozoic limestone surround the range on both sides. Our highest point is Wasson Peak, while our southern tip is known as the Tucson Mountain Chaos, for its confused hodgepodge of lava flows, volcanic breccia, layers and patches of volcanic ash, and blocks of Paleozoic limestone, all believed to have resulted from explosive eruptions, similar to that of Mt. St. Helens in 1980.

The Santa Rita Mountains:

We lay south of Tucson, and halfway to the Mexican border. As with many of the ranges surrounding Tucson, our geologic pattern includes enigmatic thrust faults, dating back 75 to 80 million years, with slices of Paleozoic sedimentary rocks sitting astride or leaning up against a Precambrian core. We peak at Mt. Wrightson at 9453 feet, and we are made up of volcanic rocks and wind-deposited sandstone, both Triassic. Because our sedimentary sequence is relatively complete and only slightly deformed, we offer more clues than most to our geologic history.

The Whetstone and Empire Mountains:

We are the southeastern portion of the Tucson ring, and we consist of relatively undeformed but quite steeply tilted Paleozoic and Mesozoic sedimentary rocks, although they are not as neatly laid out as our neighbors to the south. We Whetstones present a thick array of Paleozoic and Cretaceous strata, the most complete such sequence in southern Arizona.

Low hills of Precambrian Granite mark our northern end, while our mustard-colored southern soils are derived from volcanic ash that date to the Oligocene Era, about 25-30 million years ago. As we move northward our geology grows more complex; Precambrian Granite, Paleozoic sedimentary rocks, Mesozoic and Tertiary sedimentary, volcanic and intrusive rocks, all altered by intrusion of dikes and stocks. Erosion ensued, and the piling on of thick layers of Pliocine and Pleistocene gravel, followed by the erosion of the gravel plain.

The Rincon Mountains:

We are the northward continuation of the Whetstones and, along with the Santa Catalina Mountains, we make up the other portion of the single uplift of granitic metamorphic core complex, and we complete the circle of the Tucson ring. A part of the Saguaro National Monument (East), we are comprised of detached wedges of Precambrian gneiss, and slices of Paleozoic and Mesozoic sedimentary rocks that border the south and west sides of our bulbous granite core, which is encased in a carapace of highly sheared rock. Our notable landmarks are Mica Mountain, flanked by gneiss-schist ridges and slide blocks of Paleozoic rocks, and Rincon Peak, the other of two parallel anticline ridges.

Physical Integration: Increases strength and stamina. Releases excess water. Helps to release toxins.

Emotional Integration: Finds support during challenges. Continually looks for the blessings in obstacles. Connects more deeply to the earth.

Millennial Uses: Every place on this planet is unique; each one serves a perfect purpose within the whole. Tucson calls many beings to it now so that they can know, without distraction, why they are on the planet and what unlimited potentials speak to them.

Electrical Body Alignment: Links us to the energy of the earth and its structures.

Affirmation of Support: *"I follow my spirit immediately."*

Stone Story:
Hello brothersisterfriends,
I settle in the cactus.
I move through the mountains.
Everything warms under my touch—
all is alive, all is sacred.

My heartbeat builds and builds until
the stones erect monuments to it:
Mountains.

I circle the beauty with mountains
who lay a path of unimaginability
to any brave enough to follow it.

When you come, you fill me with water
and we together shall feed the unimaginability
to see what grows,

to see what grows.

Summary: Tucson represents the magic of land surrounded by mountains.

Turquoise

"It is easy to be free and peaceful
when you realize that you are the source of your own bliss."

We form when solutions carrying Phosphorus and Copper move along fractures in Aluminum-rich rocks. When conditions favor a reaction between these solutions in the rocks, a fine-grained, powder-blue vein of Turquoise precipitates, eventually filling the available space in the fracture. These seams, or stringers, are usually quite small, and as such most discoveries produce very limited quantities of gem material.

We were mined by the Pueblo Indians in the American Southwest long before the Spanish arrived, and relic dating indicates that we've been mined as early as the 5th century, and mining in Persia (now Iran) began far earlier.

We have also been called Callite, and our colors range from sky-blue to bluish-green to apple-green. Our hardness is 5 to 6, we have no cleavage and our specific gravity is 2.6 to 2.9. Our structure is triclinic, with crystal formation rare. Our finest, bright blue examples come from Iran, while the less perfect American Turquoise shows patterns of black or brown "spiderwebbing." Infusion of Copper makes us blue, while the addition of Iron makes us green. Our name was originally French, *turquoise*, "Turkish," due to a misconception of where Persian Turquoise was mined.

Physical Integration: Soothes the nervous system. Sharpens eyesight. Soothes the throat.

Emotional Integration: Clears away troubles. Lifts us out of our personal ruts. Embraces independence easily.

Millennial Uses: Mass media, at its best, educates the whole world at once. However, much of it is doled out as superficial entertainment that numbs the mind and spirit and promotes an unwitting conformity to the norm. As we move into the next millennium, we must learn to listen to all communications with discernment. The energy of Turquoise promotes independent thinking and a childlike detachment from struggle and pessimism.

Electrical Body Alignment: Links us to the heart of compassion while encouraging our individual truths.

Affirmation of Support: *"I choose freely what makes me happy."*

Stone Story:
The winds of change glide us along,
sometimes rough, sometimes smooth.
For me it is always just a ride.
For me, it lifts me into possibilities.
For me, it drives my spirit.
For me, it swirls my breath to the four corners of the world.
For me, it pushes me off the cliff and I land in seven worlds at once.
For you it is your choice.

Summary: Turquoise brings into the world free thinkers and doers.

(See *Stone Combination Section* for Turquoise in "Pregnancy," "Stress into Centeredness" and "World Peace")

Tree Agate

"I give thanks for the trees
that dance in the deepest earth and the highest skies.
In between, all the rest of us sigh, and breathe that wondrous union."

Another member of the Silica family, I am a visually unique Chalcedony with inclusions of Hornblende, known for my characteristic green dendrites of oxidized Manganese. I am most often found in China, the US and India, and my name is due to the plant-like appearance that is created by natural dendritic inclusions.

Physical Integration: Gives amplitude to all body movements. Strengthens the shoulders and limbs. Adapts to the seasons easily.

Emotional Integration: Immediately fulfills all needs. Finds great inner strength and calm. Lets go of stress.

Millennial Uses: In any new season (or new millennium), all of nature adjusts to the climate, the weather and the available food. Each being takes their place in that rhythm of life and the whole is served. This is the balance that Tree Agate represents. With humans, it guides us to accept, happily and freely, our own part of the earth's bounty, while continually adjusting to and contributing to the needs of the community. Tree Agate shows us how to root ourselves into the earth with strength and flexibility so we all can fulfill our needs, constantly.

Electrical Body Alignment: Connects us with sustenance for our body/mind/heart union.

Affirmation of Support: *"I live closely with all the seasons of the earth to give and receive its plenty."*

Stone Story:
Come,
rest
upon my trunk.
I grew it for you.
I grow it for all
the children of the earth and skies.

Welcome.

You don't have to talk to me.
We'll listen to the birds
who join us
and the ants, and the squirrels, and the deer, and the mice,
and the sprites (they decorate my branches).

Every day is a celebration to them
and they try to match the spark of the sun
all day long.
I watch it all.

Love.
I give love
and I feel love,
it stretches my roots and my limbs.
It shines on me
like sprites and sunshine.
It smiles that I'm rock
and I talk
like a
tree.
Love smiles at me.
That's what matters to me.
I enjoy that
so much
that I give up all my stories
to the air.
Let anyone
who has courage to dream
smell them
and draw them into
their lungs
where one day
they will shout them
to the stars!

Proud
that the earth children
tell such sweet tales.
They will bring us all
together,
trees, and rocks, and children, and animals, and sprites, and stars.
All the stories just remind us
to shine,
all day long.
The stars will mix in their faraway fables
showing us how

to shine,
all night through.

Now I feel tall.
I feel strong and long-limbed,
even though I'm a small rock.
I carry huge treesongs in me
cause I love them,
they love me.
Trees tell me to take whatever
I need to feel big
and loved.
I'm still smiling.
I give you this story
so you will know that,
to shine,
all you need to do is accept all the earth's gifts.
Let them keep you well
and share the rest—
like I'm doing now.
Love.

Summary: Tree Agate shows us how to fulfill our needs, lovingly and respectfully.

(See *Stone Combination Section* for Tree Agate in "Unimaginability" and "Violence into Compassion")

Ulexite

"I reflect all the stories of the world, so all can know wisdom."

I am among the borates, metallic elements compounded with Boron. There are two varieties, *anhydrous* (without water), which form in igneous and metamorphic deposits, and *hydrous* (with water), which form in sedimentary deposits, usually evaporites. I am Sodium Calcium Borate, with eight parts water, and I am of the hydrous variety, characteristically white, brittle, soft and easily dissolved in water. My triclinic system rarely forms distinct crystals; when present they are small, nodular, rounded or lenslike "cotton balls."

I am often called "TV Rock," for my ability to transmit light images in my fibers, and I was named after the German chemist George Ludwig Ulex (1811–1883). Typically, I am white, with a luster that is vitreous to satiny to silky luster. My hardness is minimal, at 2.5, my cleavage is perfect in one direction and good in another, and my specific gravity is a mere 1.9. Fine fibrous Ulexite occurs as seams in clay and as aggregates in a variety of Colorado locales.

Physical Integration: Promotes visual health. Regenerates the kidneys. Promotes fluid balance. Deepens breathing.

Emotional Integration: Celebrates healthy interdependency. Activates the sense of community.

Millennial Uses: Before books and universities, we learned by observing all beings around us. Ulexite guides us to becoming so invisible that we can witness anything in our environment. It promotes silent patience to absorb whatever we need to know even before we know what we need. There is a mystery and magic inherent in this stone that allows the unexpected.

Electrical Body Alignment: Allows learning from the reflection of life around us.

Affirmation of Support: *"I let go of the smallness of me to join the bigness of life."*

Stone Story:
In a hawk's flight, I see upcoming storms.
Where the plants grow, shows me the way of water.
When the squirrel doesn't know my name,
I know the winter comes early.
In a child's face, I watch the kindness of a mother.
Within the silences of a conversation, I hear your fears.
Everything in the world speaks to the silence.
So I wear the silence.
I listen.
Instead of asking spirit to fill my basket,
I watch to see where it already comes
and I am already overflowing.

Summary: Ulexite urges us to quietly learn from all others.

(See *Stone Combination Section* for Ulexite in "Relationship into All")

Watermelon Tourmaline

"When you open your heart, you never know what treasures you will find."

As with most gem Tourmalines, I am a color variation of Elbaite, the green-and-pink zoned crystal variety.

I am a family of six mineral species with similar crystal structure, but varying widely in chemical composition due to element substitutions in a complex Boron Aluminum Silicate. I occur as prismatic crystals of the trigonal system, and I develop primarily in granitic rocks, schists, and pegmatic rocks. My varieties include: Buergerite (dark brown to black with iridescence); Dravite (brown); Liddicoatite (many colors); Schorl (black); Uvite (black, dark brown, dark green); the sixth member is Elbaite, which is broken down into four specific gem colors— Indicolite (blue); Rubellite (red and pink); Verdelite, sometimes called Brazilian Emerald (green); and the extremely rare Achroite (colorless).

My structure is hexagonal, creating short to long prismatic crystals with a rounded triangular cross section, striated lengthwise. My luster is vitreous, my specific gravity is 3.4 to 3.5, and my cleavage is perfect in one direction. I am quite hard at 7 to 7.5. My name (as Tourmaline) is from the Singhalese *touramalli*, "mixed colored stones." Fine gem-quality Tourmaline comes from California, Maine, Brazil, Myanmar, and the Malagasy Republic.

Physical Integration: Sensitizes the meridians of the feet for healing work. Increases the benefits of massage. Promotes aerobic fitness. Assists with adapting to color blindness.

Emotional Integration: Adapts all resources to healthy and deep self exploration and integration. Benefits of this stone will be unique to each person experiencing it.

Millennial Uses: As a species we have developed our mental processes to a strong degree. The area of the heart lies somewhat untested. Enter Watermelon Tourmaline that embraces all levels of feelings and integrates them with pure information and finally, beneficial action. Perhaps some of the apathy of various cultures can be found in the tendency to disconnect from feelings. Watermelon Tourmaline invites us to experience all our emotions, to nurture ourselves completely in our process and then to proceed with all of our feelings to the appropriate, healthy actions.

Electrical Body Alignment: Connects us to all emotions and their unique wisdom.

Affirmation of Support: *"I compassionately allow all my feelings and then choose which ones will lead me."*

Stone Story:
Oh, hello again~
I have nothing for you
that you do not feel
in some other part of your
endless being.

Everything that I have for you, family, friends, co-creators, is this affirmation:
As you feel life, you will be rewarded with boundless awareness.

Summary: Watermelon Tourmaline presides over emotional growth and changes of heart.

(See *Stone Combination Section* for Watermelon Tourmaline in "Impatience into Presence")

Wavelite

"The wisdom of the ages comes from the heart of the earth and all the beings who feel her splendor."

We are valued for our acicular radiating aggregates of wavelight crystals. Our color ranges from white, greenish-white, yellow, to yellowish-brown, and we form as a secondary mineral in contact metamorphic rocks and epithermal veins, in phosphate and some illuminous rocks. Similar in appearance to Chalcedony, we are softer, at 3.5 to 4, and our orthohombic structure creates occasional stout to long prismatic and striated crystals.

Our specific gravity is 2.3 to 2.4, our luster is vitreous to pearly, and our cleavage is perfect, in one direction, and good in two others. Our finest specimens originate in Arkansas; other good examples derive from Pennsylvania, Colorado, England, Brazil, Bolivia, and Germany. We are named after William Wavell, a 19th century English physician who first found us.

Physical Integration: Enhances the genetic changes that adapt the species to survival. Assists with breathing disorders.

Emotional Integration: Promotes the changes that will ensure survival. Focuses the thoughts and feelings on positive planetary transformation.

Millennial Uses: To come up with the lifestyle changes necessary to thrive in the next millennium, we must explore anywhere. Wavelite represents the capability to look beyond oneself for answers, or to investigate previously avoided or unknown areas. With this stone comes a boldness of heart and purpose combined with respect.

Electrical Body Alignment: Connects us to the spiral of life and the vortices upon the earth.

Affirmation of Support: *"I explore the heights and depths to reveal the ways to promote life."*

Stone Story:
I come from the odd nook and cranny,
barely noticed by anyone at all.
Sometimes I grow in hidden places and caves.
Yet when you need me,
I explode upon the scene.
I bring all that I am, all that I have tried
and all that I have imagined.
Create a destiny that inspires!

Summary: Wavelite depicts respectful exploration of anything that answers our greatest needs.

White Moldavite
(Elestial Calcite)

"However you move through life, I will wait in the stillness of love,
to replenish you, as you wish."

Personal Story

The first time we ever saw a piece of white moldavite was at a Whole Life Expo. It felt amazing and because of its rarity, it was very, very expensive. We got the okay from our business partners to buy it, if we liked it. Just as we were about to make the purchase, the stone told us to save our money and that we would meet up with it again some other time.

During a gem show a few months later, we met a gentle crystal harvester. He liked to gather stones from the earth with respect. After talking to him a short while, Robert showed us all his treasures. One of his treasures was white moldavite.

These beauties felt incredible. It was

(con't on next page)

Most scientists who deal with minerals and stones say that I cannot be what I am. But I am. I really have no need to explain myself other than I am a miracle.

I am found in sand dune fields in the Mohave Desert near the Colorado River, in a very remote region of Western Arizona. I have been called an Elestial Calcite that is transparent and has a highly etched and natural surface texture. The texture is similar to the embayed and resorbed surface texture referred to as "alligator" textured quartz and is very similar to the green Moldavite Tektites that have become so popular.

My specimens appear to be crystal fragments with a strong crystalline structure. I am perplexing to those who have tried to study me in a linear fashion because I do not respond to normal testing methods in a logical fashion. On my deeply etched surfaces, the etched grooves do not always correspond to cleavage directions or crystal growth planes.

My essence is unmistakeably "Moldavite" and, combined with my strong transparent to white color, has given me the name, "White Moldavite."

Physical Integration: Eases pain. Softens aging process. Supports the adrenals.

Emotional Integration: Soothes the need for phobias. Relaxes unidentified stress. Supports our transitions.

Millennial Uses: All of us are evolving right now. Perhaps, with the perspective of another time, or timelessness, you will understand that. Until then, mystery will guide us. That's how it is with this stone, which inexplicably has transformed its energy into White Moldavite. In trusting this mystery, you allow gifts of White Moldavite to refresh us. It balances us instantaneously through our constant changes. As we evolve, it holds our heart with love. It acknowledges that as we advance, we still need to feel support and contentment, always. So, without explanation, White Moldavite gives us these things and it is our choice to receive.

Electrical Body Alignment: White Moldavite seeks out any weaknesses or unloved areas and embraces them.

Affirmation of Support: *"As I change and grow, I fulfill my desire for love."*

Stone Story:

At the beginning of the circle, you are born whether you remember it or not. You are created with love. As you land upon the world, you bring with you countless guardians and sacred witnesses. I am told by the Mother Earth Spirit, that you are also granted seven special allies. They walk with you and never turn their heads. They know you from root to tip and you know them in the fire of your spirit, even when your head cannot remember their names. Spirit Whispers tell me that seven great ones travel with you because you are an earthwalker. You inherit the legacy of seven from her, Mother Earth Spirit. She, too, claims seven allies and seven ages of growth. In each age, the trials and gifts of one ally will step forth and cover the world. All its children will learn the glories and the pain of that time and that great one (ally). When you find your ally, you will know it's time. I have found mine. It is the White Buffalo. I am honored to know what is asked of me now. I must give comfort to every single child of the earth—plant, animal, element or stone. I cannot take away any learnings. I will not be responsible for another's pain. Still, I will watch and when I am needed I will slip beside whoever struggles, and I will give them my smile.

Summary: White Moldavite supports us emotionally during our initiations.

(See *Stone Combination Section* for White Moldavite in "In Honor of the White Buffalo" and "Timeless Treasure")

(con't from previous page)

like being filled up with sweetness. To top it off, Robert's prices were much more accessible. Not only did we get to meet white moldavite again, but we also gained a wonderful new friend in Robert.

~ from Twintreess

Wulfenite

"I reflect your fragile fiery natures and the ensuing perfection of your being in the dream of Life."

I am a secondary molybdate mineral who forms in the zone of alteration in massive hydrothermal replacement deposits that contain significant Lead mineralization. I am yellow, orange, brown, yellowish-gray, or whitish, and am known for my brilliant hues. I am quite soft at 3 on Moh's scale, and my luster is resinous to adamantine. I have distinct cleavage in one direction and my specific gravity is extremely high, at 6.5 to 7. My system is triclinic, and my crystals are pseudo-tetragonal due to twinning, often as thin square plates in large groups.

My name is in honor of Franz Haver von Wulfen (1728-1805), the Austrian mineralogist, and my finest examples are to be found in Mexico, Arizona, New Mexico, The Congo, Morocco, Austria, and Australia.

Physical Integration: Strengthens the body's bearing. Opens closed, tight postures. Stretches out and changes repetitive motions.

Emotional Integration: Appreciates the senses. Increases healthy physical desires. Empowers us through open hearted, risk taking ventures.

Millennial Uses: If you simply tally how we have polluted this planet, it can be difficult to see how we would survive much longer. The sheer numbers of toxins around us makes us think it would take a miracle to restore us to healthy lifestyles.

Wulfenite is a miracle. It glistens with an astounding and delicate splendor...like humans beings. People live magnificently and vulnerably, sometimes closed in by the seeming tragedies of poor judgment. There is no one single way to evolve (and then to prosper) into the year 2000. Maybe there are many ways, maybe not. Likely, we are going to have to look in areas that we barely can envision now.

We might consider listening to Wulfenite, who is like us and who is not like us, to learn how to grow with every season of the earth.

Electrical Body Alignment: Unites the feet and the heart for open hearted adventures.

Affirmation of Support: *"I risk my foolishness to revel in new wisdom."*

Stone Story:
I grow in the heat and it shapes me.
What makes you grow?

Take my question to your visions,
to your dreams,
to your greatest wondering
and you will have all that you need
and much, much more.

Summary: Wulfenite shows us how to prize beauty and vulnerability to welcome in far sweeping changes and possibilities in life.

Zeolite

"I come to you to embrace all that you do not know how to love,
even your unknown denials and pains."

We are a group of several dozen minerals similar to the Feldspars, only with water added, occurring in basaltic cavities. We are widespread, but not major rock forming minerals. Chemically we are hydras tectosilicates, and we contain water in microscopic channels within a framework of Aluminum Silicate units. We are characterized by the ease with which we may be dehydrated and rehydrated, without structural alteration, and utilized for our ion exchange properties. Collectors seek such species as Analcite, Chabazite, Heulandite, Mesolite, Natrolite, Pectolite, Prehnite, and Stilbite.

Physical Integration: It offers to release inner and outer toxins. Can be embraced as a tool for affirmation, ritual, integration and transmutation.

Emotional Integration: Honors the self and all aspects of it so much that destructive behaviors fall away. Creates healthy boundaries. Happily indulges in comfortable, intimate home space.

Millennial Uses: In these times, many of us have developed environmental sensitivities. As societies, we produce more toxins than we release. As our bodies grope to adapt to this, so too does the earth's body. It produces plants and minerals to aid us naturally. Zeolite enters our lives as one of these minerals. Like our bodies, it looks beautiful and somewhat fragile, yet its capacities to transmute in the face of seeming disasters grows with every moment.

Electrical Body Alignment: Connects our excretory systems to ancient knowledge and future mysteries.

Affirmation of Support: *"I surround myself in love and beauty."*

Stone Story:

Are you afraid? When fear comes into your dreams, do you hold its hand in fascination and listen in horror as its stories grow and grow? When you feel cold with dread, do you concentrate on the pain so that one day you will be numb?

Wake up. Dreams or nightmares come to you at your own request. Fascination with fear, is still fear. And then it is more fear. Stop. Your life looms in eternity. Nothing hurts you except you. Smile upon your world, even in the darkness and you will grow taller than a wise man's dream.

Summary: Zeolite helps us to release toxic influences from our lives.

(See *Stone Combination Section* for Zeolite in "Environmental Toxins" and " Intent")

Zincite

"I cheerfully look at your weaknesses and show you the way to make them your strengths."

I am a native form of Zinc Oxide, a most rare mineral which forms alongside many others, but particularly with Willemite, Calcite, and Franklinite, in massive hydrothermal replacement deposits. I am distinctly deep red to orange-yellow or brown in color, and mineralogists believe this coloration to be the result of the inclusion of Manganese, since pure Zinc Oxide is white.

My hardness is 4, my specific gravity is 5.4 to 5.7, and my cleavage is perfect, in one direction, with additional basal parting. My luster is adamantine and my hexagonal structure creates rare crystals of pyramidal design. The premier North American locality for Zincite is in Sussex County, New Jersey, where I occur in the granular ore.

Quite a large amount of the Zincite usually seen is from Poland and is the by-product of zinc smelting.

Personal Story

We have been very fortunate in meeting some really remarkable people in our travels and through our love of stones. One of those persons, is Keran, a delightful, exploring, well-practiced herbalist. After one of our trade shows, she called us and ordered a great deal of our Vibrational jewelry pieces. Just like she has done with herbs, she has worked diligently with stones to discover their potential healing properties.

One of the stories Keran has shared with us is this: One day she was working in her garden in the hot, Georgia sun. Inadvertently, she stayed out far too long and when she walked into her house, she almost passed out

(con't on next page)

Physical Integration: Emphasizes typical mental/emotional/physical patterns, so new ones can be chosen. Works with the metabolism. Highlights whatever needs to be released from the system. Appreciates our shadow selves.

Emotional Integration: Brings forth healthy instincts to be acted upon. Increases spontaneity. Revitalizes body image.

Millennial Uses: Zincite combines an appreciation for our current technology while simultaneously encouraging simplicity in the basics of life. This stone allows us to honor ourselves just as we are and to be grateful for all the things that we produce.

Electrical Body Alignment: Joins the sense of touch with extrasensory perceptions.

Affirmation of Support: *"I am perfect in my being and in my doing."*

Stone Story:
Like the inner earth, I am formed in great heat. This heat gives me my service, my gift to share with you. I speak the language of instincts. When we speak them together, we transform the complexities of life into simple moment to moment pleasures. One day when you wonder how you will continue to survive, you will feel my essence rush up to you and together we will survey the entire world and I will say, "How can you not survive here?"

Summary: Zincite deals with passion, pleasure and warmth.

Zoisite

"Creativity comes to your center and then goes out into the world with abundance!"

We are Zoisite, and our best gem-quality crystals, transparent blue are known as Tanzanite. Our Calcium Aluminum Silicate formula often includes Iron or Manganese, and our orthorhombic structure occurs as long prismatic crystals deeply striated along their length. We are an uncommon mineral and our formation is restricted to metamorphic rocks. We can be gray, yellowish brown, greenish, pink or blue in color, most of which change color to blue when heated.

(con't from previous page)

immediately from heatstroke. Her husband ran to her and asked her what herb he should bring her. She replied that she wanted him to bring her several of the necklaces we had sold to her. Without even looking at them, she instinctively reached out and put one of them on her forehead, as she rested. It was Zincite.

Within five minutes she was so revived that she was up and making lunch for her and her husband. Keran told us later that the reason that she wanted to work with the stones (in that instance) was because they worked immediately, even faster than some herbs, and never had any side effects that she could determine.

~from Twintreess

Our luster is vitreous, but pearly on cleavage, which is good, in one direction lengthwise. Our hardness is 6 to 6.5, and our specific gravity is 2.2 to 2.4. We are named after Baron S. Zois van Edelstein (1747-1819), and can be found in Norway, Western Australia, the United States (North Carolina, California, Tennessee).

Physical Integration: Stretches chest, lungs, shoulders, moods. Youthens the entire body.

Emotional Integration: Re-energizes the inner artist. Kindles a deep respect for creativity. Renews the intimacy of familiar bonds.

Millennial Uses: Zoisite comes to all of us heralding that living is an art form. Moment to moment we can endow it with grace, enthusiasm and a constant ability to grow beyond expectations. This stone carries the heart of simple empowerment. Its energy impresses upon us that we have the most perfect glorious opportunities to birth any of our dreams, simply because we are alive.

Electrical Body Alignment: Joins the survival instinct with fortuitous grace and ease.

Affirmation of Support: *"I live my life as an artist creating exactly the colors, music and poetry that I love."*

Stone Story:
Hold my hand. Hold my heart. Whenever someone listens to my spark, I burst forth as a child. You listen now and I am brand new. I go to your dreams and I whisper, "What do you really want?" Then I point out the brush in your hand and the colors of the world. I smile as you design the life that most becomes you.

Summary: Zoisite embraces the art in life.

(See *Stone Combination Section* for Zoisite in "Bliss" and "Freedom")

Totem Stories from the Tibetan Tektites

Where lie your roots?

The earth,

the earth and all its beings.

If you can't put your arms around the whole earth,

then slide your hands around a stone.

In your palm it pulses life through you,

the same as the heartbeat of the earth.

The same rhythms worn on the surface

so that you can touch it.

Now you know it.

Smooth your forehead.

Relax.

You have touched the connection that feeds you.

You know the way that your body can keep growing.

Now all you have to explore

is how your soul

beats in the same rhythm

that gives you breath to talk about this.

Stone Combination Section

Enter the Stone Combination Adventure

Ever notice how when you need to have something done right away, it helps immensely to get lots of hands working on it? You put in your piece. Then Anna lends her help. Until finally, Brad gets in there and thinks of something that everybody else missed and slips it in at the eleventh hour, just like a hero. In short, life works very well when we combine all our incredible resources.

It's the same thing with the stones. Turquoise by itself fosters a loving, gentle independence. When you join it with an Apache Tear, that independence then emphasizes its kindly, protective nature. And like all other beings on the earth, the stones in combinations alter themselves according to the season around them.

Right now, the season is dramatic change/initiation/exponential evolution and the potential to co-create and to manifest *a new earth harmony*. Now. Therefore, the *Stone Combinations* that asked to be in this book adventure focus on personal and planetary healing. In this context, healing means integration – the ability to combine with every part of ourselves with such unconditional acceptance that we think, feel, and act whole. That individual integration automatically and always flows into all other areas of life, until we all can enjoy a new earth harmony. (Please see the "New Earth Harmony" entry for even more information).

How to Use the Stone Combination Section

Like the single stone entries, the combinations share: a Quote; a Physical Integration; an Emotional Integration; Millennial Uses; an Electrical Body Alignment; an Affirmation of Support, and sometimes, a Personal Story (Please refer to the **Tools for the Adventure**, at the beginning of the book, for more information on how to use these categories).

The *Stone Combination Section* also includes a *Tools for Manifestation* exercise/ meditation; it gives you practical examples of how to work with these combinations to utilize their services. For example, this is from the "Arms of Michael":

All of us have times when we need to feel safer and to expand further our awareness. Hold the above stones (or keep them with you) and repeat the *Affirmation of Support,* (I trust that I am totally protected and guided in all things). intentionally, several times a day, for at least a couple of days.

227

Choose to feel secure and capable in all decisions.

If and when you feel afraid, accept its presence.

Listen to it for clues about what to do.

Continue to affirm, *"I trust that I am totally protected and guided in all things."*

Journal all the times you were well guided and strong. For times of great need, place a Pyrite next to the above combination.

As you actually use the *Tools for Manifestation,* you will feel greater familiarity with how the stones work, individually and jointly. That will help you to adjust the exercises/meditations according to your own respectful intuition in order to fulfill your most immediate needs.

All the stone combinations are listed alphabetically. However there are sub-categories within the *Stone Combination Section,* as follows:

"The Angelic Line"—We devoted these combinations to the four male archangels and the female archangels, with thanks for their divine guidance on the earth: The Arms of Michael; Gabriel's Dawn; Raphael's Rays; Uriel's Wisdom; Aurora's Dream; Faith's Embrace; Hope's Call; and Mary's Wonder.

By listening to the stones, we co-created a line of combinations called, "Planetary Healing," that lists the qualities that we humans are working with and learning from in order to evolve. For example, one of the combinations is named, "Boredom into Choice." We learn from boredom and through our experience and loving acceptance we transmute boredom into choice. The stones help us to embrace our perfect lessons, instead of denying or ignoring them, so that we can evolve. That's why this group of stone combinations is called, "Planetary Healing." As we, each, embrace our feelings/our lives/our adventures, then that wisdom contributes to the consciousness of the whole and then all of us evolve and heal. The "Planetary Healing" combinations are: Boredom into Choice; Confusion into Focus; Disappointment into Responsibility; Disease into Vitality; Fear into Love; Guilt into Perfection; Impatience into Presence; Judgment into Trust; Lack into Allowability; Pain into Fulfillment; Relationship into All; Should into Acceptance; Stress into Centeredness; and Violence into Compassion.

Finally, we welcome the "Twintreess" group of stone combinations. These particular stones speak so lovingly to us that they directly help us with our personal integration. They have influenced us so powerfully that we choose to offer them, freely, to you: Bliss; Earth Light Initiation; Freedom; Immortality; Intent; Listening; Open Heart; Regeneration; Spirit Storytelling; Turkll Delight and Unimaginability. Now you can feel our hearts in this adventure…

The Origin of the Stone Combinations

We, Twintreess, have appreciated stones always. Their beauty and their stories enliven us. Even when we have held a particular rock many times, we can keep coming back to it to find new pictures or rainbows in it to love.

This appreciation led us to recording their stories and the more we did this, the more the stories expanded. It felt natural that they then guided us into placing them in formations and in combinations. Once we did that, miracles landed in our laps. Stones help us to co-create our realities. Multiple stones multiplied our abilities to manifest needs and dreams immediately.

A simple way to carry the stone combinations with us was in jewelry that we co-designed with the stones themselves. It was called *Vibrational Jewelry* since the stones were united for specific intents, not just decoration. It also allowed us an easy and beautiful way to carry the multiple stones on our bodies (and sometimes many combinations together). We have worked with each piece extensively (it's very gratifying research), and share with you now, the spark and the power of the ones that comprise the *Stone Combination Section*.

How to Use the Stone Combinations

Working with stones for wholistic integration reminds us of working with herbs. These medicinal plants have certain characteristics that they impart to almost any being ingesting them. Even so, everybody has their own somewhat particular reaction to an herb that they must explore for themselves. For instance, we adore cayenne. Pour it on and we know we're alive! Of course that's not true for everybody. If cayenne pepper tastes way too hot for you, you might be able to work with it, still, by simply carrying some of it in a medicinal pouch. What we're talking about here is utilizing its vibrational healing (like flower essences or homeopathy). The same can apply to stones; therefore, the intent you bring to working with the stones is key. It affects all the results.

Here are some suggestions for co-creating respectfully with the stones (in combinations):

♦ Regard them with admiration and handle accordingly.

♦ Carry them with you.

♦ Wear them in jewelry.

♦ Place them in formations in quiet, sacred spaces in your home.

♦ Lay written affirmations under them.

♦ If you can't get any of the stones listed, you can meditate on their names and/or visualize them and their effects in your life.

♦ Add other stones to the combinations, as needed.

Again, the following stone combinations offer themselves to you now.

The possibilities lie before you as endless as the adventures...

The Arms of Michael

"I come to you my arms as open as your heart.
Embrace me through and through.
My help is as swift as a prayer."

- ◆ *Rainbow Obsidian* is all awareness joined with unlimited possibilities.
- ◆ *Herkimer Diamond* is the light of divinity shining in all things.

Physical Integration: Aligns the spine. Promotes body/spirit awareness.

Emotional Integration: Reminds us of our free will. Brings clarity to emotions that have been confused for a long time. Grants a feeling of safety.

Millennial Uses: In many traditions, this time has been heralded as a challenging transition and time of initiation. "The Arms of Michael" stands for all the guardians and help we are receiving (and will receive) when we most need it. When crisis looms, unexpected miracles present themselves. "The Arms of Michael" asks us to be open to assistance, while simultaneously, helping ourselves. It encourages us to distinguish, amidst the chaos, what is right and true and helpful for us. Then, when assistance is offered, we can determine if and how to accept it.

Electrical Body Alignment: Links us to new visions and power.

Affirmation of Support: *"I trust that I am totally protected and guided in all things."*

Tools for Manifestation:
All of us have times when we need to feel more safe and to further expand our awareness:

Hold the above stones (or keep them with you) and repeat the *Affirmation of Support,* intentionally, several times a day, for at least a couple of days.
Choose to feel secure and capable in all decisions.
If and when you feel afraid, accept its presence.
Listen to fear for clues about what to do.
Continue to affirm, *"I trust that I am totally protected and guided in all things."*
Journal all the times you were well guided and strong.

For times of great need, place a Pyrite next to the above combination.

Aurora's Dream

"When you will yourselves to be divine, all that you see is paradise.
You are the creator, and the creation, in a never-ending spiral of knowingness."

♦ *Lapis Lazuli* is for wisdom beyond time.

♦ *Selenite* is for service and freedom combined.

♦ *Sodalite* is for inner child truth.

♦ *Russian Phenacite* is for perspective with great awe.

♦ Optional Essential Oil: *Wintergreen* clarifies both thoughts and feelings.

Physical Integration: Invites full body awareness in every limb, organ, joint, muscle and nerve. Releases headaches and focuses intuition.

Emotional Integration: Trusts intuition and "sixth sense." Promotes conviction in following spirit and truth.

Millennial Uses: In this time when our every choice seems to carry so many consequences, we live with healthy assuredness. Aurora's Dream sends us strong guidance and the confidence to trust in it (and ourselves). We are evolving and developing more and more awareness in ways that it may not be possible to measure or understand at this time. As this occurs, our guardian angels communicate with us more and more clearly. To accept that means that we can receive their wisdom more immediately.

Electrical Body Alignment: Links us to angelic knowingness and support.

Affirmation of Support: *"I am more aware of divine wisdom every day."*

Tools for Manifestation:
Sit or lay down in a sacred space where you will not be disturbed.
Surround yourself with love.
Just be in the silence.
If distracting thoughts come, just smile at them and let them pass through.
Be your own sacred witness.
Watch what happens around you.
Gaze at the sky, the clouds, the weather and any animals.
Judge nothing.
Observe life happening all around you and trust that it is occurring perfectly,
that it follows the natural ways of the seasons without question.

Bliss

"I embrace you as you embrace me. It is our nature to be reflections of each other. The joy of this creation spreads out before us, and ever deeper within."

- ◆ *Kornerupine* is knowing yourself and creating joy.
- ◆ *Chrysocolla* is the embrace of the mother spirit for all of us.
- ◆ *Zoisite* is the heart of all co-creation.
- ◆ *Herkimer Diamond* is the perfection upon all planes of existence.
- ◆ Optional Essential Oils: *Sandalwood* and *Ylang Ylang* intensify our joys and release our struggles.

Physical Integration: Helps to find new communication with the body. Enhances all the senses, through the heart.

Emotional Integration: Supports the choice of being physical and human, now. Honors all life in the present moment.

Millennial Uses: It seems true that anything we do doesn't matter, ultimately, if we lose track of our own inner and personal joy. It could be argued that we have "civilized" ourselves right out of time and space for happiness.

Bliss insists on happiness. In that insistence, it revitalizes the life force in us, until it grows and grows. Physically, emotionally, mentally and spiritually, we become stronger. When that happens, our bliss leads us into magic.

Electrical Body Alignment: Connects us to the innate love and peaceful joy of spirit.

Affirmation of Support: *"I follow my bliss and all my life is miracles."*

Tools for Manifestation:
Happiness comes to us a piece at a time.
When we cultivate its presence, it expands exponentially.
Begin to grow your happiness, by making a list of all the things that please you (big and small things, all).
Lay the Bliss Stones on the top of the list, asking it to grow.
Each day, sing the *Affirmation of Support* to it and smile.
Smile at as many things as you possibly can, every moment.
Choose to smile, continually.
When you forget, smile anyway.

Boredom into Choice

"I am the source of unlimitedness. I yearn to taste, to embrace, to revel in all things... instead of letting them slip by...."

- *Black Garnet* is the presence of all unlimitedness in all your breaths.

- *Red Garnet* is the acceptance of your free, complete choice.

- *Green Garnet* is the allowing of free, complete choice for all beings.

- *Herkimer Diamond* is consciously Being.

Physical Integration: A full grounding of the senses and the body. Clears the mind and lungs. Encourages stamina.

Emotional Integration: Increases focus and the ability to be present. Encourages confident commitment.

Millennial Uses: In many societies, now, we are flooded with numerous stimuli. Things come and go so quickly in our life, we get accustomed to wanting the next bigger and better thing, and the next and the next. Maybe we don't even see what we already have.

"Boredom into Choice" insists that we stop and see all that we do possess (materially and otherwise). It asks us to be present with our possessions, our choices, even our very beings, quietly and intentionally. Once we are calm, we can choose what we will or won't bring into our lives to bring us happiness, then we move from "reacting" to responding.

Electrical Body Alignment: Grounds us into this present moment, over and over again.

Affirmation of Support: *"I appreciate all that I have, all that I know and all that I am, right now."*

Tools for Manifestation:
All of life comes to us.
All of life passes through us.
We own all possibilities,
even when we don't acknowledge it.
Acknowledge it.
Acknowledge that infinite potential surrounds us,
every day.
Infinite potential surrounds us every day,
because that is our true essence.
It is who we are.

Say it.
Say it again.
Celebrate it in as many different ways as possible.
Accept it and know that we are fulfilled in every way.

Buddha

"Use ritual to find your own personal affirmation for this combination of stones before you wear them. Then speak your affirmation each time you touch them."

- ♦ *Pyrite* is to accept that all earth experiences are gold.

- ♦ *Labradorite* is to accept that all the earth's gold is illusion.

- ♦ Optional Essential Oil: *Peppermint* is for savoring everything.

Physical Integration: Grounds the senses. Releases old congestion. Accelerates all processes.

Emotional Integration: Cultivates calm regardless of the circumstances. Trusts in our eternal capabilities.

Millennial Uses: The question before us is, "How do we enter and live in the next millennium successfully?" Take time out of the picture and it is an eternal quest: "How do we live our lives as well as we can?"

The "Buddha" Stones soothe us and accept us so completely that we can contemplate this search, freely and honestly. In that moment of clarity, we realize that we have everything inside of us to accomplish this mission. All that remains is to find the exact way to achieve this in our own unique manner.

Electrical Body Alignment: Connects us to our infinite and earthly perfection.

Affirmation of Support: *"I accept the Buddha in my heart. I am in him and he is in me."*

Tools for Manifestation:
Every being seeks enlightenment in their own wondrous way. In our group legends, all of the actualized souls on this planet undertook vision quests or intensely focused retreats. During this time, they eliminated all distractions and simply faced themselves. They confronted the smallness of their being until they found the largeness of their spirit.

Set up a retreat of your own. Try to make it as many days as possible, or build up to several days after a few tries. Go without possessions and distractions and come out newly free.

A Celebration of Faeries

"All of us are surrounded by faeries for every need and for every desire.
Hold these stones to your heart and you will feel and hear their wishes for you, now."

- ◆ *Purple Sapphire* is for supporting unconditional love as the base for all life.

- ◆ *Labradorite* is the vision to see all of life (in all experiences) embracing you.

- ◆ *Apophyllite* is an unlimited imagination to see your dreams and then allowing them to shine through you.

- ◆ Optional Essential Oil: *Jojoba* is the honoring of the extremes of every experience and challenge with bliss.

Physical Integration: Attracts metaphysical phenomena. Increases the ability to use all physical and spiritual resources to co-create reality. Fosters flexibility.

Emotional Integration: Encourages mental and emotional versatility. Increases the sense of humor. Attracts peaceful dreams.

Millennial Uses: It may be hard to believe (in this technological age) in unseen things. Consider all the "invisible" effects that we rely upon: electricity, nuclear power, magnetics, love... How did we determine their authenticity? Someone had to look at life in a new way and then they had to observe the results of these things.

"A Celebration of Faeries" invites us to do the same: Believe in Faeries and then see what happens to you. Wait a while, because they may have to travel through years of disbelief even to come into your awareness.

Electrical Body Alignment: Links us to all levels of life, seen and unseen.

Affirmation of Support: *"I believe in magic and it rewards me with unexpected joy!"*

Tools for Manifestation:
Sometimes all that is required to transform your current reality
into your chosen one,
is that you have to remind yourself enough of your chosen life.
Take several slips of paper and write down all the most wondrous effects you would experience by welcoming in Faeries to your world.
Post your notes wherever you can see them very regularly.
When you see them, read them aloud.
Read them with relish.

Personal Story: My experience with the stone combinations in the jewelry Marilyn and Thomas make has been nothing short of miraculous. My favorite pendant right now is *"A Celebration of Faeries,"* which gave me chills when I saw it listed in their book of descriptions. It has been pure magic wearing it, and I'm reminded that the Faeries and all of Spirit is with me wherever I am. I have had people stop me and ask what it is, staring at in in awe, curious about whatever it is in the vial.

While I was working at Presents of Angels in Minnneapolis, we carried some of Twintreess' pendants and earrings, mostly the Angelic series. It was fun to watch people's eyes light up as they felt the vials and read the messages on the cards. They were inexplicably drawn to them, wondering what these stones were and why they were together. One woman I know came in, walked right to the jewelry case, pointed to "Gabriel's Dawn" and said, "I want that one." She had no idea what it was, but *knew* she had to have it. Since then she has added a few dozen others to her collection and uses them as healing tools.

I have witnessed many people purchasing the jewelry on other occasions and have found that most people feel the joy within each vial. They can tell that each one is very special, full of magic, and encloses some hidden peace/piece for which we are all searching. To me, the stone combination vials are a divine expression of something that we as humans long to find in our lives.

~from Jennifer Salness

Confusion into Focus

"I am all your choices, together in a moment.
If you feel them all simultaneously, your mind jumbles.
If you focus on NOW, on this choice before you,
everything reveals itself in natural order, in peace."

- ◆ *Green Garnet* acknowledges all parts of you, all times of your life, now.

- ◆ *Mica* is the clear reflection of you in all experiences.

- ◆ *Smoky Quartz* is the emergence of the unknown into the supposedly known structures of your life.

- ◆ *Larimar* is the conscious offering of all that you are and of all your experiences, to the universe.

Physical Integration: Access from short to long-term memory quickens and expands. Works with memory/diseases/addictions (particulary those involving blackouts).

Emotional Integration: Releases denial. Clearly faces the sources of undesirable habits. Attracts good support.

Millennial Uses: Sometimes when our challenges loom so immense before us that we feel helpless, we deny them. Then we create distractions for ourselves, so that we can work on our confusion, instead of the task at hand.

In the 20th century, many problems overwhelm us: pollution, the evaporation of the ozone layer and resulting weather changes, the destruction of the rainforest, etc., etc. "Confusion into Focus" arrives at precisely the perfect moment. It helps to eliminate the behaviors that primarily created much of our environmental/societal distress, and the maladapted actions we have developed that compounded our difficulties. Welcome to focus that faces our fears, and then goes through them to prosperity.

Electrical Body Alignment: Connects us to our fears and to the abilities to go beyond them.

Affirmation of Support: *"I embrace confusion and my strength transforms it into focus!"*

Tools for Manifestation:
The key to transformation of behaviors is intense self-observation.
First, record every time you feel confused. Just record it briefly without any observation, until you become extremely aware of every single incident of confusion. If you find yourself bored and/or annoyed with this, just give thanks for your

transmutation process and affirm, *"I embrace confusion and my strength transforms it into focus."*

Now record any and all of the feelings you have around confusion.
Just observe them.
Take the feelings and trace them back to the deepest source you can find for them.
Hold the "Confusion into Focus" Stones to you and create a new affirmation, stating your desired result.
Love yourself for all your courage and constant change.

Connecting to Your Guides

"I hear the wisdom of my guides and together we co-create a reality of unconditional love."

- ♦ *Galena* grounds us into this reality and its miracles.
- ♦ *Lapis Lazuli* opens the gateways of communication through intuition.
- ♦ *Amethyst* brings forth trust in inner truth.

Physical Integration: Lessens headaches. Releases ringing in the ears. Decreases motion sickness.

Emotional Integration: Develops completely new ways of thinking and feeling and acting. Unconditionally trusts.

Millennial Uses: All traditions upon the earth talk about guardian spirits who help the earth and its beings through various changes. "Connecting to Your Guides" allows you to feel the presence of the spirits around you. As you become acutely familiar with them, you may even hear their ancient wisdom. It is exactly this type of innate intelligence that may guide us through the tremendous earth changes, peacefully and unconditionally supported.

Electrical Body Alignment: Links us to the ancient ones who protect the earth and guide its beings.

Affirmation of Support: *"Every day I feel my guides show me the way to wisdom."*

Tools for Manifestation:
When you most need to accept this message of absolute affirmation, receive it and feel renewed:
Every flower has a deva.
Every tree grows with a sprite.
Why wouldn't humans also travel with their own guides~

Ones that adore them for the uniqueness that they are,
ones that appreciate their wild adventures,
ones that embrace their weaknesses and smile.

Find them.
They already await you.
All you have to do
is ask.

Totem Stories from the Tibetan Tektites

Isn't it amazing to have friends that you can talk to on this journey?

We enjoy it and thank you for all of it.

Maybe you don't know everything you give us,

but one day, we'll tell you all

and marvel at the adventures beneath the adventures

that we have had

and continue right on into forever...

We watch you and we watch the earth.

Your hearts are thrust out of your shells,

like a plant bursting out of a seed,

and you reach for your roots, while you stretch out to the stars.

Magnificent splendor.

Wondrous you, wondrous for you-

A time that tests your strength.

You are finding out that you can fly to the moon.

You know how to build anything,

but now you have to go back to the beginning:

How does any of your learning honor where you grew from?

How does it give back?

There at the root, you have to create enough respect to give you strength.

Strength at the root is the only way you will fly farther~

Crystal Pleiadean Pyramid Alignment

"In another dimension and in a reality within a reality that seems dreamlike, beings of the earth have been supported, loved and embraced by their star brethren. The Pleiades (The Seven Sisters) often have provided that service to the children of the earth."

"As builders and appreciators of form, the Pleiadeans have gifted all of us with tools with which we can discover the marvels of ourselves—this collection of gemstones is one of those tools."

- ◆ *Ruby* spreads unlimited life force throughout the body.

- ◆ *Sunstone* integrates awareness through instincts.

- ◆ *Golden Topaz* realigns worries and fears.

- ◆ *Emerald* timelessly shares the heart of the earth.

- ◆ *Blue Tanzanite* unconditionally loves all truth.

- ◆ *Scapulite* gives whispers, tears and laughter from the heavens.

- ◆ *Raw Diamond* sounds the perfection of all forms of life.

- ◆ Optional Essential Oil of *Lotus* creates from the inspiration of all life.

Physical Integration: Uses injuries and sickness to become ever stronger. Helps to produce spontaneous healing.

Emotional Integration: Acknowledges shadow selves and embraces them. Releases the need for limits. Aligns all parts of being.

Millennial Uses: Recently in our history/herstory of humanness, we realized that we may not be alone in the cosmos. If this is true, then incredible, unpredictable learnings may await us.

"Crystal Pleiadean Pyramid Alignment" prepares us for our future, now. It readies us for the unimaginable and teaches us to learn in brand new ways.

Electrical Body Alignment: Connects us to our own power and uses that as a bridge to other lifeforms in the universe.

Affirmation of Support: *"I open myself to unexplored territory to expand my life force and my dreams."*

Tools for Manifestation:
These stones represent crystal pyramids that allow us to align spontaneously to our

own power. Before using them, create a sacred ritual of release. It could be a sweat lodge, or a holy fire. When you feel clear and calm, bring the stones to a quiet place on the earth.

Circle them around you, while you sit very straight.

Sit through the dusk; wait until the night.

When you feel aligned, give thanks to the stars.

Personal Story: This combination is very personal to me. All my life, I have been a builder. My body instinctively knows how to make alternative, sacred structures. Most of the designs just come to me in my dreams. I decided to explore that connection even further and went to a reader who told me that she saw me constructing crystal domes on the Pleiades. She was right.

Years later, after meeting Marilyn, we were listening to our spirits and they explained the crystal domes. It seems that through sound, shape, and intent, they were designed so that when someone walked into them (if they were ready), their chakras would spontaneously align. Then they would be able to access all their infinite capacities immediately. We were advised to co-create the "Crystal Pleidean Pyramid Alignment" through seven stones that would focus the seven chakras. Now we carry the power of that technology with us. It assists us to connect with the deepest parts of our beings and supports us through all the incredible, dramatic earth changes.

~ from Thomas

Totem Stories from the Tibetan Tektites

How do you feed your soul?

By breathing?

Yes.

By smiling?

Yes.

By listening to others?

Yes.

By making friends?

Yes.

By love?

Yes.

By dancing?

Yes.

By watching the sunset?

Yes.

By honoring the earth?

Yes.

By making children?

Yes.

By taking all these moments into your soul and being all of them, every single moment, right now?

Yes.

Death

"Some long for me and some fear me.
Greet me as an equal partner in all your moments
and we soar."

- ♦ *Rainbow Hematite* is instincts and the experience of birth passions.

- ♦ *Ruby* is the power of life and death joined.

- ♦ *Kornerupine* is all emotions equally loved.

- ♦ *Galena* is knowledge released into wisdom.

- ♦ Optional Essential Oils: *Musk* and *Rose* peacefully combine very different experiences.

Physical Integration: Sharpens senses. Increases flexibility. Clears the skin. Tones the excretory system.

Emotional Integration: Reorders priorities. Releases old, unneeded patterns. Deepens the appreciation of simplicity.

Millennial Uses: As we enter the new millennium and search for how to enliven ourselves, we may have to confront our base fear—death. Until we face death and make our peace with it, we will allow all of our choices to be colored by denial. Every denial within us kills off a bit of life force, a piece at a time.

With the "Death" combination of Stones, we may embrace death as we can. It encourages us to familiarize ourselves with change and endings, until we remember that they come naturally with every single season. That realization revitalizes us and brings on the new life that is contained in each death.

Electrical Body Alignment: Links us to our core beliefs and to our immortality.

Affirmation of Support: *"Each day part of me dies and then more of me rebirths itself abundantly and joyfully."*

Tools for Manifestation:
To embrace death requires stillness and silence.
Ease your mind into gentle quiet.
Love yourself for delving into this deep journey.
Caress the above stones often.
No need to analyze or place meaning on them.
Let them touch your heart

and sigh.

Through the next few days, borrow the eyes and ears of death.

Witness.

Watch everything as a moment-to-moment flower.

Expect nothing to stay. Greet each being fully.

Listen to all things and let the words fall into the earth.

Think nothing.

After you have emptied yourself, jump back into life.

Go forth reinvigorated.

Do only the things that expand your spirit.

Be wild and always be new.

Whenever you feel fear, use this exercise to connect you with the earth.

Then recreate your life again.

Personal Story: I really enjoy the "Death" combination. For me, I like to embrace all the hidden, fearful things in life. It's very efficient. Then I don't have to waste a lot of energy in denial and with my energy freed up, I can do and be more of what I want, right now.

I had been wearing a "Death" necklace for many months. It was gorgeous and it got a lot of attention from people. When they asked me what it was, I said, "Death." Needless to say, that made them jump back several feet.

When I showed it to a friend, Lynn, and told her it was "Death," she loved it too. She told me that she had a lot of very intense things leaving her life and was wondering if she could wear it for a day to see what would happen. I didn't even hesitate; I knew that it was supposed to go with her. When Lynn brought it back to me, I almost didn't recognize it. The oil inside the vial had turned black [instead of clear] and the stones looked more bunched together. So I put it back on and offered my thanks to the necklace and sent my support so that it could continue to release any energies that needed to go.

That night when I took off Death, the oil had turned completely clear again. It was utterly amazing. I knew that it was a miracle. The next morning, a few minutes after I put it on again, I saw that it had literally exploded. I had put it in a safe place the previous night, so I knew that what had happened was that those stones had even more feelings to release, so they just blew up. It felt great (even though I had a large, oily stain on my t-shirt and sweatshirt).

To me, this is the gift of "Death." Even though it's not very popular with everyone, it provides its service and it does it freely and unconditionally.

~from Thomas

Totem Stories from the Tibetan Tektites

See yourselves through our smiles.

We feel excited because you perch yourself on the edge of one reality

while moving into a dream.

In the reality, you wept alone and you killed off so much

life inside of you that you killed off much life around you.

Still, part of you kept asking for peace.

It may be hard for peace to grow on such rough ground,

but every time you asked for harmony,

a little piece of you gave up your roughness

in exchange for a seed of compassion.

The seeds give you all possibilities.

All your tears feed the new plants.

Disappointment into Responsibility

*"I look for everyone and everything to save me and to give me my life fulfillment.
Then when it does not work, I am left with myself,*
 the source,
finally ready to claim my life
and to begin living it."

- ◆ *Hematite* is for recognizing our creating of reality now.

- ◆ *Tiger Ore* creates the fire to jump into life and adventure.

- ◆ *Cats-eye* is to see miracles in everyday reality.

- ◆ *Sodalite* is constant affirmations of the unique expansiveness of our own resources.

Physical Integration: Toning and firming of the immune system. Balancing of the sinuses. Clearer thinking and receiving of stimuli.

Emotional Integration: Develops self determination. Releases co-dependency. Appreciates wisdom.

Millennial Uses: As we converge on the 2000's, we assess our achievements and our disappointments. With many situations reaching crisis level, it can be easy to focus on the "should have's". However, to grow, we have to break out of the cycle of shame, so that we can empower ourselves to act.

"Disappointment into Responsibility" insists that we just face all of our actions, right now, immediately. When we claim them, we automatically invite in all of our strengths to change situations, as need be. These stones welcome us to co-creation by supporting us with feelings of acceptance and trust. In that atmosphere, we call forth the miracles inside of ourselves, asking to be born.

Electrical Body Alignment: Connects us to our inadequacies and our capabilities and then joins them to acceptance.

Affirmation of Support: *"I easily accept myself and my life and change it as I wish, when I wish."*

Tools for Manifestation:
Ask each one of these stones (one at a time) to be a part of your life and to open up their hearts and service to you.
Write down Hematite, Tiger Ore, Cats-eye, and Sodalite each, on their own piece of paper.

Once a day meditate quietly and invite one of the stones to visit you.
After the meditation, record anything that occurs to you from that stone.
Once the papers are filled up, file them away.

Only bring them out when you feel disappointed and then drink in their guidance.
(Add to your lists, as you wish).

Disease into Vitality

"I give away my power, my body,
to find my spirit—
intact, free, and immortal."

- ◆ *Red Calcite* clears confusion at the core.

- ◆ *Strawberry Quartz* is the desire to be the unique miracles we already are.

- ◆ *Malachite* is the natural cycles of earth inside and outside of us.

- ◆ *Azurite* is unlimited creativity expressing itself.

Physical Integration: Empowers the body to freely flow with every experience. Allows the innate, constant regeneration of all parts of the body.

Emotional Integration: Presents the opportunity to receive the blessing of every disease, and to grow with it, through it, and then beyond it.

Millennial Uses: As we grow technologically, we replace old, life threatening diseases with new ones. Even with all our achievements and timesaving devices, we have not improved the quality or vigor of life. "Disease into Vitality" asks us to review all of our activities to see how much they contribute to and/or take away from our energy. Then we can face the true "cost" of our choices and eliminate the undue stress that compromises our full vitality.

Electrical Body Alignment: Links us to the natural, continual regeneration of body/ mind/spirit.

Affirmation of Support: *"My body regenerates itself continually and I celebrate with zest and delight."*

Tools for Manifestation:
  Begin a journal just for your body.
  Record anything that happens to it, along with all of the accompanying feelings.
  Let your body speak for itself.
  Appreciate its immediate wisdom.
  Schedule one hour (at least) every week to do something to honor your physicalness.
  Let it be whatever you most need or want and respectfully release any expectations about this.

This practice will align you with the constant renewal that occurs in every cell of your being and welcomes you to affirming life, utterly.

Welcome vitality!

Personal Story: Since the services of the stones expand powerfully in combination, I enjoy wearing multiple combinations at once. Whenever I do this, I always ask the stones which ones want to be worn together with me. One day, I had an "Immortality" necklace on. So I asked it which other necklace would be a good match. It told me, "Disease into Vitality." That made me pause because I just don't get sick. Ever. Did I really need to wear that one? Regardless, I put it on and then I glanced at the quote that comes with the "Disease into Vitality" piece and I knew why it was a good match for me and "Immortality":

"I give away my power, my body,
to find my spirit—
intact, free, and immortal."

~from Marilyn

Earth Light Initiation

"All moments come together now.
Every choice is life and death.
We choose...more!"

- ♦ *Black Tourmaline* is choosing to be present over and over again.

- ♦ *Smoky Quartz* is accepting that we are our perfection now.

- ♦ *Topaz* is the wisdom of the ages flowing through us.

- ♦ *Sapphire* is life's questions and answers breathing in us.

Physical Integration: Strengthens and regenerates bones. Clears the skin. Accelerates the elimination processes.

Emotional Integration: Finds renewal after lengthy challenges. Supports core, respectful beliefs. Honors and expresses truth immediately and fully.

Millennial Uses: This is it! Many prophecies have declared this time as a moment of planetary initiation. We are living it. We are being initiated into an evolution of being that has not been recorded before now.

"Earth Light Initiation" welcomes the challenge; it welcomes all our free choices within it. We may create this timeless time as a great adventure of complete fulfillment.

All these stones together remind us that we are entering unimaginability. Since we can't know what to expect, we free ourselves just to be more of the perfection that we inherently are.

Electrical Body Alignment: Links us to death and rebirth and the source of freedom.

Affirmation of Support: *"I choose to use every challenge as fuel for my freedom and power."*

Tools for Manifestation:
There are many ways to meet an initiation, here are some possibilities:
1. Stop using negative language. Comment on the usefulness of every person and happening.
2. When you feel fearful, write down what you fear. Be eloquent. Burn the paper and delight in your fears flying away with the smoke.
3. Always give thanks for everything. At the end of each day, list all the things for which you give thanks.
4. Support someone else in their difficulties.
5. Laugh often.
6. Laugh some more.

Environmental Toxins

"I respect all beings and all space; therefore, I live in a clear, safe and bountiful world."

- ◆ *Smoky Quartz* encourages us to live all parts of life consciously and gratefully.
- ◆ *Purple Fluorite* empowers us to create sacred space within and around us.
- ◆ *Zeolite* immediately releases the need to be attached to struggle.

Physical Integration: Responds wholistically to all toxins. Activates strength reserves appropriately. Increases body awareness. Sharpens instincts.

Emotional Integration: Strengthens conscious, joyful discrimination. Intensifies experiences and gratefulness. Encourages free, thoughtful choices.

Millennial Uses: We have advanced so quickly that we live in a world of unsafe waste products. "Environmental Toxins" reminds us that no being can thrive in its own garbage. It entreats us to go to the source of our discomfort—a disregard for the earth and for all life.

   This stone combination points out that we must begin again and show respect for all beings, in our every act. Then, polluting our home would be unimaginable.

Electrical Body Alignment: Links us to respect.

Affirmation of Support: *"I honor life in every thought, feeling and act."*

Tools for Manifestation:
   Create an altar, a place of holiness, in your home.
   Lay upon it the most special items you can find.
   Place things there that invoke
   awe,
   wonder,
   amazement,
   contentment,
   renewal,
   hope,
   inspiration.

Let your altar be in your heart every day.

Personal Story: I was very curious about what this stone combination would do. How would I release toxins from my body while wearing these stones?

One day, I put it on and went to work. All day long I was restless. The dogs barked too loud. The phone rang too much and I paced every time I answered it. Then I went home and felt very irritable with Thomas. The next thing I knew I spilled my guts and ended up telling him things that had been on my mind for quite awhile, but hadn't been able to talk about. Wave after wave of emotion ran through me.

By the time I went to bed, I relaxed. I had lived a whole lifetime in one day. Then I remembered the "Environmental Toxins" necklace. For me, I realized that the toxins that I had released were the old thoughts and pent-up feelings that were poisoning me from the inside out. It wasn't what I expected would happen; it was even better.

~ from Marilyn

Personal Story: I, also, was very curious about this vial of stones when I made it. However, I seemed to forget it about it for some reason soon after (even though I constantly looked forward to using it. I know that may seem a contradiction in terms but it clearly expresses they way I felt and also, to me, seems to put words to the kind of "set up" that Spirit has in store for us that we have decided to not be aware of yet- even though we are).

One day during the building of a triple dome/pyramid home we were building for a friend of ours, the time finally came for the plumbers to be on site for the intermediate plumbing installations. I was not really looking forward to the day (although I am not in time) because I knew that my body had the tendency to react strongly to the glues that the plumbers used in their work. There were times in my life when breathing those fumes would, for a short period of time, send me flat on my back for days if not longer. I have since decided that I do not need that type of physical learning any more.

So when the plumbers showed up on the job, I did my best to just breathe normally and let the different smells and forms of life flow through me and back into the earth. It was impossible for me not to be in the direct line of the fumes much of the day and the day after. I found my body experiencing many unpleasant effects and decided that I wanted to take further measures to change my environment to a more nurturing one for my body and spirit. That's when I remembered "Environmental Toxins."

I put the vial on the next day (the plumbers were back also) and decided to just listen to my body all day long (like I usually do) and acknowledge its experience, whatever that may be. A funny thing happened in that I seemed to just forget about the fumes and also about the vial I was wearing, and I had a pleasant, clear workday. Towards the end of the day, it kind of hit me that the fumes were as strong as the last two days, I had a build-up of them in my system, AND I was having a pleasant experience. My hand went to the "Environmental Toxins" vial I was wearing and I knew that spirit had answered my call for assistance in responding in relation with my chosen environment, instead of reacting to it out of fear.

~from Thomas

Faith's Embrace

*"Guardianship is a sacred task. Take my hand and we will learn
beyond fear that each moment, we may choose love."*

- ◆ *Silver* is for the mirrors in life that show us truth.

- ◆ *Moonstone* is for safe passage in every home.

- ◆ *Gold* is to express all feelings immediately.

- ◆ *Aventurine* is for joy, inside and out.

- ◆ Optional Essential Oils: *Jojoba* and *Sage* create clear, safe spaces to be in.

Physical Integration: Supports the thyroid and the metabolism. Increases flexibility.

Emotional Integration: Creates a safe space for all feelings to be released. Continually frees the self from attachments.

Millennial Uses: As we evolve into the future, each person will experience exactly the adversities that ultimately will free and strengthen them, according to their own needs and capabilities. The service of "Faith's Embrace" is that it loves us as we face up to every part of our journey, fully. This frees us to love everything, starting with ourselves. As we feel strong enough, we can share our unconditional love and support with all others. Then we live in a peaceful, enduring world.

Electrical Body Alignment: Connects us with our guardian angels.

Affirmation of Support: *"I am supported, utterly, in all that I am."*

Tools for Manifestation:
For one full day, focus on Silver. Meditate upon it.
Note its presence wherever you go.
Gaze upon it fully.
Appreciate it.
Imagine yourself glittering in Silver.
Absorb it into your being and know its love.

Do the same with Moonstone, then Gold, then Aventurine.

Repeat this until you intimately feel each, single stone being.
Now, you're ready to journey with them into unknown worlds.
Now dedicate one full week to Silver, then Moonstone, then Gold, then Aventurine.

Expand your ways of joining with them.
Welcome the delight that they gift your world.
Go forth in love and support.

Personal Story: I don't have a single-event-story about "Faith's Embrace." I just know that when I first saw it, I loved it. I have worn this combination many times. I have taken it with me on trips, because it helps me to feel secure. When I have been lonely, I put it on and my heart fills with a calming silence that helps me to celebrate solitude. I know that when I wear "Faith's Embrace," I am connected to others in a gentle, respectful way.

~from Marilyn

Fear into Love

*"Go through your fears and
you arrive at the natural state of life—
love."*

- *Brookite* connects our breaths with all consciousness and life force.

- *Kornerupine* initiates us fully into life upon the earth.

- *Neon Blue Apatite* regenerates our bodies through the soul's bliss.

- *Danburite* allows all energies to pass through us, presenting us only with what we need.

Physical Integration: Gently adjusts bone misalignments. Increases the body's sensitivity to physical stimuli. Increases all parts of the body's abilities to communicate and to record its senses.

Emotional Integration: Clears the mind and heart. Focuses on love. Embraces fear as a teaching.

Millennial Uses: To enter the future ultimately represents each individual's story of evolvement and self-actualization. This array of stones brings us right to our core and to the base of all our dysfunctions — fear. When we embrace fear as intimately as we do any other feeling, then we ARE unconditional love. Then we automatically free ourselves from all fears. Then we operate from and with love in all things.

"Fear into Love" brings us into the future, now.

Electrical Body Alignment: Connects us to our powers of transmutation and co-creatorship.

Affirmation of Support: *"I embrace all my fears as they bring me more fully into life and love, now."*

Tools for Manifestation:
When you experience fear, stop (whenever feasible).
Breathe very deeply.
Open up the body.
Widen the eyes.
Float in the sensation.
Connect all the breaths in a circle;
at the end of each exhale, inhale without pause.
Chant "Fear into Love" repeatedly.
Witness the miracles.

Focused Grounding

"Rush into life
and find yourself breathful!"

- ♦ *Hematite* reminds us that our bodies are continual miracles.

- ♦ *Pyrite* celebrates the passionate drama of human existence.

- ♦ *Herkimer Diamond* allows us to see ourselves and to witness delight.

Physical Integration: Tones the entire body. Exercises the laugh muscles.

Emotional Integration: Gives focus and organizations to thoughts and feelings. Easily establishes priorities. Continually releases habits, to make way for new possibilities.

Millennial Uses: When we live in the present moment, all other moments present themselves within now.

Electrical Body Alignment: Links us to our moment of birth.

Affirmation of Support: *"I am here now. I choose to be here now and I fully choose all that I am doing and being."*

Tools for Manifestation:
Sound is a vibration that immediately transforms its environment.
To honor the energy of Hematite, chant "EEE," then "AAH," then "EYE."
To honor the energy of Pyrite, chant "EYE," repeatedly.
To honor the energy of Herkimer Diamond, chant "EYE," then "AAH."

Create your life with focused grounding.

Freedom

"I visit you in every breath.
I live in every experience.
My heart beats within all of your choices.
You touch me whenever you reach your hand
through the unknown and recognize
yourself."

- ◆ *Silica* is the unbelievable lightness of being.

- ◆ *Green Malachite* is the acceptance, the welcoming, and the living of all experiences.

- ◆ *Zoisite* is joining into the co-creation of the universe consciously.

- ◆ *Aventurine* is a single point of knowingness scattered in all directions.

- ◆ Optional Essential Oils: *Rosemary* and *Clary* cleanse the senses and perceptions.

Physical Integration: Sharpens the senses. Increases balance, strength and flexibility. Releases aging.

Emotional Integration: Changes habits and ingrained patterns. Promotes curiosity and generosity.

Millennial Uses: Many structures and governments seem to be breaking down, signaling wide-sweeping changes. Lots of change joins us with the core of our existence—freedom. Freedom means constant, continual change. This calls forth the unknown and maybe there is no predictable means of nurturing ourselves in that process. All we can do is to align with freedom and choose our decisions, moment-to-moment...which may be its own best reward.

Electrical Body Alignment: Links us to free will on every level.

Affirmation of Support: *"I celebrate my complete freedom."*

Tools for Manifestation:
Affirm "I am Freedom, rooting into the earth, while stretching to the stars."
Stand with your feet widely spread and firmly on the ground.
Dig in your toes and feel yourself rooted fully into the earth.
Bend over and touch your hands to the ground.
Inhale the luxury of being close to the earth.

Slowly, raise your arms and your eyes to the sky.
Stretch above, root below, and breathe in the middle.

You have granted yourself freedom.

Gabriel's Dawn

"I settle into your being.
I nest myself deep inside of you,
as much as you like.
And then, when I expand, I bring forth the joy of all things united in birth.
Every cell in you awakens to a fresh day, but it is not only a day,
it is forever.
I enter and we join
in your breath and bliss."

♦ *Russian Phenacite* is the focus through which our joy springs.

♦ *Moldavite* is the inclusion of the universe, heartily.

♦ *Herkimer Diamond* is the magic of childlike vision.

♦ *Kornerupine* loves it all, for the joy of it.

Physical Integration: Increases the flexibility of the limbs. Softens the spine. Decreases tight, unnatural postures.

Emotional Integration: Strengthens the desire to leap into the unknown. Heightens creativity. Fosters trust.

Millennial Uses: "Gabriel's Dawn" is dedicated to the archangel, Gabriel. All traditions and times of the earth have honored the spirits that have protected, guided and loved us. In emergencies, we have turned to these beings, intensely and hopefully. "Gabriel's Dawn" awakens the qualities of the angels that live within us. To call upon them is to integrate our highest hopes into our realities.

Electrical Body Alignment: Links us to cellular memories and awakening.

Affirmation of Support: *"I awaken to all of life and I glow with its enchantment."*

Tools for Manifestation:
At the end of the day, light a fire.
Enjoy its flames.
Revel in the warmth.
As the smoke arises, see everything that happened today, flying away.
Let all thoughts and concerns soar away. (Name them if you wish and bid them good-bye).
Once you feel empty, sigh deeply and proclaim,

263

"I release everything into the night, so I can awaken all of myself in the next day."

Now you are Gabriel's Dawn.

Personal Story: We're moment-to-moment kind of people, so we don't often have special memories. However, for some reason, we do remember the very first stone combination that we ever co-created, "Gabriel's Dawn." We were listening to the stones and they just formed this union. It came to us very easily and we wrote it down, knowing that it was very powerful.

"Gabriel's Dawn" became the first *Vibrational Jewelry* piece ever to come out of our hands, and it was perfect (still is).

~ from Twintreess

Personal Story: My experience with Twintreess jewelry and stone combinations began with a visit to a small store devoted to angels. As someone who never wore jewelry, I have rarely looked inside a jewelry case until this day. I felt literally pulled to the case where I saw a green vial called "Gabriel's Dawn." There were others in the collection, but my eyes were only drawn to this one piece. Holding the vial and reading its message, I knew the necklace would be going home with me.

Now I am the proud owner of 26 vials. I wear a different necklace every day, asking for the support I need in that moment. The vials assist me in my meditation, my hands-on healing, and in my dreamtime (under my pillow).

These stones are a gift from Mother Earth, their alchemy supporting human growth and evolution. Wearing them reminds me of the potential for miracles——the hope, joy and magic that I wish to manifest in my everyday life.

~from MaryAnn Graziano

Guilt into Perfection

"I watch my actions — the core of my life, and separate myself from them in shame, until I can choose my innate perfection."

- ♦ *Mica* is observing all things to witness miracles.
- ♦ *Moonstone* is total empathy for all emotions and dreams.
- ♦ *Rhodonite* is the commitment to choosing unconditional love while on earth.
- ♦ *Phenacite* is reveling in the present, here and now.

Physical Integration: Deepens breathing. Invigorates the appetite. Eases chronic conditions.

Emotional Integration: Relaxes moods. Releases the need for addictions.

Millennial Uses: In the 20th century, we have aspired greatly to recording achievements and failures in a linear, scientific fashion. In the 21st century, "Guilt into Perfection" persuades us to reconsider our parameters. All that we are cannot be measured in data. We are whole, unlimited beings. As we embrace that, we find new respect for the earth and all ways of life. We release disease (the lack of unity in body/mind/spirit) and explode with new power.

Electrical Body Alignment: Links us to our inexplicable perfection.

Affirmation of Support: *"I think perfectly, I feel perfectly, I live perfectly."*

Tools for Manifestation:

If you have the above stones, lay them in front of you.
Close your eyes. Hold Mica to your body (or hold its name to your body). Imagine glitter falling all around you. Let all worries escape with the glitter.

Hold Moonstone to your body (or hold its name to your body). Imagine a full woman-in-the-moon smiling on you. As her face grows closer and closer to yours, tell her all your pains, which burn away in the brightness of her beams.

Hold Rhodonite to your body (or hold its name to your body). Imagine lots of gorgeous valentines landing next to you. See your name on all of them. Know you are very well loved.

Hold Phenacite to your heart (or hold its name to your heart). Imagine it gently entering your heart. It's smoothing the wrinkles. See the glitter, the moon and the valentines all there with the Phenacite. Accept all the feelings.

Celebrate your incredible, audacious capacity to be human and to feel every single possibility.

Hope's Call

"I call like a long silver trumpet,
overpowering to some—
whispers to others.
However loudly you wish it,
I proclaim your presence to all of the world."

- ♦ *Pyrite* is to get your attention and full wakefulness.

- ♦ *Rubellite* is for the immortality of beauty.

- ♦ *Rhodochrosite* is because a heart must change constantly.

- ♦ *Lepidolite* is because you have arrived.

Physical Integration: Supports the heart. Quickens movement without risk of injury.

Emotional Integration: Learns from all movements and habits that beauty is also a cycle of life. Celebrates all your being!

Millennial Uses: In some ways, the human race has seemed like the curse of the 20th century. All earth's beings adapt to her seasons, except for humans. Before we can transform that reality, we must acknowledge it as it is. We must declare all that we have been on the planet and all that we do upon it right now.

Then "Hope's Call" steps in and welcomes people to the earth. It declares the miracle of humankind. All life forms are incredible, just by being.

"Hope's Call" reminds us of this, over and over again, loudly, delightedly.

Electrical Body Alignment: Connects us to the center of Being.

Affirmation of Support: *"I declare myself as a miracle!"*

Tools for Manifestation:
Find some things that have brought you great joy.
Give them away!
You're making room in your heart for new magic.

Your heart is new magic.

Impatience into Presence

"I listen to all the voices that are asking to be expressed.
I care for them all.
I care enough to find the roads to their expression."

- ◆ *Chrysocolla* is the road to the earth, where all comes from, in blessing.

- ◆ *Tourmalated Quartz* is the insistence on giving voice to every feeling without judgment.

- ◆ *Watermelon Tourmaline* is opening the heart to all life, joyously, intentionally.

- ◆ *Lepidolite with Rubellite Inclusions* is the realization and welcoming of your perfect path in the world.

Physical Integration: The reordering of the senses and tactile memories. Nurtures the thyroid and the pituitary.

Emotional Integration: Creates new mind structures with acceptance. Releases phobias. Channels creativity with joy.

Millennial Uses: We continually and exponentially increase the amount of measurable data available on the planet, which works well with our minds, but not so well with our emotions. Everything accelerates around us, which makes us feel like we must keep pace, regardless of our feelings. "Impatience into Presence" allows us to be us, transmuting our dysfunction into function. We come alive in all moments.

Electrical Body Alignment: Connects us with timelessness.

Affirmation of Support: *"I live in the Now."*

Tools for Manifestation:
Give up the word, "should," completely, right now.
Throw yourself a party to celebrate your freedom.

Immortality

"I am the central sun arising within you.
Each time I set, I beam forth more life.
We sweep each other into a song of conscious acceptance and commitment:
We remember all life, now, and it rejoices in us!"

- *Fluorite* is the instant cleansing and release of all karma.

- *Tourmalated Quartz* is complete acceptance of the earth and of your body upon it.

- *Phenacite* is the stillness of a single point of being.

- *Selenite* is the echo of love in all life.

- Optional Essential Oils: *Rose* and *Bergamot* celebrate joy and beauty.

Physical Integration: Tones the nervous system. Aligns body/mind/heart/spirit.

Emotional Integration: Understands and realizes perfection. Releases scattering of energy.

Millennial Uses: All our beliefs are learned expectations and behaviors. As we evolve to our full actualization, everything that we have been taught may not apply. Maybe we will exist beyond known parameters. "Immortality" demands that we reassess everything that comprises our beings: Evaluate even the strongest realities — challenge them. Live beyond them.

By our nature, we are immortal beings. Try that one on.

Electrical Body Alignment: Links us to truth and universal reality.

Affirmation of Support: *"I love the unlimitedness of life."*

Tools for Manifestation:
Place a piece of Fluorite on your lower abdomen.
Place a piece of Tourmalated Quartz on your diaphragm.
Place a piece of Phenacite on your heart.
Place a piece of Selenite on your forehead.
Review all the beliefs that you have ever held. Let the feeling of them flow through your body and drift away. You are in your freedom. With great intent, create an affirmation that honors the core of your life.

In Honor of the White Buffalo

"At the end of all fear, there is change.
At the end of all change,
is fearless regeneration."

- *White Moldavite* fills in the holes of experience with whole nurturance.

- *Raw Yellow Diamond* instills courage to go through every experience until all that is left is truth.

- *Copper* adds instantaneous alchemy!

Physical Integration: Sharpens the senses. Supports the joints, particularly the knees. Enhances memory.

Emotional Integration: Creates new senses and new ways of being for a new earth. Increases compassion. Delights in all the seasons of the earth.

Millennial Uses: According to some of the ancient prophecies, we live in apocalyptic times. Within those prophecies lie the promise of forewarnings and assistance (before the crises arrive). The birth of the White Buffalo calf (a few years ago in Wisconsin) is one of the signs of assistance and transformation.

"In Honor of the White Buffalo" accepts the signs, the transitions and our own empowerment within that. We can look for catastrophes and/or we can look for the divine help that arrives, simultaneously. These stones remind us to welcome all of our support, with gratitude. That welcoming gratitude opens the doors to new possibilities and correspondingly, changes the prophecies. As it has been said, "The job of a good prophecy is to alert everyone (in advance) so that it doesn't come true."

Electrical Body Alignment: Links us to focusing intuition enough to be used in practical realities.

Affirmation of Support: *"I honor all my guides and support and send my unlimited support to the earth and all its beings."*

Tools for Manifestation:
Begin the day calmly.
If you continue to feel tension, meditate until you find your own unswerving peace.
As you wish, surround yourself with a glorious, white light.
For the rest of the day, notice all the signs of new life (children, puppies, plant seeds, etc).
and each time you note them, give thanks.

You align with Miracle, the White Buffalo, in peaceful joy.

Personal Story: With the stone combination, "Intent," I wear "In Honor of the White Buffalo." When I wear both I "see" so clearly. I see what others are doing and where they are going and I am also seeing myself more clearly. I am doing what is needed to put myself and others in place for the change that is to come. I have in the past felt strongly for the Native traditions and now it seems to be magnified. I feel connected beyond this realm (time & space) when I wear both these stone combinations.

~from Jeanice Braun

Infinite Intimacy
Partners in Life
(the Male version)

"Through you I know the infinity of intimacy with all life."

- *Gold* spreads the warmth of passion and all encompassing life force.

- *Ruby* encourages blissful risks into adventure.

- *Citrine* aligns creativity and the recording of knowledge and learning for all.

- Essential Oil of *Myrrh* embraces life force, for its own sake.

Physical Integration: Expands circulation. Increases aerobic capacity.

Emotional Integration: Combines creativity, passion, and discovers how to use them. Stimulates spontaneity.

Millennial Uses: In order to create world peace, we must begin with individual inner peace. Then we extend it outward to our most intimate partners; from there we learn to co-create a harmonious global community. "Infinite Intimacy" increases our open-heartedness and our opportunities to risk loneliness for a deep, unending connection to loved ones and then, to all.

The Male version of "Infinite Intimacy" specifically supports honest, immediate communication and expression.

Joint Electrical Body Alignment: Integrates the body, mind and heart into a spiritual dance that honors the uniqueness and interconnectedness of life and of the passion for life.

Affirmation of Support: *"I love all parts of myself; therefore I love all."*

Tools for Manifestation:
In every life we meet at least one other person that helps us touch the depths of ourselves and the greatest feelings of life. When you meet that perfect mirror of self, put your heart and this necklace into their hand and smile, saying, "Through you, I know the infinity of intimacy with all life."

Personal Story: When the "Infinite Intimacy" necklaces were created, I got very excited. I felt them asking me to wear a female version, Thomas a male version, and then we could exchange them and wear each other's.

So I wore the female "Infinite Intimacy." My lucid dreamtime increased. I felt in tune with the seasons, particularly the full moon. Overall, I felt more sensitive and regenerated and it was absolutely wonderful.

Next I wore the male version. Every day, I found more energy and more drive. I got more work done and I felt calm, instead of overloaded. Then I started playing with various combinations, according to whatever my body and the stones wanted to do each day. Sometimes I wore two male necklaces; sometimes I wore two females, or any combination thereof.

They all felt great. I experienced more of myself and my hidden strengths and I knew how to use them. In short, I felt empowered. I had become intimate with myself and I knew all sorts of possibilities rested within that. About this time, I realized I didn't need to exchange my necklaces with anyone (although I look forward to that, too). These stones helped me to be my own partner in life and I feel very grateful.

~from Marilyn

Infinite Intimacy
Partners in Life
(the Female version)

"Through you I know the infinity of intimacy with all life."

- *Silver* generously accepts all things.
- *Emerald* follows the heart in all moments.
- *Blue Tanzanite* sees and speaks the truth freely and completely.
- Essential Oil of *Peony* adds grace and enlightenment.

Physical Integration: Supports the endocrine system. Protects the breasts. Maintains a health urinary tract.

Emotional Integration: Moves the emotions past stagnation into freedom. Aligns all the senses with the heart.

Millennial Uses: In order to create world peace, we must begin with individual inner peace. Then we can extend it outward to our most intimate partners; from there we learn to co-create a harmonious global community. "Infinite Intimacy" increases our open heartedness and our opportunities to risk loneliness for a deep, unending connection to loved ones and then, to all.

The female version of "Infinite Intimacy" instigates nourishing communication and regenerative actions.

Joint Electrical Body Alignment: Integrates body, mind and heart into a spiritual dance that honors the uniqueness and interconnectedness of life and of the passion for life.

Affirmation of Support: *"I love all part of myself; therefore I love all."*

Tools for Manifestation:
In every life we meet at least one other person that helps us touch the depths of ourselves and the greatest feelings of life. When you meet that perfect mirror of self, put your heart and this necklace into their hand and smile, saying, "Through you, I know the infinity of intimacy with all life."

Intent

"I am the source of magic in your body.
We are free beings
and we choose who and what we are
with each breath.
I come to you, clearly, consciously, and ask,
'What are you choosing?'"

- *Galena* is the acknowledged voice of body/mind/spirit.

- *Zeolite* is the bridge between intent and acting upon it in the world.

- *Brookite* is the determination of all your commitment from all of your lives and guides.

- *Kunzite* is the remembrance that you are made of love and in love, always.

Physical Integration: Balances eating and sleeping patterns. Increases ability to access immediate energy.

Emotional Integration: Automatically, continually, releases the need for distractions and addictions. Spontaneously expresses feelings. Attracts support for clear priorities.

Millennial Uses: In times of great challenges, the resources we finally have to meet these obstacles are our personal strengths: freedom, love, trust, generosity, etc. Intent is the bridge between these core powers and our actions.

"Intent" calls us into action that is motivated clearly, timelessly, and respectfully. It focuses on the underlying intention of all decisions. In that core place, we may enact and/ or change anything quickly to meet the needs of our truth.

Electrical Body Alignment: Links us to full and free responsibility.

Affirmation of Support: *"I intentionally express my truth."*

Tools for Manifestation:
On slips of paper, write the most basic intents you have for your own life.
With respect, place the paper slips under some Galena, Zeolite, Brookite, Kunzite. Leave them there.
Visualize that the stones are anchoring your intents into a powerful, loving reality.

When you feel especially troubled, pick up one of the rocks and carry that intent with you for a day.

Place the corresponding rock next to you while you sleep.
Now you have further integrated your intent with your conscious and unconscious selves.

Judgment into Trust

"I seek to make myself perfect by finding imperfection in everything else,
until I am in a harsh, unforgiving world.
With only my judgments for love,
I must reach out for a new, unconditional world
where I, and everyone else, belong."

- *Smoky Quartz* is embracing all qualities of life as another quality of love.

- *Bloodstone* is courage to go into the heart and to follow it completely.

- *Selenite* is acceptance of the depth and uniqueness of all life forms.

- *Apophyllite* is laughter from the heart to celebrate it all.

Physical Integration: Eases the joints/bones. Tones the digestive system. Strengthens the liver. Releases body smells.

Emotional Integration: Challenges old defenses and offers nurturance in the process.

Millennial Uses: In the 20th century, we have advanced our technologies tremendously and, almost exclusively, it has been through our mental capabilities. In the process, we often disassociate from our emotional sides, thereby increasing our linear, dispassionate abilities to disassociate from others in destructive ways.

"Judgment into Trust" traces the separation between our heads and our hearts. Once this is acknowledged, it embraces all our processes and all our being. Whenever we are fully loved in any area, it gives us the support to integrate everything within us. That leaves us free to develop trust.

Trust reaches into unknown innocence and creates a connected, nurturing world.

Electrical Body Alignment: Links us to our original innocence.

Affirmation of Support: *"I let go of judgment and find my world unconditionally loving."*

Tools for Manifestation:
Take a day and go play with children.
Be spontaneous.
Be free.
Exhilarate yourself.
Let them show you the ways to follow your heart moment-to-moment.

Lack into Allowability

"I see the world around me,
it holds me in,
the corners restrict me...
and I am learning to see the nurturance of that embrace, as well."

- *Kornerupine* is opening your core to the core of all.

- *Aventurine* is embracing the adventure of a body, mind and spirit.

- *Green Topaz* is all knowingness entering your being consciously.

- *Green Apophyllite* is union with all divinity and spirit guides.

Physical Integration: Increases bodily sensations. Loosens rigid postures. Releases the need for chronic conditions.

Emotional Integration: Fosters generosity. Releases painful self restrictions. Embraces love.

Millennial Uses: In this transitional time, we have had difficulty imagining the full bounty of the earth. That doesn't make the earth less full or less plentiful. "Lack into Allowability" embraces all of our qualities, including the miserly ones. Even in our moments of difficulty, if we would accept the abundance around us, we could feel adequate to every situation. Then we could help produce enough for everyone and, always, enough to share.

Electrical Body Alignment: Connects us to the unlimitedness of the earth.

Affirmation of Support: *"I live in prosperity and I am surrounded by prosperity, constantly."*

Tools for Manifestation:
Meditate upon Kornerupine.
Ask it for guidance to opening your heart.
When you receive the answer, act upon it with love.

Meditate upon Aventurine.
Ask it for guidance to living with great verve and excitement.
When you receive the answer, act upon it daily.

Meditate upon Green Topaz.
Ask it for guidance to gaining wisdom.

When you receive the answer, share it with others.

Meditate upon Green Apophyllite.
Ask it for guidance to see and to hear divine messengers.
When you receive the answer, carry it in your heart.

Listening

"All the voices of all life, enter me now
because I am ever love.
It is all there is, and then in willingness,
I hear more."

- ♦ *Aquamarine* is the whisper of spirit transformed into interdimensional presence.

- ♦ *Selenite* is the delicate strength of joyful surrender.

- ♦ *Phenacite* is the explorer's adventure, the certainty of the unknown.

- ♦ *Lepidolite* is the freedom of simply being.

Physical Integration: Encourages easier release through the sinuses. Sharpens hearing and smell. Regenerates the feet.

Emotional Integration: Appreciates stillness. Develops an affinity for nature and its rhythms. Honors the ups and downs of life.

Millennial Uses: "Listening" teaches us listening as an artform: True listening links physical hearing with the heart and following its wisdom. True listening nurtures spontaneity, trust and unconditional acceptance. It allows us to approach any situation, like a child, empty of expectations and completely ready to learn anything.

"Listening" lets us know that listening is a chosen way of life that gives everything we ever imagined.

Electrical Body Alignment: Connects hearing to the heart, to respect.

Affirmation of Support: "I listen."

Tools for Manifestation:
Meditate upon the following quotation,
"In the beginner's mind there are many possibilities; in the expert's mind there are few...
This is the real secret of the arts: Always be a beginner."
~S. Suzuki

Mary's Wonder

"Heaven is a dream planted in an earth garden.
When you pass through the doorway,
you see what you have imagined
and all is real."

- ◆ *Zebra Jasper* is seeing the extremes of life expression and accepting them.

- ◆ *Snowflake Obsidian* is the challenge of growth.

- ◆ *Herkimer Diamond* is the clarity that recognizes truth.

- ◆ *Rainbow Hematite* is all of your energy resources activated spontaneously.

Physical Integration: Integrates the hemispheres of the brain. Offers support for the spine and the chakras. Finds postures that open the body/mind/spirit.

Emotional Integration: Encourages childlike awe. Nurtures innocence. Expresses spontaneously.

Millennial Uses: To enter a new millennium, wholly and happily, maybe we have to be simply timeless. The truths that always serve us are timeless. "Mary's Wonder" teaches us to be children over and over again. And in that innocence we continually regain our purity.

Electrical Body Alignment: Links us to our innocence.

Affirmation of Support: *"I live in my truth and marvel at the harmony of the world."*

Tools for Manifestation:
Do everything you can to remember yourself as a child.
Bring out old pictures and souvenirs.
Then plan a day where you choose to be a child (in a respectful manner).
Play at everything.
Fill yourself with so much awe that it spills over into many, many days.

New Earth Harmony

"We stones come from the earth
at the exact moment
to support you,
to hold you close to the earth cycles.
Come feel free and loved in our embrace."

- ♦ *Purple Sapphire* is the base for creating a new reality on every level.

- ♦ *Labradorite* is the absolute knowing that you are supported by life, always.

- ♦ Optional Essential Oil: *Jojoba* is for honoring the extremes of every experience and challenge, with bliss.

Physical Integration: Expands the union of the heart and the brain. Activates the cellular knowledge and instincts that allow us to be more a part of life in every way.

Emotional Integration: Acknowledges our areas of denial and shadow. Inspires us to love and feel loved. Connects us to the earth.

Millennial Uses: How do we peacefully, happily, join with the future? That answer may rest in our ability to intuit and then to envision our potential. Both the future and our core capabilities come to our daily realities as mysteries—stories that walk in the distance, beyond our complete understanding, until we journey wisely enough to stand beside them as equals. Until then, what will we do?

In other times, we have relied upon shamans and visionaries to paint us a picture, something we can direct our energies toward, something tangible in an intangible world. In tribal communities, those shamans and visionaries used many tools to listen to the earth (the source of sustenance for our bodies) for signs of what would be. With their talents and honed attention, they discovered something powerful: All beings upon the earth have consciousness. Each consciousness unfolds a beautiful, utterly unique, earthstory. All the stories intertwine, creating life. We co-create the seasons through joining our distinctive essences with all beings, harmoniously.

Therefore, the cycles of time (life) are us. To know the upcoming seasons, we must align ourselves, respectfully, intentionally, constantly, with our core selves and with all of nature. If we lose our direction, we can listen to the story of another. We can see all possibilities in the path of the winds, or in the shriek of a crow, or an eclipse of the moon, or in the patient forming of a crystal.

"New Earth Harmony" whispers to us of all these truths, therefore it supports us, as a piece/peace of life, to choose our perfect place in ourselves, and then in all times and spaces. These stones have united their cores to show us the direction to aligning with our basic, loving nature and with the total abundance of the earth and of life. They present themselves as a shamanic tool for any who have forgotten themselves and their life-given power to join with all seasons, now.

Electrical Body Alignment: Links us to the life force in all beings.

Affirmation of Support: *"I align my perfection with all of life to co-create the new earth harmony, now."*

Tools for Manifestation:
Carry Purple Sapphire in your heart.
Let it rest there, sharing its glorious consciousness, freely.
Accept it.
Accept it as an earth brother or sister that chooses to co-create a new season of harmony with you, happily and perfectly.
Allow its gifts of excitement, creativity, newness
to replenish you, as needed.
Hone your shamanic attention and trust that the sageness of this stone fulfills you now (and later) according to the grand scheme of life.
Give thanks for the bounty of the earth and all its children.

Carry Labradorite with you in your heart.
Walk with it silently so that you can hear its love.
Nourish yourself with it.
Regenerate so completely that you beam as a source of inspiration.
Share that story with others.
When some do not listen, love them as they find their **own** direction.
Walk on in gratitude and in the completeness of a being who is led by the peace of the earth.

Welcome to the new earth harmony~

Open Heart

"I listen in the silence, I watch in the dark.
I record with the voice, I breathe with spirit.
In all of this,
I find everything
and if there are questions,
I will be the answer."

- *Mustard Seed* is faith in self and all reflections of self, in the world.

- *Danburite* is the breath of all life forms, crystallized in a sigh.

- *Apophyllite* is the star family that is present always on the earth.

- *Moonstone* is facing your emotions and creating the wonder in life.

- Optional Essential Oils: *Peony* and *Lotus* encourage grace, beauty and enlightenment.

Physical Integration: Eases and deepens breaths. Balances appetites and desires.

Emotional Integration: Calms, soothes, nurtures. Develops healthy, joyous freedom. Maintains inner peace.

Millennial Uses: As we embark on a new millennium, the earth also changes and grows and as a conscious being, chooses how that change will appear. We (Twintreess) feel that she has and is expanding her heart. With her unlimited consciousness, she grows so that there is unconditional space for all beings upon her to choose their own direction and how they will share that with the whole.

"Open Heart" offers itself as a gift of the earth (and of her blossoming heart) to us. If we fear the future, we can hold these stones close to us and they will brace our hearts in any storm or season. They teach us that the storms (like fear) clear away the old brush and debris (distractions) in the woods (humans, as a mass consciousness). All parts of weather grow something—some thing that needs to stand in its ideal place and time in order to complete the great purpose of spirit.

Each being in "Open Heart" shares the story of how the earth elements exquisitely formed them. If we choose to open our hearts, we will know how we were formed and how we can continue to transform ourselves with the earth's blessings.

Electrical Body Alignment: Connects us to the feelings of beings and the heart of life.

Affirmation of Support: *"I open my heart and all feelings come to me as love."*

Tools for Manifestation:

There are as many ways to open an heart, as there are lifeforms (even more). Accept this list as a gift of our open hearts, which means that it is offered freely. Change the list to suit you to your own singular ways and seasons:

1. Surround yourself with loving, supportive people.

2. Be a sacred witness to every part of your life. Just observe yourself and all your feelings in each and every moment. Ask yourself to allow learning and possibilities in all of your emotions.

3. Whenever you feel something, celebrate it. Give thanks! Repeat the *Affirmation of Support.* Know that you are fulfilling the human potential of your being.

4. Send love letters. Include yourself.

5. Run around a beautiful park and get your heart pumping.

6. Put mustard on your food to energize it (and your body) with faith.

7. Place a glass of water in sunlight. Lay a Danburite next to or in the glass. Drink it slowly, absorbing all the minerals and elements and earth elementals.

8. Lay down in a soft meadow at dusk. Place a small Apophyllite in the center of your forehead. Witness the sunset giving way to the moon and the stars. Feel surrounded by family.

9. Put a Moonstone on your person. Take a short vacation. Let it guide you.

10. Make a very complete list of everything you have ever dreamed of doing. Be wild in your imaginings. Paint pictures on the list. Add photos, glitter, feathers to it. Love it and admire it utterly.

11. In a sacred manner, burn the list and set its spirit (and you) free to create any magic possible, or impossible.

We support you~

Pain into Fulfillment

"No matter what I do, I am not satisfied with myself,
I crowd my world with distractions to hide my discomforts,
until it builds into undeniable pain.
There, I can face myself, without other distractions,
and choose to accept who I am,
as I am,
now,
and always."

- ◆ *Snowflake Obsidian* is grounded trust in reality and dreams.
- ◆ *Chrysocolla* is unconditional acceptance and daily support.
- ◆ *Blue Lace Agate* is new, calm thoughts and affirmations.
- ◆ *Kunzite* is seeing the face of love in every experience.

Physical Integration: Regenerates the body by night and revitalizes its energy by day.

Emotional Integration: Discovers and honors life's purpose. Feels and then speaks and acts with loving acceptance.

Millennial Uses: Pain signals us that something is out of place. If we feel pain, then maybe we are out of sync with our truth. "Pain into Fulfillment" guides us right on through the hurt. The journey through it can reduce us to our essence; it realigns us.

These stones ground us in our bodies, so we cannot live in denial. Then they assist us by helping us to breathe fully into the pain (of any feared change) that will birth us as free, aligned beings.

Electrical Body Alignment: Links us to our divine place as co-creators.

Affirmation of Support: *"When I feel pain, I loosen my body. I breathe and set myself free to receive it as love."*

Tools for Manifestation:
Go to someone in pain.
Offer just to be with them and to support them, respectfully.

At the end of the day, find a stone that has offered to release the hurt.
Bury it in the earth.

Breathe freely.
Breathe deeply.
Breathe clearly.
Breathe love.

Perfect Weight

*"I embrace my perfect weight
and live in a glorious, free body
that fills my needs
and my desires."*

- *Apache Tear* embraces the shadow side and releases the need to be attached to it in any form.

- *Rutilated Quartz* integrates aligned healthy communication between head, heart, body and spirit.

- *Copper* adds unexpected, immediate, alchemical magic.

- *Rose Quartz* exemplifies the grace and beauty in every body just as it is right now.

Physical Integration: Balances the metabolism and the fat/muscle ratio. Increases suppleness of the skin. Enhances digestion. Improves absorption of vitamins and minerals.

Emotional Integration: Asserts happy individuality. Finds and appreciates the beauty in all forms. Lets go of unnecessary control and defensiveness. Flows with the rhythms of life.

Millennial Uses: During the 20th century, some cultures separated themselves from the earth. Sometimes this shows itself as growing dissatisfaction with our bodies ("I don't feel comfortable in my skin.") and leads to an inability to meet our needs and wishes. Sometimes we respond further by feeding ourselves according to this distorted sense of our desires.

"Perfect Weight" asks us to respect ourselves, right now, without hesitation. The way to balance is through the center path, where we do not value ourselves just according to our shapes. Embrace "Perfect Weight" and we can express unconditional love for life and fuel ourselves with great sacredness. Then our bodies will reflect that honoring. With comfort in our bodies, we will find it even easier to love and we then create an enduring cycle of respect with life.

Electrical Body Alignment: Links us to the perfect, immortal, genetic blueprint of life.

Affirmation of Support: *"I honor my body in everything I am and everything that I do. I love its beauty."*

Tools for Manifestation:

Every night for a week (at least), lay a soft Rose Quartz next to your pillow.
Just before falling to sleep, hug yourself.
Embrace your wonderful curves.
Touch the Rose Quartz and declare,
"I go to sleep in beauty and I awake in even more beauty."

Change the declaration to anything that inspires you, just keep it the same each night.
At the end of the week, you will find that your body responds to the loving suggestion.
It will transform.
You will release inner blocks to receiving the magnificence of you and the splendor of the gift of life.

Repeat this exercise for as many weeks as you wish.

Pregnancy

"I accept the natural creativity and power
that flows through me
with utter vitality,
now."

- ◆ *Realgar* is to go beyond the fear of life and death and to embrace it.

- ◆ *Sunstone* is for supporting the vitality of all the organs working harmoniously.

- ◆ *Golden Topaz* is for assistance with directly communicating with the body/mind.

- ◆ *Bloodstone* is to honor the strength of the heart physically/emotionally/ spiritually.

- ◆ *Turquoise* is to create free choices without regret.

- ◆ *Iolite* is to see the path and to act upon it.

- ◆ *Purple Fluorite* is to release unnecessary inner and outer influences.

- ◆ Optional Essential Oil: *Myrrh* honors creativity in all its forms.

Physical Integration: Restores and regenerates the energy centers of the body. Integrates body/mind/heart for unified action and manifestation.

Emotional Integration: Focuses on the acceptance of the body as it is and affirms its natural powers and miracles.

Millennial Uses: It has been prophesied that in times of great stress, we would experience infertility. With "Pregnancy," we learn that when we have moments of such disconnection with the earth, we fear the future. We fear bringing children into the world.

Fear alerts us to our misconceptions about life. It shows us how to connect beyond ourselves, to the greater cycles of life. "Pregnancy" relaxes us enough so that we slip seamlessly back into rhythm. Then we embrace all moments of life. The unknown and the unexpected offers itself as an adventure and a partnership with love.

Electrical Body Alignment: Connects us to the Creator.

Affirmation of Support: *"I love all the children of my heart, my body and my spirit."*

Tools for Manifestation:
Choose to explore this exercise for a few months (or more).
Every day, note the temperature, the direction of the wind, the amount of sunlight and the activity of the animals around you.

Every night, observe the cycles of the moon.
Watch the stars as they move across the sky from night to night.
Feel the wind, the temperature and the movement of the animals around you.

Note that as environmental conditions change, different types of life forms flourish.
If you wish, record those in a journal.
Dedicate a poem or a song to those beings.

Raphael's Rays

"I whisper in your ear and there is poetry.
I touch your heart and there is dance.
You reach for me and we are heaven."

- ♦ *Labradorite* is the perfection of all, manifested in form.

- ♦ *Larimar* is the creativity of thought and feeling merged.

- ♦ *Kunzite* is the delicate power of an open heart.

- ♦ *Lepidolite* is the joy of all love expressed through doing and being.

- ♦ Optional Essential Oils: *Peppermint* and *Peony* clears old thinking for the new.

Physical Integration: Soothes the nervous system. Balances the metabolism. Frees up enough physical, emotional and mental energy to manifest wishes.

Emotional Integration: Attracts supportive relationships. Brings out the inner artist. Increases beauty. Deepens satisfaction with life.

Millennial Uses: When we feel the most stressed, we sometimes have to call on divine guidance to see new meanings in everything so that we can imbue ourselves with enough hope to go on. "Raphael's Rays" is dedicated to the archangel, Raphael, who gifts us with the inspiration to treasure everything, with all of our heart. Through him, we learn that every difficulty translates into some new wonder, in the language of spirit. For instance, Obstacle equals Stamina. Fear equals Alertness. Raphael urges us into the innate romanticism that is within the fullest reality of life.

It's up to us to find as many ways as possible to express the romance and the reality, ~ with beauty, grace and love.

Electrical Body Alignment: Connects us to core creativity, beauty and knowingness.

Affirmation of Support: *"I walk with beauty in all my being."*

Tools for Manifestation:
Use the examples of

"Obstacle = Stamina"
"Fear = Alertness"

to create your own statements in the language of spirit and share them with love.

Relationship into All

"I look for the perfection that I have not yet met.
I look for it and I find
whatever I need,
always and forever."

- ◆ *Rubellite* is exploring beauty in life, poetry in motion.
- ◆ *Red Jasper* is the immediate expression of desires.
- ◆ *Uxelite* is the divine mirror of all experiences.
- ◆ *Danburite* is recognizing your heart in all beings.

Physical Integration: Supports the spine, particularly the lower back. Fortifies the blood and overall vitality. Enhances kidney function.

Emotional Integration: Improves the ability to express one's self honestly and spontaneously. Honors the body and all of its needs. Increases empathy. Exudes charm.

Millennial Uses: One of the "curses" of the modern age, is the endless drive to compete, to best everyone else. Why do we do this? So that we will know our own uniqueness and our singular importance? This unsatisfying competitiveness derives itself from a basic unhappiness with the self.

"Relationship into All" invites us into a vital, ever changing relationship with ourselves. It invites us to embrace ourselves as our primary love. From there, we unfold our happiness into all other bonds. We live, enchanted with ourselves and with everyone else, just as we/they are.

Electrical Body Alignment: Links us with the power to fulfill all our needs.

Affirmation of Support: *"I am the source of my own satisfaction."*

Tools for Manifestation:
Find the most honoring, respectful, glorious way to please yourself.
Do it.
Enjoy your bliss.
Revel in it.
Plant the joy in your memory and call upon it whenever you doubt yourself.

Regeneration

"I am the power of the sun and the moon holding themselves in love.
I am the season of all things immediately accepted at their birth.
I receive the abundance of the ages and I pass it on to you.
We shine and reflect as one beam of light."

- ◆ *Kornerupine* is ancient remembering of instantaneous perfection.

- ◆ *Herkimer Diamond* is instantaneous alchemy of past, present, and future, joined.

- ◆ *Lapis Lazuli* all knowing and gentle compassion.

- ◆ *Rutilated Quartz* is electrical flow of the mental, emotional, physical and spiritual bodies.

- ◆ Optional Essential Oils: *Mugwort* and *Myrrh* spark the mysteries of life.

Physical Integration: Facilitates natural sleep patterns. Promotes vitality.

Emotional Integration: Naturally flows with the cycles of life. Decreases resistance. Honors leisure time.

Millennial Uses: When you disconnect from the beauty of your surroundings (as we have done through the manipulation of our environment), you feel great, unappeasable desires. "Regeneration" calls us back to connecting with all life, where all of our needs are met. Then we enter the natural cycle of abundance where every lifeform on the planet fuels each other. In that space, we open ourselves, so abundantly that everything we do refreshes, refuels, and regenerates us into the amazing beings we are.

Electrical Body Alignment: Connects us to every moment of birth.

Affirmation of Support: *"I honor myself enough to work, to play and to enjoy everything in its perfect timing."*

Tools for Manifestation:
Without thinking about it, list four animals that inspire you greatly.
Post any pictures of them that you can.
Familiarize yourself with all of their habits, until you feel like them.
Invite their spirits to visit you and grace your life.

Now take the first animal and link it with the service of Kornerupine—ancient remembrance of instantaneous perfection.

How does it relate to this quality?

How do they complement each other?

How does the animal carry Kornerupine's gifts into the world?

Meditate upon the two of them and find out how to link them both in your memory as one.

Consider the first animal to be the ally of Kornerupine and its gifts.

Link animals 2-4, with Herkimer Diamond, Lapis Lazuli and Rutilated Quartz in order.

Now you have animal allies for the stones who offer themselves to regeneration.

When you feel tired, breathe in the essences of these stones, move like their corresponding animals, and revel in your ever deepening kinship with life.

Personal Story: I was quite attached to the stone combination necklace I obtained at Festival of the Little People '97, it was "Regeneration." I say was, because it decided to disperse itself not too long ago. This piece helped me through much change in my physical life. When I was feeling down or felt I needed assistance in my form I asked it to help and soon I was back to my old self. I relied on this piece much and when it left I was sad and felt a little lonely. After I was hurt in an accident, I really missed it, and then I was sent the message that I did not need it because I had worn it so often it is now part of me and all I need to do is call and it will be there to help. I thank the piece everyday and I don't know what I would have done if I had not been introduced to that combination of rocks.

~from Jeanice Braun

Shamanic Dream

"Welcome in to all of my dreams.
When, I, the shaman, bring you into all of them (even the wildest ones),
you walk in reality."

- ♦ *Brookite* is all your energy focused to a point of miracles.

- ♦ *Aragonite* is reason and intuition merged.

- ♦ *Herkimer Diamond* is the clarity to see it all happening.

- ♦ *Hawaiian Calcite* is the ability to birth more and more imaginings.

- ♦ *Copper Shavings* represent the Great Mystery.

Physical Integration: Increases sight, intuition and cellular memories. Uses the body's innate wisdom in day-to-day reality. Slows down movements to include more grace, strength, balance and stamina.

Emotional Integration: Increases the vividness of life. Relaxes judgments. Opens the heart. Sharpens the mind and simultaneously uses fear to cultivate more balanced awareness.

Millennial Uses: Some things present themselves as inexplicable tools for our enlightenment, with exquisitely precise timing. There are no words for this. There are no words for "Shamanic Dream." We leave it to your experience and Great Mystery and we give thanks.

Electrical Body Alignment: Connects us to mystery and reality, combined.

Affirmation of Support: *"I honor the sacred mystery in life by giving it my heart."*

Tools for Manifestation:
Go back to every word in this page.
Accept it as wisdom meant specifically for you.
All the clues are present to find the wisdom that touches your heart.
Now go and make your own shamanic dream.

Should into Acceptance

"I think about the right-ness and the need to understand,
while hoping that my heart will accept me,
anyway,
any way."

- *Gold* is actively seeking hidden treasure.

- *Sunstone* is warming of possibilities, fulfilled in dreams.

- *Cinnamon Quartz* is the hope of all times residing in now.

- *Aragonite* is the release of everything into freedom.

Physical Integration: Nurtures everything. Warms any stagnations. Releases infections.

Emotional Integration: Freely develops and sustains independent values. Embraces the diversity of the planet. Seeks out supportive, free thinking, compassionate teachers.

Millennial Uses: Science has invented communications that encircle the globe, easily. Sometimes, mass media has portrayed life in a homogenous fashion that gets embraced as a single standard to emulate. "Should into Acceptance" reminds us that we can celebrate all the differences between us as a way to celebrate life. By learning acceptance, we drop the judgment that encourages us to use our dissimilarities as a reason for hate and destruction.

Electrical Body Alignment: Connects us to our core of love.

Affirmation of Support: *"I give up judgment and I gain love."*

Tools for Manifestation:
Every day for a month, listen to everything you say.
Give up the word, "should."
At the end of the month, record how much your life has changed.

Spiral of Life

"Welcome to the regeneration of the sea.
On this magical earth, we are surrounded, completely, by the power of the water,
inside and out."

- ◆ *Blue Green Algae* gifts us with the joy of the most magical places on the planet.

- ◆ *Butterstone* links us with the power of the past, the hope of the future and the abundance of the now.

- ◆ *Hawaiian Calcite* offers us the signs and the voices of other worlds.

- ◆ *Phenacite* manifests the dreamtime in our sacred visions.

Physical Integration: Unites all our senses with intuition. Regenerates the body completely. Builds up stamina.

Emotional Integration: Embraces our weaknesses into strengths. Channels stress into constructive energy. Allows the flexibility to be fast or slow, or to be loud or quiet, as needed.

Millennial Uses: We possess incredible amounts of information, both old and new, on virtually every topic imaginable. We have amassed this storehouse of data, because now is the time to use it. "Spiral of Life" increases our physical and emotional energy so that we can activate our knowledge into immediate, powerful, life-enhancing action.

This union of stones and plants teaches us patience and inspiration while we learn to find the ways that will serve us now. "Spiral of Life" whispers to us of wisdom, not just knowledge. In every season, we explore lots of paths, but in truth, we must select one that enlivens us and aligns us to the season of now.

"Spiral of Life" honors the ancient learning and the new discoveries, which know that all ways must change within the spirals of life.

Electrical Body Alignment: Connects us to the eternal cycles and growth of life.

Affirmation of Support: *"I live empowered by what I have learned from the wise ones."*

Tools for Manifestation:

Each of us is born with our own special genius. Sometimes we spend a lifetime finding out what that is. This moment is for finding and using it now.
1. List, record or note your favorite world philosophies and their basic tenets.
2. Give thanks for how they have shaped you.
3. List, record or note the newest technologies and information that inspire you.

4. Give thanks for their inspiration.
5. Place the "Spiral of Life" next to you. Hold your hands, fingertips together, as if in prayer. Meditate upon the wisdom of the world.
6. When you light upon a piece of wisdom that you wish to absorb into your life, sound a note with a simple instrument: a drum, a gong, a chime, or even a glass of water that you can gently strike.
7. Repeat the meditation when you're ready to create more of your own personal tradition.
8. Give thanks for your own way of life.

Personal Story: I tried blue-green algae once. For some reason or another I didn't notice any real difference, which surprised me because I have enjoyed kelp very much. (Isn't one seaweed like another?) So when I wore a "Spiral of Life" vial, I didn't know what to expect. One thing was certain, I had a very, very full day in front of me. Armed with a list that would take me 2-3 days to finish and not much sleep, I decided to get at it.

I just kept plugging away. A little way through the list, I realized I didn't feel tired. Later on, I discovered that the further down I got on the list, I was actually picking up speed. Then with great surprise, I saw that I had everything done! It was so amazing and I felt so good, that I started projects that had been on the back burner for a long time. All of a sudden while I was organizing the bookshelf, I remembered that I was wearing the "Spiral of Life." I laughed. I didn't take it off for several days so I could catch up on a lot of extra work.

~from Marilyn

Spirit Storytelling

"We speak the whispers
in the quiet magic you sometimes hear.
We lie in tree shadows, in gnomes scurrying,
and always in the dusk and the dawn.
We are your family of
guides from all other worlds."

- ◆ *Black Garnet* is embracing all experience, all emotion, unconditionally.

- ◆ *Kornerupine* is the initiation of all lifetimes in every choice.

- ◆ *Botswana Agate* is hearing and seeing the magic of your spirit family.

- ◆ *Rutilated Quartz* is living in all dimensions simultaneously.

Physical Integration: Releases stiff body postures.   Facilitates dream memories.

Emotional Integration: Introduces more clairvoyance and clairaudience. Promotes the sense of belonging. Relaxes reflexive judgments and invites open hearted exploration into new areas.

Millennial Uses: In some ages, people have listened to the life around them and learned. In this century, people have turned away from listening to the land and have learned through the tools of science. All things on the earth (people too) move in perfect cycles and balance. Now we come full circle with the opportunity to combine the ways of the earth and the ways of science. "Spirit Storytelling" invites us to go to this integration supported by our spirit families to accept their quiet help. It reminds us that just because something apparently can't be measured by our physical senses or scientific methods, doesn't mean that it doesn't exist.

In the core of us, we know beyond words and explanations, that certain things live so far beyond the reach of our means that we have to believe in them in order for us to grow.

Electrical Body Alignment: Links us to our spirit families and their support.

Affirmation of Support: *"I am surrounded by loving spirits and I witness their support in my life."*

Tools for Manifestation:
1. Hold a Black Garnet next to you. Embody yourself in this reality, joyfully.
2. Hold a Kornerupine next to your heart. Whisper encouragements to yourself.
3. Carry a Botswana Agate with you. Just believe.

4. Hold a Rutilated Quartz to your forehead. Let your expectations fly away peacefully.

Know that you are surrounded by divine beings.
Accept this and feel unshakable calm.
Schedule a time away from work and any distractions (for at least two days).
Take the support of your spirit family with you. Invite them to join you out loud and in love.

Stress into Centeredness

"I am life coming at you from all directions.
Wait for me in expectancy
and lose your expectations."

♦ *Black Kyanite* is demonstrating that all experience is divine.

♦ *Coral* is expanding the breath through the emotions, not just around them.

♦ *Turquoise* is detachment from limits—the freedom to fly.

♦ *Fluorite* is easing into the new earth vibration and smiling.

Physical Integration: Integrates the hemispheres and the meridians of the body. Empowers the brain to receive and release more stimuli. Relaxes the joints and the nerves and pain.

Emotional Integration: Utilizes stress as an immediate reflex and then releases it easily. Remains unaffected by others' worries. Promotes a very focused love of self.

Millennial Uses: In this information age, we have flooded our waking moments (and more) with fast paced stimuli. We become so inundated, that we no longer know or remember that we, ourselves, can control what we do or don't accept, along with when, how and why.

"Stress into Centeredness" is designed to support us in all the stages of self-empowerment. We may overwhelm ourselves, but even this eventually forces us back to our core essence of simple peace. Balance.

We are creatures of balance, even when we don't acknowledge that. Our true nature brings us to that, over and over again. It's simply delightful to know that, along the way, we can choose our experiences and any help that we desire.

Electrical Body Alignment: Connects us to our center and our place of power.

Affirmation of Support: *"I act from my loving power."*

Tools for Manifestation:
Take a well loved stone and hold it in your hand.
Run it gently up your right leg and then stop at the center of your body.
Pause it there. Sigh deeply.
Do the same with your left leg.
Run it gently down your right hand and right arm.
Then place it at the center of your body.

Pause it there. Sigh deeply.
Do the same with your left hand and left arm.
Run it gently from the top of your face to the center of your chest.
Breathe exquisitely.
Then tone a long, full, "Ahhhh."
Sing the tone until you vibrate the peace
for which you always have been designed.

For partners: Do the same and then repeat on the back side of each other's body.
Share the peace.

Personal Story: We were at our very first trade show, just enjoying ourselves and sharing our wares with people. This woman and her son came up to our booth. She had heard that we had stones in Vibrational jewelry that could help people with various challenges.

Though the woman was quite young, her hands were shaking violently. She said to us, "I have a great deal of stress in my life. Can you recommend anything?" Then she put her trembling hand up on the shelf, clutching one of the pieces of jewelry. It seemed very brave for her to be so forthright and so open, so we just suggested she relax and breathe for a minute.

Then the woman calmed down rapidly and said, "I feel much, much better. I think these stones are helping. What is the name of this piece?" She lifted up her hand and looked down at what she had been holding so tightly and the jewelry label read, "Stress into Centeredness."

~from Twintreess

Timeless Treasure

"I reach into your heart
and all ways and all times of life come to you now
so that you may accept the unlimitedness of you.
Whatever you need or wish, breathes in you and in your imagination now.
Thank you."

- *Platinum* fills you with all knowingness.

- *Dioptase* readies your heart to receive yourself and all knowingness.

- *Phenacite* gives away the old need to be less than perfection.

- *Holly Berry Agate* connects you to your guidance and life as you never have felt them before.

- *White Moldavite* always accepts you, as spirit clothed in perfect form, now.

Physical Integration: Increases the awareness of body/mind/spirit/all and expands your senses and gifts to receive this union.

Emotional Integration: Welcomes all parts of selves and all dimensions, lovingly into Now. Aligns inner peace with universal harmony. Reminds us of life's perfection.

Millennial Uses: Currently, the most widely accepted means of exchange between people for goods and services is money. That system evolved as a means for people to receive, equitably, what they needed. As we enter the next millennium, we have had the opportunity to review the effectiveness of this system and have determined that we likely require a more harmonious distribution of the world's wealth.

"Timeless Treasure" reminds us that people exchange much more than money, goods and services. Each of us gives our essence into life until all the gifts of love and all knowingness from all ages enter the consciousness where they avail themselves to anyone, freely, timelessly.

Electrical Body Alignment: Connects us to our inherent value.

Affirmation of Support: *"I am a treasure of the universe."*

Tools for Manifestation:
Write down whatever you need and desire to fulfill yourself.
Make the list as long or as short as you wish.
Choose its length according to whatever makes you feel excited and reinvigorated.
Gather with a good group of friends who also have their own wish lists.

Agree to exchange the lists with open hearted enthusiasm and welcoming.

Barter with your friends to fulfill your needs and desires.

If everything on your list was not met, then exchange it with more friends.

Set up more gatherings to trade and to relish in each other's company.

Acknowledge the great talents of all assembled (including yourself).

For your own joy, pick one new skill that you would like to acquire (and then would barter with).

Learn the skill and revel in your own growing awareness, power and strength.

Personal Story: One night I placed "Timeless Treasure" next to me before I went to sleep. As I was drifting off, I opened myself up to feeling timeless (during a very busy time in my life). When I woke up the next morning, I heard, "Re-claim your energy." Before I could think about it, I just started seeing all these instances where I had committed myself, but that I no longer was involved in actively (nor wanted to be). I would picture the situation, smile at it and say, "I re-claim my energy." I found myself doing this with things and people who had been out of my life for a long time. The more I did it, the stronger I felt. Pretty soon, I was glowing.

Then I realized that "Re-claim your energy," came from "Timeless Treasure." In a single instant I realized that it is never too late (or too soon) to treasure my time and my energy. I felt honored and honoring of everything.

~from Marilyn

Transformation, Prosperity and the Goddess

"Every moment in each earthchild's life carries
the seed,
the stalk
and the flower of utter power and perfection."

- *Rainbow Hematite* brings the rich, unending vitality of the earth's core.

- *Ruby* gives us the grace to receive all abundance with unlimitedness.

- *Aventurine* combines luck, laughter and life.

- *Holly Berry Agate* softens and blesses every struggle.

Physical Integration: Tones the hearing. Attunes us to the earth. Adapts our body's cravings to fill, automatically, our needs, according to the seasons.

Emotional Integration: Increases the ability to give and to receive from others. Warms the heart. Guides us to inexplicable wisdom at the appropriate moment.

Millennial Uses: There are many traditions (that we are becoming more aware of) which honor the earth and act upon that. We seek the clarity of those ways, as they innately understood how to transform and prosper according to the planet's cycles.

Welcome to "Transformation, Prosperity and the Goddess," as one way to enter the ever growing heart of the earth.

Electrical Body Alignment: Links us to the sentient consciousness of the earth.

Affirmation of Support: *"I am a prosperous child of the abundant, mother earth."*

Tools for Manifestation:
Prepare yourself and then enter an environment that is as devoid of sensory input as possible (like a sensory deprivation tank).
Think of yourself as proceeding into a void, a womb, that will birth you.
Accept that you will transform before leaving the void.
Center all of yourself within your breathing.
Let each inhale and each exhale flow through you, very consciously.
Think breathing.
Feel breathing.
When you are ready to leave the room, find one thing to concentrate your essence on, then go somewhere quiet and peaceful and focus on your subject until you choose to enter the world again, with renewed clarity and full attention.
You have received gifts that will continue to unfold in your life at exactly the perfect moment.

Turkll Delight

"I come to you, now.
I bring all my magic and intent.
I give it freely
because there is no other way to give,
I smile as you jump, hearing me say,
'I am the troll of your dreams!'"

- *Tourmalated Quartz* is born from deep within the earth, and with all her love, she shoots out into the universe.

- *Black Coral* is embracing all fears into bliss, into unlimitedness.

- *Pyrite/Fool's Gold* is the eternal magical fool within, with all the gold.

- *Sugilite* is the expectancy to deliver all our dreams upon the earth, now and always.

- Optional Essential Oil: *Ylang Ylang* sharpens our senses, sweetly.

Physical Integration: Increases groundedness. Strengthens circulation and aerobic capacity. Decreases the need for sleep.

Emotional Integration: Appreciates all parts of being human. Invents life as an adventure. Immediately manifests desires.

Millennial Uses: For every task that is before us, there is a spirit guardian to assist us with it. Celebrate it! With "Turkll Delight," investigate all the possibilities. Why not give all these guardians jobs that fit their services? Devas help with plants. Sprites help with trees. Gnomes and trolls help with day-to-day work.

These stones shout at us, "You are supported, not just in who you are, but in everything you do, as well!" We are guided beyond our capacity to comprehend it and that is the gift of life to each of us.

Electrical Body Alignment: Connects with the rewards of life.

Affirmation of Support: *"I receive everything I need, and more, to help me with everything I must do."*

Tools for Manifestation:
Ask Tourmalated Quartz to enter your life, lovingly.
Invite it to root you deeply into the earth experience. (Dig your toes in the mud).
Ask Black Coral to enter your life, lovingly.

Invite it to light up your shadows to be admired for its service to the whole of you (Write a comic strip about you).
Ask Pyrite to enter your life, lovingly.
Invite it to show you every gift you have received (Go look for buried treasure).
Ask Sugilite to enter your life, lovingly.
Invite it to send help to fulfill your most magnificent dreams. (Take a fun trip).
What else can you do to make it easy to receive your magical wishes?

Personal Story: For the past two years, I have been wearing a pair of stone combination earrings (not two of the same kind) made by Twintreess. I am not someone who knows a great deal about gemstones and crystals, except what I occasionally hear from friends. I don't feel energy like some people I know and so the phenomenon of how these stone combinations land on my ears mostly every day is something that I don't quite understand. I love dangling stuff from my ears, and generally feel "undressed" when I don't wear earrings. Clearly, I own lots of fun and interesting baubbles, many of whom were given to me by friends ... which makes them even more special. So why do I wear these two earrings 90% of the time?

I have a "logical" answer for this: these earrings are great for any kind of outfit, not startling dressy but "catchy" for mostly any kind of outfit. But, more than that, they draw me in. They choose me as I look at my array. They are my friends and I love them. Somehow all the other decorations have lost their specialness and pale beside my "Turkll Delight" and "Faith's Embrace" stone combination earrings.

~from Ursela Gurau

Unimaginability

*"We live through words,
until we are beyond them.
Imagination carries us
through the worlds.
Beyond there,
be unimaginability..."*

- ◆ *Calcite* prepares us for the new earth vibrations through our experiences.

- ◆ *Tree Agate* is all aspirations released and creating miracles.

- ◆ *Rhodochrosite* speaks the language of love in form and formlessness.

- ◆ *Moldavite* is simple cellular knowing.

- ◆ Optional Essential Oil: *Star Anise* embraces all life.

Physical Integration: Transforms the body! Revitalizes appearance. Balances metabolism to needs.

Emotional Integration: Releases knowledge to open to unimaginable wisdom. Catalyzes core changes of beliefs. Centers on trust and freedom. Sparks the power of visualization.

Millennial Uses: How will we enter the future? Is that even possible? How can we predict how we will choose or act in the unknown?

"Unimaginability" enters our consciousness at the precise, clearest moment and leads us without leading anything. Deep within timeless knowing, we feel that life truly lives beyond words. Our attempts to name this powerful mystery we walk in, doesn't describe it. It is simply our way to have a safe world to travel in with expectations that we can prepare for in any circumstance. That controlled safety may be leaking the life out of us and killing us gently, one piece at a time. That doesn't prepare us for the "future," it positions us to die quietly and predictably.

We can ready ourselves for a new reality, but it may feel unreal to us. Our senses have not been taught to measure our timeless, immortal, unlimited beingness. Some scientific methods say that if something cannot be measured, it does not exist. How then can we acknowledge love, happiness or genius? Simple. Declare yourself to be unimaginable. Stand in unimaginability. Rather than preparing yourself for what you can already see, watch the unimaginable come to you for an adventure.

Electrical Body Alignment: Connects us to great mystery.

Affirmation of Support: "*I respect the unimaginable, inexplicable love in life.*"

Tools of Manifestation:

Our bodies have been trained to expect to witness a certain reality (even when that's not what is actually there) and then to act upon that. We tend to react to our environment from prior programming and, truthfully, we sleepwalk through our lives, barely noticing it, let alone savoring its richness. To change your reactions to something, we just have to change something:

1. Get a soothing massage, with one of the stones in "Unimaginability." Relax your stiffnesses. Ease your defensiveness. Let your heart glow.

2. Do something pleasantly unexpected. Look for every chance to alter how you name things. When a friend asks you how old you are, reply with the age you want to be right now. When someone asks you, "How are you?" Tell them briefly, but truthfully. When you want something, say so respectfully and free yourself and everybody else from that hidden feeling. Experience unimaginability.

Personal Story: Sometimes, when traveling around the country, we would hold groups and gatherings for specific reasons and intent. At some, we would ask everyone to participate in a manifestation circle where one individual would sit in the center of a circle of other people and clearly and concisely state a succinct phrase asking for what he/she wanted to manifest in his/her life, now.

I remember the first time I sat in the center of a circle and what I asked for. It was simple, unimaginability. It made no sense to me to ask for something that already was or had been thought of or imagined. I simply wanted more; more of the divine. And I always get it. That's the fun part.

This is an important combination of stones (Unimaginability) for me. It is so strong that I have never had to wear it, because it lives with me. Spirit is always teaching us (very clearly through crystal and rock lifeforms) that tools are meant to be integrated and then released so their essence is always with us as more life force rather than a dependency or an attachment that keeps creating a continual need.

For some reason, the Tree Agate and the Moldavite, together, in this combination, speak loudly to me. I don't know why and I am not inspired to find out why. I just hold them together in my heart and am enriched and give thanks.

~from Thomas

Uriel's Wisdom

"Let us walk together, hand in hand,
upon the earth and see all there is~
love, creating perfection."

- ♦ *Moss Agate* is the sweetness of the earth inside of us.

- ♦ *Rutilated Quartz* is the communication of our guides in everyday events.

- ♦ *Moldavite* is seeing with the eyes of our heart.

- ♦ *Angelite* is the peace of knowingness.

- ♦ Optional Essential Oils: *Calendula* and *Heather* activate openness and healing.

Physical Integration: Regenerates the organs. Clarifies dream messages. Ages gracefully.

Emotional Integration: Releases unnecessary stimuli and stress. Unconditionally accepts others. Cultivates the art of simplicity. Appreciates the gifts (not just the challenges) of solitude.

Millennial Uses: In our desires to have more and more, we have plundered the earth and each other. When we get the goods we want, often, we don't feel satiated. In fact, the desire fuels itself into almost uncontrollable greed.

"Uriel's Wisdom" emphasizes the sweetness of simplicity. Instead of driving endlessly for more possessions, we can value ourselves and how to be with ourselves, calmly. When we don't use materialism to distract us from self intimacy and quiet, we relax. We loosen our grip on our wants. They automatically fade away, because we allow our essences to feed and to enrich ourselves in ways that belongings cannot. "Uriel's Wisdom" shows us that the way to happiness is to detach from things that we own (and that own us) and walk into a satisfying world of self love and exploration.

Electrical Body Alignment: Connects us to being, instead of doing.

Affirmation of Support: *"I have value because I am a worthwhile being."*

Tools for Manifestation:
Rather than include an extra tool here, we will simplify this space.
Do what you are already doing: Read this book. Enter its being.
Give it your fullness and enjoy~

Violence into Compassion

"I express my needs and desires immediately.
I search for the connection that will bring me love and satisfaction.
My heart longs to remember family."

- *Agate* focuses on self-determination, resources and stamina.

- *Bloodstone* develops practical empathy.

- *Rose Quartz* softens the limits and soothes frustration.

- *Lepidolite* allows for unlimited expression of hope.

Physical Integration: Releases imbalances of energy and limits. Releases excess heat from the organs.

Emotional Integration: Directly remembers unlimitedness.

Millennial Uses: At this time, many of the cultures of the world live in their "heads," disassociated from feelings and from the consequences of their actions. Sometimes when the pain of that disassociation grows, we explode with violence.

"Violence into Compassion" soothes us. It asks us to be nurturing with all the elements of self. Compassion starts with ourselves and grows. As a society, when we can own our feelings, then we will find the appropriate channels to express them.

Electrical Body Alignment: Connects us to the depths of feelings.

Affirmation of Support: *"I welcome compassion into every part of my being."*

Tools for Manifestation:
Built-up anger can produce violence.
Practice releasing frustration, as it happens, when it happens.
There are many ways to redirect its energy in a way that satisfies, instead of builds.
   1. Punch a pillow.
   2. Scream alone in a room where no one will be disturbed.
   3. Run until you're exhausted.
   4. Do something physical until you are worn out.

World Peace

"Whatever we meet on our path,
we see it as a part of ourselves
and greet it in peace."

- ◆ *Magnetite* insists that we honor life now.

- ◆ *Lithium Crystals* embrace our calm center of being.

- ◆ *Turquoise* frees us from loneliness and pain.

- ◆ *Amethyst* unifies all life unconditionally.

Physical Integration: Smoothes rough skin. Eases stiff muscles. Increases flexibility. Relaxes the immune system.

Emotional Integration: Decreases defensiveness. Establishes healthy priorities and boundaries. Fulfills the needs of self immediately and peacefully.

Millennial Uses: We go into the 2000's with enough destructive weaponry to kill the world many times over. This forces us to practice peace, because war could mean absolutely no survivors.

"World Peace" accepts us as we are, violent and calm, both. Peace means living at the center of the self and loving who we are. Then we can walk through any circumstances, unaffected, because our core always remains intact. We have all that we need, there is nothing to fight.

"World Peace" so thoroughly accepts us that we naturally want to share our bliss with others. When we do that, we find that everyone else is basically just like us. They have needs and hopes and gifts to give and receive. "World Peace" allows us to accept all beings and offers them help to fulfill themselves.

Electrical Body Alignment: Links us to total empathy.

Affirmation of Support: *"I dedicate my world to peace."*

Tools for Manifestation:
  Every day take something from your world that gives you great fulfillment.
  Enjoy it and dedicate that happiness to world peace.

World Peace Exercise: Create one new way of doing things in your life that gives ease and efficiency (even if you feel resistant to it at first). Visualize this new action and breathe very deeply saying, "I accept myself completely."
  Peace begins wherever we go through any differences and choose to trust.

Totem Stories from the Tibetan Tektites

You have so much to do because you have so much to give.

This is the time when it will mean so much.

All the seasons of the earth come together now.

They rise inside of you until you cannot deny it any longer.

You are being swept into timelessness.

You are being thrown into abundance.

You are being cast into peace.

You are being plunged into all growth.

You are ready.

You just don't feel it

cause that kind of surety

comes after the test.

The only way for your feelings

and your true magnificence to match

is for you to leap into your unknown.

You're the only one who can make that a reality.

Still you have so many standing right beside you,

sighing with you,

celebrating with you.

Yes.

We are some of the many.

We are your totems, too.

We come to you as friends.

We offer ourselves as friends, not just for this adventure,

but for all of them.

To us friendship means that we fill all of each other's lifetimes.

That's what we have been offering you all along.

Can you feel our hearts next to yours?

We have invited you into our everything.

Will you join us?

Will you let us walk beside you while you make peace with the earth?

This book is just the beginning.

These pages were for us to become family, even before you noticed.

Now the reality adventure begins.

When you put down this book, realize that you speak all the languages

by listening.

With that gift, you can meet all the children of this earth.

You can see your eyes in their faces looking back at you.

All dreams come true

right now.

REFERENCES

National Audobon Society Field Guide
to North American Rocks and Minerals
Chanticleer Press Edition
Alfred A Knopf, Inc., 1975

Mineral Collector's Handbook
Barry Krause
Sterling Publishing Co., Inc., 1996

Rocks, Minerals, Gems, Crystals, Fossils
The Complete Collector's Companion
Harriet Stewart-Jones, Editor
Chartwell Books, Inc., 1995

Crystal & Gem
Dr. R. F. Symes and Dr. R. R. Harding
Eyewitness Books
Alfred A. Knopf, Inc., 1991

The Smithsonian Treasury
Minerals and Gems
John Sampson White
Smithsonian Institution Press, 1991

An Illustrated Guide To Rocks & Minerals
Michael O'Donoghue, Editor

Jewelry

Well, now you have met the stone beings who wanted to be introduced to you. You have heard from their hearts about how they offer their qualities to us and to all of life. This is the point where you head down the road to a new adventure. You can take this information and you can make miracles from it. Think of it…as you go through your life you can use the language of the stones to realize that lifeforms around you speak to you and share their incredible, unending gifts with you. The rest of the conversation is up to you. You can go forth and listen to everything anew, and you can share your unique magic, too. From there, the possibilities exist way beyond words. We send you unconditional support on your next journey and all the multitudes of others that yet have to be birthed.

As for us, we continue to listen to the stones and we keep finding more and more expansive ways to do that. One of the ways we carry the wisdom of the stones with us is through the Vibrational Jewelry they asked us to co-create. The Stone Combinations come directly from listening to the stones and then placing them (singly and in combination) and their energies in jewelry that we wear on our bodies to directly remind us to integrate their innate earth intelligence in all that we do. Wearing the stones brings us unimaginable adventures. If you would like to join us in that, please contact us (our address is in a section after this, called, "about us"). You would be very welcome. We sell these pieces (and we can customize them, as you and the stones wish) with great joy and intent. We listen to every single stone that goes into the jewelry (they teach us much) and that is our piece to share with you with love.

It's truly an adventure that grows way beyond us and keeps on going. The more we grow and listen to the stones, the more new combinations and Vibrational jewelry keep forming and the more we join with all of life. It's a miracle and you're invited.

tones

The stones have given us even more possibilities: As we listen to and record their wondrous life stories, people come out of nowhere to share very unique stones with us. They tell us (the people and the stones) that it's time for us to gather together these very incredible stones and pass them onto others to learn from and to enjoy.

So we have welcomed these stone beings into our space with great respect and consciousness. We place them alongside us while we work (lots of them have watched us put this book together. Feels like they smiled the whole time.), we carry them in our pockets, and we lay beside them while we sleep so that together we slip into the dreamtime. That's where we meet them as teachers and shamans of every perfect kind.

Every single stone being is listened to and greatly admired (we believe that they do the same for us).

After we have lived and learned with each of these unusual stones, they told us that most of them had come to us to give us abundance. We thanked them and went about our life. Then they told us that they had come to give us money, as well; we were to sell them. Like the MacEarl crystals, they offered themselves so that we could afford to write this book, on their behalf. Of course, we said, "Yes."

So we pass on their offer to you. Write, call or e-mail us and we will tell you, happily, what stones are living with us now that are for sale and could join your life. Their hearts and their services utterly expand everything. We accept that, and for our human part, we share it with you with trust, great joy and unconditional love as we all gather together to do business in new ways in the new millenium.

About Us

Hi! We're Twintreess, we're the hosts of this adventure and we've really enjoyed being here with you. Thank you for joining us. We'd like to introduce ourselves now. Maybe you're wondering why we didn't do that earlier. Well, first of all, it's mostly the stones' book and secondly, if we talked about ourselves at the beginning, you might think that we were experts and/or that our words should carry extra meaning.

Actually, we thought you just might like to have this adventure yourself, without any unnecessary interference. So, why introduce us at all, then? Well, for one thing, we'd love to hear from you some time (write us at the address below please). The biggest reason is the same as the one above: We don't want you to be influenced by us too much in this book. And that can be a subtle thing (influence, not us). Since we're co-creators of Stones Alive!, our hearts and fingerprints are all over these pages, even when we intended to be invisible. So we decided to tell you how we came to bring you this adventure. Once you know that, maybe you'll be able to find the parts in the book that come directly from us and then just take that for what it's worth- our experiences, not necessarily yours. However, we do want you to know that we share our experiences, freely; that's how we all evolve.

Hello! We are Twintreess, sometimes also called Marilyn and Thomas. That may sound confusing but it's completely simple. When we, Marilyn and Thomas, come together, we form another being that our spirits call, Twintreess. The incredible part is that, as Twintreess, our beings expand exponentially. We found out that our combined hearts hear the stories of all life around us. (Or as our guide, Grandma Birdie told us, we're spirit storytellers). We listen to all beings, especially the ones who have appeared to be silent around humans: stones, plants, animals, stars, elementals, etc. That makes our life glorious. To be able to hear the infinite wisdom of all life forms makes us fall in love with everything, all over, every day.

One of the most pleasant miracles of the listening (what we call the spirit storytelling) was discovering that the nature beings around us didn't want to yell at us for being destructive, selfish humans; they totally embraced us as their earth family. They honored us more than we knew how to honor ourselves. They understood [as beings still close to nature often do], that each of us provides a perfect piece to the overall plan of life on the earth, and in some grand way somehow, it was impossible for us to waver from that. In short, our teachers, -the plants, the animals, the stones, etc.- affirmed us utterly, as we were and as we are.

That felt so heavenly that we found ourselves writing down the words of the beings around us. After filling several notebooks, we were told that these were books that were to be shared with other humans who couldn't hear the earth spirits without a little guidance. So be it.

So now we are authors, speakers, publishers, ritualists, CD producers, event organizers, Vibrational jewelry co-creators, crystal musical instrument inventors, sacred structure builders and more. People keep asking us what do we do? What they seem to mean, is what's the common link in all this? The spirit storytelling. Listening to our spirits brings us to every activity we're in. We enter things according to the design of the cycles of life all around us. They give us the wisdom to share. Our part in that is to keep choosing to open our hearts, every day, every night, even when we don't want to do it. For us, this listening is a practice of our life. Our joy comes in sharing it with you. Thanks for listening.

Want to get to know us a little better? Write any time. We'd love to hear your story. If you want we'll send you a catalog of our latest adventures– gatherings, more books, Vibrational jewelry, sacred geometry construction, whatever we can co-create together respectfully…

Twintreess

AhhhMuse/Twintreess
800-585-9389
twintreess@juno.com
www.ahhhmuse.com

treehousepress@juno.com

www.turkii.com

Thanks for listening.

Other Titles from Twintreess

naturespeak

Etheric Songs from the Children of Earth

The Heart of Matter

Ogallalah de Oro: My Life with Humans

Meditations in Regeneration

Nurturance of the Soul: Ad/rift in A/maze!

Windows on Other Worlds

The Rituals of Manifestation Deck

One Voice, Many Bodies- meditational music CD